# CONTENTS

# 1    RESPONSIBILITIES

Some of the requirements of persons doing electrical wiring are as follows:

## THE ELECTRICAL CONTRACTOR

The Electrical Contractor must:

— Obtain permits for all of his work.

— Do all work according to code.

— Not work under a permit issued to the owner or another Contractor.

— Not take out a permit for work done by someone else.

— Not hire uncertified men on a job basis to work under his certificate. (these men are then really contracting without proper Certification).

— Not undertake to do work which exceeds his certification.

— Make sure that all electrical equipment is properly certified before it is connected. See below for a list of equipment certification marks acceptable in the province of BC.

— Declare in writing to the Electrical Inspector when the work is ready for inspection.

— Not cover any wiring until acceptable arrangements have been made with the Inspection Office.

## THE STUDENT

The student who will familiarize himself with the information contained in this book will find it easier to write the official Government examination for a Restricted Certificate of Qualification. Try the sample examination located on page 139.

The Government Examiner will supply you with an official Code book, a set of Bulletins a copy of the Regulations, and all the paper you will need to write the exam. Do not bring your own. Just bring a pen, pencil, a calculator and a clear thinking head.

The student should understand:

— He must be a mature adult with at least 3 years experience in the installation and maintenance of electrical equipment or have special training satisfactory to the Chief Inspector before he may write the official examination. Documentary proof, required by the Chief Inspector, may consist of a certificate of achievement from a training school, i.e. Apprenticeship certificate or letters from employers stating level of responsibility and training received; and

— He must obtain at least 70% on the official examination. If he fails, he must wait thirty days before he may write again. This depends on the mark he receives on the examination; and

— Once he has passed the exam he is issued a Certificate of Qualification. This means he may now do electrical work for an electrical contractor but before he can function as an electrical contractor himself he must first obtain a contractors license from Safety Engineering Services. Application forms are available at any provincial electrical inspection office; and

— After hours of study and agony over the exam, you face the Inspector in the field with each installation you do. If your work is good and your cooperation is good, you will have no problem. If it is not good, the Board of Examiners may want to talk to you about it - may even want to give you a vacation (suspend your Certificate) for a period of time; and

— After two failures, it appears the thing to do is to become interested in some other trade - plumbing maybe.

## THE HOMEOWNER

The homeowner:

— Must obtain an electrical permit for all electrical work he does, including the wiring for ranges, dryers, furnace, extra outlets, etc. The rules require an electrical permit for any additional wiring, any alteration, and any new wiring. It is like a building permit; it permits the holder to install certain electrical wiring and equipment in his own home. This permit must be obtained before any electrical work is begun.

May be required to answer a few questions asked by the local Electrical Inspector to show a certain level of competency before a permit is issued but that should not be difficult provided you have read through this book. The Inspector cannot do the planning and layout work for you. The purpose of this book is to walk you through the whole installation and prepare you with good answers so that you should not have any difficulty with the Inspector in obtaining a permit or with his inspection of your work.

Should note two things about that permit: First, that it has an expiry date. This means that you are expected to complete your work within the time allowed. An extension is usually possible by permission of the Inspector. Second, that you assume legal responsibility for all the electrical work you do. Again, these things are not difficult if you follow the instructions given in this book.

— Must do all the work himself — he may not allow anyone to do any of the work covered by the permit issued to him.

May do the wiring in his own home only. This is the basis on which a permit is issued to an owner. He may not install the wiring, any wiring, in his own building if it is to be rented or sold. He may obtain an electrical permit only for his own personal dwelling. He must do all the work himself. No one, other than his immediate family, such as a father, brother, son, may do any of the electrical work under this permit. It has nothing to do with payment for work done. Even an Electrical Contractor could not work under a permit issued to an owner. Treat it as you would your drivers license.

— Must do all the work according to the electrical code.

— Must notify, in writing, the Electrical Inspector when the work is ready for inspection. He must not request an inspection before he is, in fact, ready. The Inspector may charge a re-inspection permit fee if he finds the work is not ready or if it has been improperly installed.

— Complete the entire installation including all fixtures, switches, plates, etc. before he may have a final certificate of approval.

## 2 - C.S.A. CERTIFICATION - Rule 2-024

CSA is no longer the only testing and labeling agency acceptable in BC. There are now ten certification agencies. Each of these agencies performs prescribed tests to insure the electrical equipment and appliances sold in this province are manufactured according to a rigid set of standards. Following is a list of the certification marks used by these agencies.

**CGA, Canadian Gas Association** - This is what to look for on gas appliances such as furnaces, dryers, cooking stoves etc. If this label is in place it usually means both the gas and the electrics are certified for use in Canada.

**CSA Canadian Standards Association** - This is the old reliable and very familiar certification label. Until recently, this label, and the provincial label, were the only two labels acceptable in this province. This label is still acceptable just as it always was on almost everything electrical.

**ETL Inchcape Testing Service** - This label is not as well known here in Canada but we can expect to see it on an ever increasing number of electrical devices.

Note the small "c" outside and to the left of the circle. This means that equipment with this label is acceptable for use in Canada. If an electrical device has this label look for the small "c". If it is not there the device is **not acceptable for use in Canada.**

**Warnock Hersey** - This certification mark already appears on heating equipment. We can expect to find it on a broad range of electrical devices in the future.

**UL Underwriters Laboratories** - This is a major testing agency in the United States.

Note the small "c" outside and to the left of the circle. This means that equipment with this label is acceptable for use in Canada. If an electrical device has this label look for the small "c". If it is not there the device is acceptable for use in the United States **but it is not acceptable for use in Canada.**

**ULC Underwriters Laboratories of Canada** - This certification marking is used mainly on fire protection equipment. You will find it on smoke alarms used in single family homes.

The next three approval markings, **Met, Entela and O-TL**, are from the latest agencies accredited by the Standards Council of Canada to approve electrical equipment for connection and use in Canada.

Note that in each case there is a small "c" outside and to the left of the certification mark. Without that small "c" these marks are not acceptable in Canada.

| BC Government Approval Label |
|---|

**BC Provincial Government marking.** - This marking is applied to electrical equipment which for one reason or another must be tested for acceptance in the field. This would include specialty items which have been brought in as settlers effects or items imported on a one time basis. This label indicates the equipment has been examined and found to be acceptable for use in Canada.

**Certification markings** are very important for your safety. Each electrical device in your home, from the main service panel to the cover plate on the light switch, must bear one of these markings to show it has been properly tested and is certified. It may be tempting to pick up that cheap, uncertified, light fixture in Mexico or elsewhere, or that under the counter electrical gizmo at a fraction of the cost for the same thing back home but don't do it. It may be a fire hazard or an electrical shock hazard. Manufacturing to a safe standard and submitting that equipment to a laboratory for rigid tests is an expensive process but it is your assurance that that device meets certain minimum standards. Always look for one of the above certification marks on all electrical equipment you purchase. If you do not find any of these markings bring the device to the attention of the store manager.

# 3  ELECTRICAL INSPECTIONS — WHEN TO CALL FOR INSPECTION.

## ROUGH WIRING INSPECTION

Before calling for an inspection of the rough wiring make sure that:

1. **The electrical service** equipment is in place.  The service conduit or cable, the meter base, service panel and the service grounding cables should all be installed, where it is practicable to do so, for the rough wiring inspection.

   Note    If you are using service conduit, not cable, the conductors need not be installed for the rough wiring inspection, but the conduit, and all its fittings, wherever practicable, must be in place.

2. **All branch circuit cables** are in place and properly strapped and protected from driven nails.  Don't forget, all joints, splices and ground wire connections to boxes must be completed as far as possible.

**Avoid Costly Rejections and Delays.**

   Before calling for inspection of the rough wiring check your work very carefully as an Inspector would do his inspection.  Check every detail.  If you have followed the instructions in this book you should do well.

Caution -  Do not cover any wiring, not even with insulation, until it has been inspected and is approved for covering.

   Note -  In some rural areas a sketch map may be necessary to help the Inspector find your premises.  Also, if a key is required, provide instructions on where to find it.

## FINAL INSPECTION

I. **For this inspection your installation must be entirely complete.**  It's a good idea to check it carefully as an Inspector would do his inspection.  Use this book as you go through your installation to check off each item.  Look for forgotten or unfinished parts.  Check for such things as circuit breaker ratings, tie-bars, circuit directory, grounding connections etc..  Look for open KO holes or junction boxes and unfinished outlets.  Don't forget, if any of the appliances such as a dish washer is not going in just yet you must terminate the supply cable in a fixed junction box, (the box must be fastened in place) and must be complete, with cover, until that appliance is actually installed.

2 **Electrical Permit - Check also if your permit covers all you have installed.**

   The Inspector is one of the good guys.  His concern is that your installation is safe and that it meets minimum code requirements.  That is, alter all, exactly what you want too.

# 4    ELECTRICAL INSPECTION OFFICES

**HEAD OFFICE**    Director, Electrical Safety Branch
3rd Floor, 750 Pacific Blvd.Vancouver
V6B 5E7  Tel  660-6262
Fax 660-6661

## REGIONAL OFFICES

**Vancouver Island**...C. Webber .................................. 250 741 5920
250-741 5914
155 Skinner Street
Nanaimo, BC,  V9R 5E8
Fax: 250 741 5929

**Lower Mainland** ....C. Webber ........................... 604 852-5270
155 Skinner Street
Nanaimo, BC, V9R 5E8
Fax 250-741 5929

**Interior** ................... J. MacMillan ..................... 250 565 6105
3740 Opie Crescent
Prince George, BC V2N 4P7
Fax: 250 565 7281

**Northern** ................ J. MacMillan......................... 250 565 6105
3740 Opie Crescent
Prince George, BC V2N 4P7
Fax: 250 565 7281

## FIELD OFFICES

**Abbotsford**...............Office phone ...............................604 852 5270
#1B - 33820 S. Fraser Way
V2S 5G7
Fax: 604 852 5469

**Campbell River** .....Office phone .............................. 250 286 7653
#115 - 1180 Ironwood Street
V9W 5P7
Fax: 250 286 7573

**Chilliwack** ..............Office phone ............................. 604 795-8402
45850 D Yale Rd.
V2P 2N9
Fax  604 795 8627

**Coquitlam** ...............Office phone ............................. 604 927 2041
24 - 2773 Barnet Hwy.
V3B 1C2
Fax  927-2047

**Courtenay** ...............Office phone ............................. 250 897 7530
2500 Cliff Ave.
V9N 5M6
Fax  250 334 1209

**Cranbrook** ..............Office phone .......................... 250 426-1277
1 - 100 Cranbrook St. N.
V1C 3P9
Fax  250 426-1253

**Dawson Creek** ........Office phone ............................. 250 784-2380
Prov. Blg. 101 -  1201 - 103 Ave.
V1G 4J2
Fax  250 784-2211

**Duncan** ...................Office phone ............................. 250 746-1324
5785 Duncan St.
V9L 5G2
Fax  250 746-1401

**Ft. St. John** .............Office phone ............................. 250 787-3230
10600 - 100 St.
V1J 4L6
Fax 250 787-3210

**Kamloops** .................Office phone ............................. 250 828-4530
440 - 546 St. Paul St.
V2C 5T1
Fax  250 828-4769

**Kelowna** .................Office Phone .............................. 250 861 7313
1913 Kent Rd.
V1Y 7S6
Fax: 250 861 7349

**Langley** ...................Office phone ........................... 604 530 7107
20635 Fraser Hwy.
V3A 4G4
Fax: 604 533-3142

**Merrit** ......................Office phone ............................. 250 378-9376
2176 Quilchena Ave.
V0K 2B0
Fax: 250 378-9346
Govt. Agent

**Nanaimo** ...................Office phone .............................. 250 741-5920
155 Skinner Street
V9R 5E8
Fax: 250 741-5929

**Nelson** .....................Office phone ............................. 250 354-6544
310 Ward St.
V1L 5S4
Fax: 250 354-6102

**Penticton** .................Office phone ............................. 250 490-8294
#103 3547Skaha Lake Rd.
V2A 7K2
Fax: 250 490-8299

**Powell River** ...........Office phone ..............................604 485-3622
6953 Albernie St.
V8A 2B8
Fax: 604 485-3627
Govt Agent

**Prince George** ....Office phone ............................. 250 565-6105
3740 Opie Cres.
V2N 4P7
Fax: 250 565-7281

**Prince Rupert** ........Office phone ............................. 250 624-7417
201 - 3rd Ave. W.
V8J 1L2
Fax: 250 624-7411
Govt. Agent

**Quesnel** ...................Office phone ............................. 250 992-4240
#102 - 350 Barlow Ave.
V2J 2C1
Fax: 250 992-4314

**Richmond** ................Office phone ........................... 604 660-9433
148 - 10451 Shellbridge Way
V6X 2W8
Fax: 604 660-0187

**Salmon Arm** ...........Office phone ........................... 250 832-1688
681 Marine Pk. Dr.
P.O. Box 100, Station Main
V1E 4S4
Fax: 250 832-1607

**Sechelt** ...................Office phone ........................... 604 885-5616
Box 950, 102 Toredo Sq.
V0N 3A0
Fax: 604 885-3710

**Smithers** .................Office phone ........................... 250 847-7202
1020 Murray St   Bag 5000
V0J 2N0
Fax: 250 847-7232

**Sqamish** .................Office phone ........................... 604 892-3221
Box 1008, 1360 Pemberton Ave.
V0N 3G0
Fax: 604 892-2342

**Terrace** ...................Office phone ........................... 250 638-6564
109 - 3220 Eby St.
V8G 5K8
Fax: 250 638-6519

**Vanderhoof** ............Office phone ........................... 250 567-6307
189 Stewart Street E.
V0J 3A0
Fax: 250 567-6303

**Vernon** ....................Office phone ......................... 250 549-5596/7
3201- 30th. St.
V1T 9G3
Fax: 250 549-5508

**Victoria** ...................Office phone ........................... 250 952 4444
4248 Glanford Ave.
V8W 9N8
Fax: 250 952 4458

**Williams Lake** ........Office phone ........................... 250 398-4481
112 - 540 Borland St.
V2G 1R8
Fax: 250 398-4208

District Inspectors may be reached by telephone daily from 8:30 am
to 9:30 am only, except for those days when they are inspecting in
outlying areas.

## The following Cities and Municipalities administer their own electrical inspection service:

**City of Burnaby**     F.Ghafari, Supervisor................. 604 294 7130
4949 Canada Way,
V5G 1M2
Fax: 604 294-7986
Office hours 11:15 am to 12:00 noon.

**Maple Ridge**        Contact Pieter M.Den Uly R.B.O.604 467 7313
11995 Haney Place,
V2X 6A9
Fax: 604 467-7331
Office hours 8:30 am to 9:15 am; and
3:30 pm to 4:30 pm.

**City of N. Van.**     J. Ball .....................................Chief Inspector
141 West 14th. St.
V7N 2K7
Tel: 604 983 7355
Fax: 604 985-0576
Office hours  8:30 to 9:30 am; & 3:30 to 4:30pm
24 hour inspection request 604 985 5448

Leave your company name, permit number, type of inspection
request and address at which inspection is required.

**Dist of N. Van.**..........M. Usselman, .........................Chief Inspector
355 West Queens Rd.
V7L 4K1
Tel.  604 990-2480
Fax: 604 984-9683
Office hours  8:30 to 9:45 am

**City of Surrey** ........Jim Barker  ..............Chief Inspector
14245 - 56th. Ave.
V3A 3A2
Tel:  604 591-4240
Fax: 604 591-4440
Office hours  8:30 to 9:00am; and
4:00 to 4:30 pm.

**City of Vancouver**  Ark Tsisserev .......................Chief Inspector
453 West 12th. Ave.
V5Y 1V4
Tel:  604 873-7603
Fax: 604 873-7100
Office hours  8:30 to 9:15 am; and
1:00 to 1:45 pm.
24 hour inspection request 604 873 7159

Leave your company name , permit number, type of inspection
request and address at which inspection is required.

**City of Victoria**     D. Stevenson, .......................Chief Inspector
1 Centennial Square,
V8W 1P6
Tel: 250 361-0343
Fax: 250 385-1128
Office hours  8:30 to 10:00 am; and
1:00 to 2:00 pm.

**West Vancouver** Len Rhodes, .................Chief Inspector
750 - 17th. St.
V7V 3T3
Tel: 604 925-7040
Fax: 604 925-7006
Office hours  8:30 to 9:30 am; and
4:00 to 4:30 pm.

All requests must be phoned in.  A Registered Contractor
Authorization form is required before final inspection.

# 5    SERVICE SIZE - Rule 8-200

We must begin with the electrical service box. It may appear to be very difficult to install a new electrical service in your house but it need not be so. If you read these instructions carefully it should be easy and enjoyable and what's more, you should save a bundle.

The rules permit a service as large as we like but not as small as we like. There is a definite minimum size we must have if it is going to be passed by the Inspector.

Service size is based on two things.

1. **Calculated Load** - This is the sum of all the loads after certain demand factors are applied. For an average 90 m² (968 sq.ft.) house with electric range and dryer but with gas or oil heating, the service demand load consists of 5000 watts for what the Code calls basic load, plus 6000 watts for the range plus another 1000 watts for a 4000 watt dryer. Total is 12000 watts. To find amperes we need to divide the 12000 watts by the service voltage. 12000 watts divided by 240 volts is 50 amps. Don't forget this is **CALCULATED amperage** not **MINIMUM service size and there is a BIG difference.**

2. **Minimum Service Size** — This is based on floor area.

   **60 amp.** — For any house with **LESS THAN** 80 m² (861 sq.ft.) floor area. This includes the areas of all the floors except the basement. Basement floor area is ignored completely for this purpose.

   **100 amp.** — For any house with 80 m² (861 sq. ft.) **OR MORE** floor area. As above, this includes all floors except the basement.

   **Note** — Even if the actual load is, say 30 amps, the minimum size service permitted is 100 amps if the floor area is 80 m² or more. This extra capacity is for future load.

   The table on page 12 has been developed to simplify the service size calculation. The table shows a progressive load - in other words, any service size given in any column assumes all the loads shown above that value are going to be used.

   For example, a 90 m² (no basement) house with no electrical appliances such as a range, dryer, water heater or electric heating would require a 100 amp service. The material required for this service is listed under B, page 8.

   If the 90 m² no basement house had a 12,000 watt range, 4000 watt dryer, 3800 watt water heater, the service size would still be only 100 amps. This is the minimum size service for this floor area. The material required for this service is listed under B, page 8.

   If the 90 m² no basement house had a 12000 watt range, a 4000 watt dryer, a 3800 watt water heater and a 15000 watt. electric hot water boiler the service size would need to be minimum 117.1 amps. The material required for this service is listed under C, page 8.

   Once you have determined the correct list of material for your house, measure the lengths required for your job. You can use the following lists when shopping for the materials you will require.

# LISTS of MATERIAL

## Remember you need twice as much hot conductor length as neutral conductor.

**A**  **Service Size - 60 amps.**   Note - may be used only if the total floor area, above ground, is less than 80 m² (861 sq. ft.).

| | |
|---|---|
| Service switch, fuse or breaker rating ---------- | 60 amps. |
| Hot conductors------------------------------------------------- | 2 - #6 R90XLPE copper (black, red or blue) |
| Neutral conductor ------------------------------------ | 1 - #6 R90XLPE copper (white or natural grey) |
| Service raceway ------------------------------------ | 1 inch. or use #6 copper TECK cable. |
| Meter base rating ------------------------------------ | 100 amps. |
| Service grounding conductor --------------------- | #6 (or larger) bare copper. |
| Service panel size (See also chart page 44) --- | 16 circuits (minimum) |

This panel may supply all the normal outlets in this small house and a central gas or oil furnace.

---

**B**  **Service Size - 100 amps.**

| | |
|---|---|
| Service switch, fuse or breaker rating ...............100 amps |
| Hot conductors ....................................................2 - #3 R90XLPE copper (black, red or blue) |
| Neutral conductor - (See Note 3 below) ..............1 - #6 R90XLPE copper (white or natural grey) |
| Service raceway | 1¼ inch. or use #3 copper TECK cable.See also Note 2 below. |
| Meter base rating ................................................100 amps |
| Service grounding conductor ............................#6 bare copper, see page 48 for details. |
| Service panel size (See also chart on page 44) ...24 circuits |

**Note 1**  This panel may supply all the normal outlets in the house and a central electric furnace, an electric boiler or baseboard heaters.

**Note 2**  A 1 inch (27) would be acceptable for this 100 ampere service but the list above shows 1¼ inch conduit. A 1¼ inch conduit will permit a service upgrade to 150 amps at minimum expense later, when large loads are added.

**C**  **Service Size - 120 Amps.**

| | |
|---|---|
| Service circuit breaker rating ............................125 amps. (For fused service switch see note 4.) |
| Hot conductors ...................................................2 - #2 R90XLPE copper (black, red or blue) |
| Neutral conductor - (See Note 3 below) .............1 - #6 R90XLPE copper (white or natural grey) |
| Service conduit ...................................................1¼ inch. or use #2 copper TECK cable. |
| Meter base rating................................................200 amp. |
| Service grounding conductor ............................#6 bare copper, see page 48 for details. |
| Service panel size (See also chart on page 44) .. 24 circuits |

**Note**  This panel may supply all the normal outlets in the house and a central electric furnace or electric boiler. If heating is with electric baseboards you will need more than 24 branch circuits, see list D below.

**D**  **Same as C above except:**

Service Panel Size - (See also chart on page 44).............. 30 circuits

Note   This panel may supply all the normal outlets in the house and a central electric furnace, an electric boiler or electric baseboard heaters.

**E    Service Size - 150 Amps.**

Service circuit breaker rating ...........................150 amps. (For fused service switch see note 4.)
Hot conductors ...............................................2 - #1/0 R90XLPE copper (black, red or blue)
Neutral conductor - (See Note 3 below) ...........1 - #4 R90XLPE copper (white or natural grey)
Service conduit ...............................................1¼ inch. or use #1/0 copper TECK cable.
Meter base rating ..........................................200 amp.
Service grounding conductor ...........................#4 bare copper, see page 48 for details.
Service panel size (See also chart on page 44) ...30 circuits

Note   This panel may supply all the normal outlets in the house and a central electric furnace or electric boiler.  If heating is with electric baseboards you will need more than 30 branch circuits, see list F below.

**F    Same as E above except:**

Service Panel Size (See also chart page 44)........   40 circuits.

Note   This panel may supply all the normal outlets in the house and a central electrical furnace, an electric boiler or electric baseboard heaters.

**G    Service Size - 200 Amps.**

Service circuit breaker rating ...........................200 amps. (For fused service switch see note 4.)
Hot conductors ...............................................2 - #2/0 R90XLPE copper (black, red or blue)
Neutral conductor - (See Note 3 below) ...........1 - #3 R90XLPE copper (white or natural grey)
Service conduit ...............................................1½ inch. or use #2/0 copper TECK cable.
Meter base rating ..........................................200 amps.
Service grounding conductor ...........................#3 bare copper.  See page 48 for details.
Service panel size (See also chart on page 44) ... 30 circuits.

Note   This panel may supply all the normal outlets in the house and a central electric furnace or electric boiler.  If heating is with electric baseboards the 30 circuit panelboard is too small.  You will need to install a 40 circuit panelboard.  See also the chart on "Minimum circuits required" on page 44.

**NOTES     NOTES          NOTES**

1   **Spare Circuits - 2 Required -** Rule 8-108(2) requires that there be at least two spare circuits left in the panel after you have connected all the circuits you have installed.  These two circuits are for future use.  See also page 42 under (c) "How Many Circuits Do I Need".

2   **Minimum Panel Size -** The above lists give the minimum panel size required by code in each case, however, this may not be enough for your installation.  Make sure that you have a sufficient number of circuit spaces available in your panel.  See also under (c) "How Many Circuits Do I Need", on page 42 and the chart on page 44.

3   **Reduced Size Neutral Conductor -** The Lists of Material above show a reduced size neutral as permitted by Rule 4-022 however BC Bulletin 4-1-0 suggests that a larger size neutral may be required.

It should be noted that Rule 4-022 was not amended for use in BC.  This means the rule is acceptable as it is and that it may be applied as it is in the Code Book.  The difficulty in writing this book is that only the Rules in the Code have official status and in any conflict between a Rule and a Bulletin the Rule must take precedence.  The Bulletin is subject to the rule, it cannot amend the rule.  There appears to be a conflict between Rule 4-022 and BC Bulletin 4-1-0.  Check with your local Electrical

Inspector for a final decision. If there are special considerations he will recognize them and will rule accordingly.

The above lists of material are based on the literal interpretation of Rule 4-022 which permits the service neutral conductor to be smaller than the hot service conductors. The smaller service neutral conductor, in some cases, will also allow a smaller size service conduit to be used. There is no point in installing a large service neutral conductor, and the larger conduit, when it is recognized, by the Code, that the extra capacity is useless, it can never be used.

**Neutral Terminal in the 200 amp Meter Base** - If you are installing a 200 ampere service, check the neutral terminal in the meter base to insure it is suitable for use with a #3 neutral conductor. The neutral terminal in most modern 200 ampere meter bases are approved for use with #3 conductors but you should check this detail when you buy that meter base.

## Information for the STUDENT

**200 Ampere Service** - The footnotes for Table 2, page 277 in the Code, were revised to permit 2/0 90° copper conductors to be used for a 200 amp service as shown in the "Lists of Material" above. This smaller conductor now permits 1½ conduit to be used for a 200 ampere service. The neutral service conductor need only be as large as the service grounding conductor, and in this case, Table 17 requires a #3 copper conductor for service grounding.

**Bare Neutral** - Rules 4-020, & 6-308 - Each list of material refers to an **insulated neutral** conductor, however, the rules do not require the neutral to be insulated; it may be bare. Using a bare neutral will save a bit of money and it is easier to form into the desired shape to make connections. Note that a bare neutral, if of copper, may be run in PVC conduit. The Code, however, does not allow us to reduce our service conduit size even though the bare neutral is smaller than an insulated neutral, Rule 12-1014(4)(e).

Where a bare neutral enters a meter base, or switch, or a panel, it must be insulated to prevent contact with live parts. In most cases it should be possible to train this bare conductor so that there is no danger of inadvertent contact with live parts. However, where it is not possible to prevent inadvertent contact with live parts the bare conductor must be insulated. Apply a layer of electrical tape throughout the length of the exposed section. This layer of tape should be equal to the thickness of the insulation on the hot conductors.

## Reduced size neutral - some details

While there is general agreement, in the electrical trade, that a full size neutral conductor is wasteful because it cannot possibly ever be used, there is disagreement on how much reduction should be permitted. The following explanation will help the student understand why the Code will permit the service neutral to be considerably smaller than the hot service conductors.

### Consider the following:

It is argued that Rule 8-200 specifies a minimum size for service conductors for residences and the point is stressed that this includes the neutral, therefore, as the argument goes, we may not reduce the neutral below the minimum size stated in that rule. It should be noted that almost the same words are used in Rule 8-202, 8-204 & 8-208. Each of these Rules deals with different buildings and each states "the minimum ampacity of service conductors" may not be smaller than permitted in that rule. In each case the "service conductors" includes the neutral conductor, therefore, as the argument goes, we may not apply Rule 4-022 in any of those cases either. The effect of this interpretation is that we may never reduce the neutral conductor for any service. In fact, most of these rules refer to both "service" and "feeder" conductors and therefore, this interpretation would not allow a reduced neutral in a feeder either.

It should be noted that one of the basic rules of interpretation is that a specific rule supercedes or overrides a general rule. Rule 4-022 is such a specific rule. Rule 8-200 is specific in that it refers to "service conductors" as opposed to "branch circuit conductors" but Rule 4-022 is more specific in that it refers to the neutral conductor only. Then notice, it refers to the neutral conductor in the service. It should also be noted that this rule does not limit the application to commercial buildings nor does it limit it in any way to services above 100 amperes. Rule 4-022 says that we do not need a full size neutral in a residential service. The rule says it need only be large enough to carry all the load connected to the neutral. It goes on to say that this load must be determined by the minimum demands required by Rule 8-200.

In a residence the loads connected to the neutral consist of lights, plugs, and in some cases a few range cooking top elements. The oven, electric heating, dryer, water heater and sauna loads are all not connected to the neutral. Applying all the demand factors permitted by the rules the calculated load on the neutral for a 969 sq. ft. (90 m$^2$) house would be 5000 watts. This is 20.8 amperes. Therefore, according to code. the connected load on the neutral in this house is 20.8 amperes. The smallest size neutral specified in the above lists is #6. A #6 - R90 copper conductor may carry 65 amperes. This leave 65 - 20.8 = 44.2 amperes, or 200% spare neutral capacity. Even if we added a 12 kw range, and it would be incorrect to do so because, at worst case only about half the total range load is connected to the neutral, the service neutral load would still be less than the #6 copper service neutral could safely carry. Without a valid reason there is no point in providing an 80 ampere neutral for a 20.8 ampere load. The important thing to remember is that the service neutral must be at least the same size as the service grounding conductor according to Rule 4-022. Don't waste your money on a full size neutral and conduit when it is simply not possible to ever use it in a residence. Spend your money on things that can be used to improve your installation. Install more lights and better control of them, more plug outlets along the kitchen counter, more plugs in the basement areas, the workshop areas, the exterior of the house, and the garden areas. That is a much better investment.

## Service Sizing Table for Single Family House

This Table gives the minimum service ampacity required in each case.
The letter after each ampere rating indicates which list of materials to use.

| Connected Load | If total, of all floor areas except basement, is less than 80 m² (861 sq. ft.) | | If total, of all floor areas except basement, is between 80m² than 90 m² (969 sq. ft.) | | If floor area is between 90 m² and 180 m² (1937 sq. ft.) | If floor area is between 180 m² and 270 m² (2906 sq. ft.) | If floor area is between 270 m² and 360 m² (3875 sq. ft.) |
|---|---|---|---|---|---|---|---|
| | No basement house | With any size basement | No basement house | With any size basemen | See Notes 2 & 5 | See Note 2 | See Note 2 |
| **Basic Load** only See Note 3 | 60 Amps A | 60 Amps A | 100 Amps B | 100 amps B | See Notes 2 & 5 | See Note 2 | See Note 2 |
| **Plus range** (up to 12 KW rating) | 60 Amps A / 60 Amps A | 60 Amps A / 60 Amps A | 100 Amps B / 100 Amps B | 100 Amps B / 100 Amps B | 100 Amps B / 100 Amps B | 100 Amps B / 100 Amps B | 100 Amps B / 100 Amps B |
| **Plus 4 KW dryer** | 60 Amps A | 60 Amps A | 100 Amps B | 100 Amps B | 100 Amps B | 100 Amps B | 100 Amps B |
| **Plus 3 KW water heater** See Note 8 | 60 Amps A | 60 Amps A | 100 Amps B | 100 Amps B | 100 Amps B | 100 Amps B | 100 Amps B |
| **Plus heating with** electric hot air furnace **or** electric hot water boiler | | | | | | | |
| 10 kw | 96.1 amps B | 100.3 amps B | 96.1 amps B | 100.3 amps B | 100.3 amps B | *104.5 amps C | 108.6 amps C |
| 15 kw | 117.1 amps C | *121.3 amps E | 117.1 amps C | *121.3 amps E | *121.3 amps E | 125.5 amps E | 129.6 amps E |
| 18 kw | 130.1 amps E | 134.3 amps E | 130.1 amps E | 134.3 amps E | 134.3 amps E | 138.5 amps E | 142.6 amps E |
| 20 kw | 138.1 amps E | 142.3 amps E | 138.1 amps E | 142.3 amps E | 142.3 amps E | 146.5 amps E | *150.6 amps E |
| 24 kw | | | *156.1 amps G | 160.3 amps G | 160.3 amps G | 164.5 amps G | 168.6 amps G |
| 27 kw | | | 169.1 amps G | 173.3 amps G | 173.3 amps G | 177.5 amps G | 181.6 amps G |
| 30 kw | | | | | 185.3 amps G | 189.5 amps G | 193.6 amps G |
| Or if using **Baseboard heaters** The sum of all heater ratings | | | | | | | |
| 4 kw | 69.8 amps B | 100.0 amps B | 100.0 amps B | 100.0 amps B | 100.0 amps B | 100.0 amps B | 100.0 amps B |
| 5 kw | 74.0 amps B | 100.0 amps B | 100.0 amps B | 100.0 amps B | 100.0 amps B | 100.0 amps B | 100.0 amps B |
| 6 kw | 78.1 amps B | 100.0 amps B | 100.0 amps B | 100.0 amps B | 100.0 amps B | 100.0 amps B | 100.0 amps B |
| 7 kw | 82.3 amps B | 100.0 amps B | 100.0 amps B | 100.0 amps B | 100.0 amps B | 100.0 amps B | 100.0 amps B |
| 8 kw | 86.5 amps B | 100.0 amps B | 100.0 amps B | 100.0 amps B | 100.0 amps B | 100.0 amps B | 100.0 amps B |
| 9 kw | 90.6 amps B | 100.0 amps B | 100.0 amps B | 100.0 amps B | 100.0 amps B | *103.1 amps B | *103.1 amps B |
| 10 kw | 94.8 amps B | 100.0 amps B | 100.0 amps B | 100.0 amps B | 100.0 amps B | *103.1 amps D | 107.3 amps D |
| 11 kw | 97.9 amps B | *102.1 amps D | 100.0 amps B | *102.1 amps D | *102.1 amps D | 106.3 amps D | 110.4 amps D |
| 12 kw | *101.0 amps D | 105.2 amps D | *101.0 amps D | 105.2 amps D | 105.2 amps D | 109.4 amps D | 113.5 amps D |
| 13 kw | *104.2 amps D | 108.3 amps D | *104.2 amps D | 108.3 amps D | 108.3 amps D | 112.5 amps D | 116.7 amps D |
| 14 kw | 107.3 amps D | 111.5 amps D | 107.3 amps D | 111.5 amps D | 111.5 amps D | 115.6 amps D | 119.8 amps D |
| 15 kw | 110.4 amps D | 114.6 amps D | 110.4 amps D | 114.6 amps D | 114.6 amps D | 118.8 amps D | *122.9 amps E |
| 16 kw | 113.5 amps D | 117.7 amps D | 113.5 amps D | 117.7 amps D | 117.7 amps D | *121.9 amps E | 126.0 amps F |
| 17 kw | 116.7 amps D | 120.8 amps E | 116.7 amps D | *120.8 amps E | *120.8 amps E | *125.0 amps E | 129.2 amps F |
| 18 kw | 119.8 amps D | 124.0 amps E | 119.9 amps D | *124.0 amps E | *124.0 amps E | 128.1 amps F | 132.3 amps F |
| 19 kw | *122.9 amps E | 127.1 amps F | *122.9 amps E | 127.1 amps F | 127.1 amps F | 131.3 amps F | 135.4 amps F |
| 20 kw | 126.0 amps F | 130.2 amps F | 126.0 amps F | 130.2 amps F | 130.2 amps F | 134.4 amps F | 138.5 amps F |

# These notes refer to references on the Table.

**Notes**

**(I)**  **Remember,** this table gives the **minimum service sizes permitted** under the rules. Services of higher rating may be installed and sometimes may be an advantage for future load additions.

**(2)**  **The floor areas** in all these columns must include the floor area of an in-house garage, (if there is one) but does not include an open carport. Calculate your floor area by adding basement floor area at 75% and the other floor areas at 100%.

**(3)**  **Basic load** - This includes:
- — All lighting outlets
- — All l5 amp plug outlets
- — Hot air furnace (standard) gas or oil burning type.
- — Any appliance of less than 1500 watts (this is the same as 12.5 amps at 120 volts) each. This includes loads such as a garburator, freezer, toaster, etc. but does not include **fixed** (permanently wired not plug in type) electric heating.

**(4)**  **\* Some amperages shown** on the table are marked with an asterisk. This means that the next smaller standard size service **is** acceptable in this case because it is within 5% of the required minimum size shown. Please note, special permission is not required. This is your choice now under the Code, Rule 8-106(1). Therefore the ampacity of the service switch, or circuit breaker, and the branch circuit panel, may be reduced to the next smaller standard size **but the number of the branch circuit positions in that panel must be as indicated, it may not be reduced.** For example if you require a 105.2 amp service you could use a 100 amp service but the total number of branch circuit positions in your one or more panels must be at least 24.

**(5)**  If your floor area is 90.1 m$^2$ we must use the column marked "90 m$^2$ to 180 m$^2$".

**(6)**  **The table may not show** the exact rating of your electrical load - in that case you may take the next larger size or calculate in detail, as described on the next page.

**(7)**  **Motor loads** - A hot air furnace requires a fan motor and a hot water heating system requires a motor to circulate the heated water. These motors are small, they require approximately 7 amps at 120 volts. This is included in the values given in the table.

**(8)**  **6 kw Water Heater** - This does not include an electric water heater for a hot tub or spa. Most water heater tanks are equipped with 2 - 3 kw heater elements. While this is 6000 watts in total, the switching arrangement in the thermostat is such that only one 3 kw element is working at any one time. It is a flip-flop switching arrangement. Under normal water use the lower 3 kw element will heat the water. When the demand for hot water becomes too great for the lower element the thermostat disconnects the lower heater element and connects only the upper heater element. The upper element will heat the water in only the top part of the tank, this provides rapid recovery of hot water. When the demand for hot water decreases the thermostat will switch back to the lower heater element again.

**(9)**  **7600 Watt Water Heaters** - This tank has 2 - 3800 watt heater elements, total wattage is 7600. With the flip-flop thermostat, as described above, the maximum load on this tank is 3800 watts. This is 800 watts more than allowed for in the table. For service calculations we add only 25% of this 800 watts. The additional load is only 200 watts. In an exam this is important - even this little bit - but on the job - - - well, it's not even one ampere more.

**Swimming pool, Hot tub or spa** - Electric water heaters for these loads are not included in the table. These must be added at 100% of their rating, Rule 8-200(l)(a)(v).

**(10)**  **Sauna (Electric heating)**- Rule 62-102 says this must be added as fixed electric space heating.

**If you are using gas or oil** (not electricity) to heat your house but sauna water is heated by electricity, enter the table with the full rating of this sauna heater as if it were an electric baseboard heater. For example, if you are installing a 4.5 kw sauna you would enter the table as if it was a 5 kw baseboard heater then read across under the correct floor area. Baseboard heaters are listed in the lower left corner of the table.

**If you are also using electric baseboard heaters as well as a sauna,** then simply add the sauna kw load to the total baseboard heater load before you enter the table.

**If your are also using an central electric hot air furnace as well as a sauna** use the table for all the other loads, then add the sauna load. All the values given in the table are in amperes, therefore, we need to convert the sauna load to amps as well. Do this by dividing the sauna watts by 240 volts (make sure the sauna heater is connected for 240 volts) then add this to the other load amps. Total amps is the minimum service size. Then use the list of materials on page 8.

**(11)**  **Built-in Vacuum Cleaning System** - Most of these systems will draw 12.5 amps or less at 120 volts. In that case they are included in the basic load shown in the table. Those units which draw more than 12.5 amps at 120 volts must be added at 25% of their rating but remember to take only half of the amperage because the service is calculated at 240 volts and the vacuum motor is connected for 120 volts. For example, if your service should be 125 amp according to the above table and you want to add a 14.0 amp vacuum cleaner system, it would look like this:

Other load -------------------------------------------------------------------- 125.00 amps.
Vacuum system ---- 25% of 14 divided by 2 = 0.25 X 7 =     1.75 amps
                                    Total        =     126.75 amps

Hardly worth the effort but it could mean that the next size larger service conductors may need to be used.

Now we know how large the service must be.  For the next step, refer to the lists of material on page 8.

# DETAILED CALCULATION FORM  (for student use)

Use the following format.  Fill in the blanks as required to describe your installation.  This calculation gives minimum size service required.  Then refer to the appropriate List of Materials on page 8.

**Step 1  Basic Load**  Rule 8-200(1)

1st. 90 m$^2$  floor area......................................................................................................... =   5000 watts
Next 90 m$^2$  floor area or portion thereof ............ (Add 1000 watts) ......................................... =_____ watts
Next 90 m$^2$  floor area or portion thereof ............ (Add 1000 watts) ......................................... =_____ watts

**Note (1)** Floor area in this case must include 75% of the basement floor area plus 100% of all other living floor areas on all floors.  All floor areas are inside, actual, floor area measurements.

**Note (2)** This basic load includes all lighting and plug outlet loads.  It includes oil or gas furnace and any other appliances such as built-in vacuum systems (which are rated 12.5 amps or less), swimming pool pump motors, most workshop motors, compactor motors, garburators, air conditioners, each individually rated at not more than 1500 watts (this is 12.5 amps at 120 volts) but  does not include any fixed electric space heating.

**Step 2  Appliances**

**Range** (For a 12 kw, or smaller, range) - add 6000 watts ........................................................ =_____ watts
    **Plus** - (If it is greater than 12 kw, add) 40% of that part which is in excess of 12 kw ......................... =_____ watts
        Note - 6000 watts is not a percentage of the range rating - it would be 6000 watts for any size range up to 12 kw.

**2nd. Range** - Add 25% of its wattage. (25% of 12000 for a 12 kw range) ................................... =_____ watts
        (See Appendix to Rule 8-200, Page 367 in your Code book.)
**Dryer** - Add 25% of its rating if a range is provided for ................................................................ =_____ watts
**Water heater** - Add 25% of rating if a range is provided for........................................................ =_____ watts

**Note -** If this is all the load we have, i.e. if heating is with gas or oil and there is no other large load such as electric sauna etc. Then we must determine minimum service size here as follows:

**(a)** **If the floor area is less than 80 m$^2$**, this includes the area of all the floors but does not include the basement.  Basement floor area is ignored completely for this determination.  **Then** - minimum service size must be 60 amps.  Now see List of Material, page 8.

**(b)** **If the floor area is 80 m$^2$** or more, for this determination, as in (a) above, we may ignore completely the basement floor area.  **Then** - minimum service size must be 100 amp.  Now see List of Material, page 8.

**Step 3  Sauna** - (The Code calls this space heating).

Add sauna load at 100% to other loads if house heating is not with electricity ......................... =_____ watts
If the house is electrically heated see under specific type of heating below.

**Step 4  Electric Baseboard Heating & Sauna**

Baseboard heaters  - add watts of all heaters .............. =_____ watts
Sauna heater ................................................................ =_____ watts

                                            Total = _____ watts
1st. 10 kw must be added at 100% (Rule 62-116)....................................................... =_____ watts
All the balance may be added at 75% ........................................................................ =_____ watts

                                                        Total =_____ watts

Thus far all our calculations are based on watts because that is what many of the demand factors in the Code are based on.  The balance of our calculations, however, are based on amperes, not watts.  At this point it is best to convert the total watts we have gotten so far into amperes, then we can complete the balance of our calculation using only amperes.

**Note** **If you are installing both electric heating and air-conditioning** Rule 8-106(4) does not specifically require an interlocking switch. It says simply "where it is known" that both electric heating and air conditioning systems "will not be used simultaneously" we need add only one of these loads, either the electric heating load or the air-conditioning load, whichever is larger. However, some Inspectors may feel that the words "where it is known" means that either a changeover switch must be installed so that only one of these loads **can be used** at any one time, or that both loads must be added as shown above. The best approach is to add both loads then check if that will bump your service up one size larger. If it does install the larger service or check with your Inspector.

$$\frac{\text{Total watts}}{\text{240 volts}} = \text{.............................................} \underline{\hspace{2cm}} \text{ amps}$$

The following loads are usually added directly in amperes.

## Step 5  Electric Hot Air Furnace & Sauna

Add 100% of furnace nameplate rating ................ = _____ amps

Add sauna at 75% of its nameplate rating ............ = _____ amps

## Step 6  Air Conditioning at 100% .......................... = _____ amps.  See Note above.

Total amps ............................. = _____ amps ....................................... _____ amps

Minimum  service size is _____ amps

Now consult the List of Materials on page 8.

### EXAMPLE 1

Calculate the service size for a house which has a floor area of 120 m$^2$ (1291 sq. ft.) on the main floor and 60 m$^2$ (646 sq. ft.) in the basement, (m$^2$ x 10.76 = sq. ft.). The electrical load consists of a 14 kw. range upstairs and a 12 kw range in the basement, 4 kw. dryer, 3 kw. water heater, 3 kw. sauna and 11 kw. electric baseboard heating. There is also a 12 amp A/C unit. Calculate service size.

**Basic Load** - Floor area = 120 m$^2$ main floor at 100%  =    120 m$^2$

60 m$^2$ basement at 75%  =     45 m$^2$

Total  =     165 m$^2$

First 90 m$^2$ .....................................................................................5000 watts

Next 75 m$^2$......................................................................................1000 watts

165 m$^2$

First range .......................................................... 6000 watts

Plus 40% of 14 kw -12 kw  = ....................................... 800 watts

2nd range at 25% of rating ...................................... 3000 watts

Dryer,  25% of 4000 watts .......................................... 1000 watts

Water heater,  25% of 3000 watts  ............................... 750 watts

Electric heating & sauna = 11  kw. plus 3  kw. = 14  kw.

First 10  kw. at 100% ................................................. 10000 watts

Balance,  4  kw. at 75% ................................................ 3000 watts

Total  =      30550 watts

$$\frac{30550}{240} = \text{.....................................................................} 127.3 \text{ amps}$$

**A/C Unit** is 12 amp - Add this at 100% of its rating .......................................... 12.0  amps

Minimum service size required      139.3 amps

Now refer to the lists of material on page 8. For this service use list F.

Our load is 139 amps. This is greater than list C, which is 120 amps, but less than E, which is 150 amps. We may use list E but because heating is with electric baseboards our panel size must be according to list F.

**CAUTION** - Don't ignore the note regarding the panel. The panel for list E may not supply baseboard heaters - but that is what this question requires. Therefore, we must use list F because we need a 40 circuit panel for this load.

## SUB-FEEDER SIZES   to 2nd. PANEL

It is often an advantage to install a second panel near the kitchen load. The size of panels and feeders and other details are dealt with on page 45.

# 6  SERVICE CONDUCTOR TYPES - Rules 12-100 & 12-102

(a)  **Copper Conductors or Aluminum Conductors** - The service conductor may be either copper or aluminum. Aluminum conductor installation requires great care. This special procedure is not covered in this book.

(b)  **Service Conductor Insulation** - Service conductors are subject to extreme temperature changes. For this reason the Code requires a different marking on the insulation of service conductors. See Footnote #31 for Table 19. It requires that we look for surface printed markings on service conductors to show they are certified for use where **exposed to the weather**. Look for a marking such as "Outdoor use" or similar wording. The old "Minus 40°C" or "-40°C" marking is no longer required although you may still find it on old cable inventory. To my knowledge only the RW90 insulated conductor has the marking required for conductors which must be formed into drip loops at an entrance cap. If you have difficulty locating properly marked conductors for your service do not just ignore the requirement, consult with your local inspector.

The reason for this restriction is that service conductors, which are connected to overhead lines, are exposed to very low temperatures and to sunlight. Both conditions can destroy the insulation on your service conductors unless they are certified for this application. Accidental contact with a conductor who's insulation has begun to deteriorate could result in severe electrical shock.

Note -  This does not apply to the conductors of an underground service because no part of the conductors in an underground service are exposed to the weather.

**White Striped Neutral Conductor** - Bulletin 4-2-0 advises that new almost white conductors are acceptable for the neutral conductor in your service. These new neutral conductors are not completely white or completely grey, they have white stripes along the length of the cable. This was necessary to overcome the deteriorating effects of ultra-violet radiation where these conductors are exposed to the weather at the entrance cap. These conductors are now acceptable for use as a neutral conductor.

# 7 HYDRO SERVICE WIRES to the HOUSE

**(a)**     **Consult Hydro** - Rules 6-112, 6-116, 6-206

Before any work is done the power utility should be consulted to determine which pole the service will be from.  This is very important.  The entrance cap must be properly located with respect to the Hydro pole.

There are a number of details to watch out for when locating the service entrance cap:

**A**   **Entrance Cap above Line Insulator** - Rule 6-116(b) requires the entrance cap to be located between 6 in. and 12 inches **above** the line insulator.  This is to prevent water from migrating along the service conductors to the meter base.  See also page 21 for more details  on this requirement.

**B**   **Roof Crossing** - Rule 12-312 - Fire fighting operations require ready access to and free movement on roofs.  Check with your Electrical Inspector before crossing any more than the overhang of the roof of any building.

The illustration below shows some service locations which are acceptable and some which may not be acceptable.

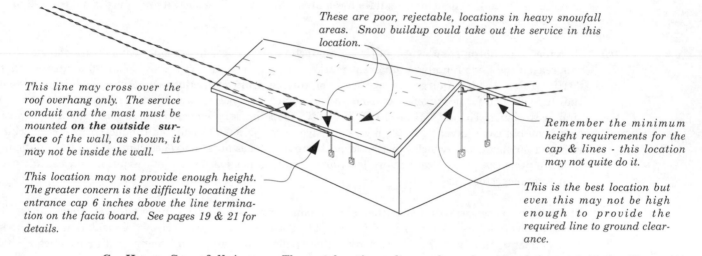

*These are poor, rejectable, locations in heavy snowfall areas.  Snow buildup could take out the service in this location.*

*This line may cross over the roof overhang only.  The service conduit and the mast must be mounted **on the outside surface** of the wall, as shown, it may not be inside the wall.*

*This location may not provide enough height. The greater concern is the difficulty locating the entrance cap 6 inches above the line termination on the facia board.  See pages 19 & 21 for details.*

*Remember the minimum height requirements for the cap & lines - this location may not quite do it.*

*This is the best location but even this may not be high enough to provide the required line to ground clearance.*

**C**   **Heavy Snowfall Areas** - The two locations shown along the side of the roof, in the illustration above, may not be acceptable in heavy snowfall areas.  Check with your local Inspector.

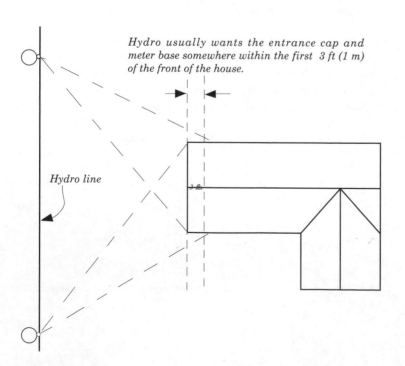

*Hydro usually wants the entrance cap and meter base somewhere within the first  3 ft (1 m) of the front of the house.*

*Hydro line*

Hydro usually wants the service entrance cap and meter base to be somewhere in that first 10 feet, 9 inches of the building facing the line, as shown.  If it just cannot be located in this part of the house you should check first with Hydro before locating it further back.  Cost is usually an important factor but if money is no object I suppose the service could be located almost anywhere on the house; well almost.

**Note** - The front of the house could be the back of the house if the power lines are located in the lane. It refers to the side or end of the house which faces the power lines.

**(b)** **Minimum Line to Ground Clearances - Rule 6-112(2)**

The line insulator, shown on page 20, is required by Hydro for their service drop. It must be installed high enough to provide the following minimum clearances:

|  | Meters | Feet |
|---|---|---|
| Any Public roadway | 5.5 | 18.04 |
| Across a readily accessible roof, Rule 12-310 | 2.5 | 8.20 |
| Across residential driveways | 4.0 | 13.12 |
| Across walkways, ground accessible to pedestrians only | 3.5 | 11.48 |
| Sundeck, (this is the same as a flat roof) | 2.5 | 8.20 |

## The line clearances required look like this:

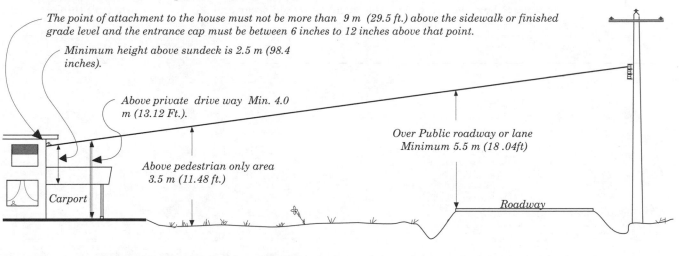

*The point of attachment to the house must not be more than 9 m (29.5 ft.) above the sidewalk or finished grade level and the entrance cap must be between 6 inches to 12 inches above that point.*

*Minimum height above sundeck is 2.5 m (98.4 inches).*

*Above private drive way Min. 4.0 m (13.12 Ft.).*

*Above pedestrian only area 3.5 m (11.48 ft.)*

*Over Public roadway or lane Minimum 5.5 m (18 .04ft)*

*Carport*

*Roadway*

**(c)** **Hydro Line Attachment to House** - Rule 2-108, 6-112 & 6-116

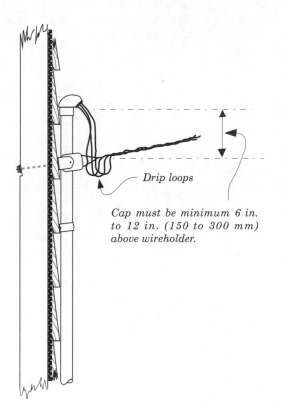

*Drip loops*

*Cap must be minimum 6 in. to 12 in. (150 to 300 mm) above wireholder.*

Hydro requires that you provide and install an insulator on your building for their line crew to attach their service cable. This wireholder must:

—Be insulated type, even for triplex cable.

—Be located within 24 in. of the entrance cap so that proper drip loops can be formed with 750 mm (29.5 inch) leads you must leave hanging out of the entrance cap, Rule 6-302(3). See the illustration below.

—Be high enough to maintain all the line to ground clearances given above but must not be located lower than 14.8 feet, (4.5 m) or higher than 29.5 ft (9 m) above the sidewalk or grade level..

—Be carefully located so that the 1 m (39.4 in.) line to window and door clearances can be maintained. See illustration on page 22.

—Be sufficiently well anchored in a structural member of the building to withstand the pull of the lines in a storm.

Note  Rule 6-112(6) requires that the wire holder must be bolt type as shown above.  It may not be lag-screw type.

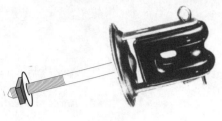

This means , of course, that if a tree falls across the line to your house or if an overheight 70 ton truck comes hurtling down the road and hooks onto the Hydro lines to your house you are safe - your wire holder is designed to withstand these kinds of stress. . . . . . It is possible the stress will pull out the  wall but you can count on that bolt to not let go of the 2 x 4 stud.  (It's best to choose a wall that could be pulled out without it taking down the whole house with it.)

**Note -** The construction of the wire holder is an important detail.  It must be a type which is designed to hold the lines so they cannot fall to the ground even if the porcelain insulation material on the insulator should break.

The wire holder in the illustration above has a pin holding the porcelain insulator in place.  This pin will continue to hold the line even if the porcelain should break and fall away.  These guys think of everything.

# 8    SERVICE ENTRANCE CAP - For overhead services only.

**(a)**    **Consult Hydro** - Rules 6-112, 6-116(a), 6-206

Before beginning the installation of your electrical service be sure to obtain from your local power supply authority (Ontario Hydro or equivalent in your area) the correct location of the pole from which you will receive service.  Your service head must be properly located with respect to the Hydro service pole.

**(b)**    **Type of Cap to Use** - Rule 6-114

There are a number of different caps permissible depending on the type of service conduit or cable you

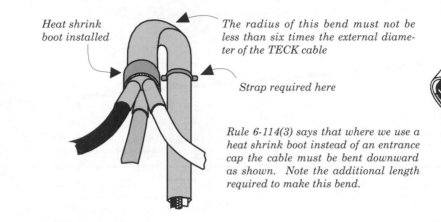

*Heat shrink boot installed*

*The radius of this bend must not be less than six times the external diameter of the TECK cable*

*Strap required here*

*Rule 6-114(3) says that where we use a heat shrink boot instead of an entrance cap the cable must be bent downward as shown.  Note the additional length required to make this bend.*

use.  See under specific type.

**(c)**    **Height of Entrance Cap** - Rule 6-112

There are two things to watch for:

1st. -- That you can obtain the minimum line clearances, given on page 19,

**AND**

2nd. - Rule 6-116(b) says the entrance cap must be higher than the wire holder which supports the Hydro line.  This rule says the cap must be between 150 mm and 300 mm (between 6 & 12 in.) above the Hydro line insulator as shown on page 19.  See also under "Drip loops" below.

If, in your case, it is difficult to locate the cap above the line insulator you should check with your local Inspector first before you ignore this rule.

### Some background Information for the student.

Rule 6-116(b) was originally designed to prevent water travelling down the Hydro service line to the splices at the entrance cap and there, at the splice, find its way into the conductor itself.  Water in this location (actually around the conductor strands inside the conductor insulation) would be drawn along by capillary action between the conductor strands and on down to the meter base where it would collect and do all kinds of nasty things.

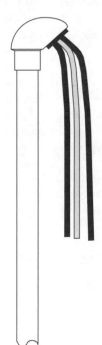

**(d)**    **Drip Loops** - Rule 6-302(3)

This Rule requires that you leave at least 750 mm (29.5 in.) of service conductor hanging out of the entrance cap so that drip loops can be formed as shown on page 19.

This long length may seem wasteful and sometimes is, but that's what the rule requires.  The purpose is to provide sufficient length for Hydro crews to form acceptable drip loops that will prevent water following the service conductors into the service conduit and down into the service equipment as described above.

**(e)    Location of Entrance Cap** - Rule 6-112(3)

This is an "out of reach" rule.  The entrance cap must be placed so that **all** open conductors (conductors not in conduit or in a cable) are above the window.  If they are below or alongside the window, or if they run in front of the window, as shown below, they must be at least 1 m (39.37 in.) away from the window.

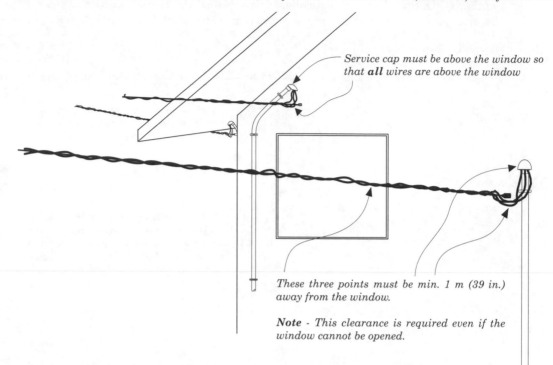

*Service cap must be above the window so that **all** wires are above the window*

*These three points must be min. 1 m (39 in.) away from the window.*

*Note - This clearance is required even if the window cannot be opened.*

This rule applies to all windows **even those which cannot be opened.**

Note  1    **A long drip loop** is not approved.  Locate the entrance cap within 24 in. of the point of attachment of the service drop wires.  Hydro service drop leads should contact the building at one point only.  Except by special permission these service drop leads may not be run along the building through two or more line insulators to get to the cap location.

2    **Snow Slides** - Many services have been pulled out or have been severely damaged by snow sliding off a roof during the winter months.  It is important that the entrance cap be very carefully located so that such slides cannot harm the service conduit and the Hydro service lines.  The gable end of the roof is the preferred location for the entrance cap.  The illustrations on pages 18 shows a number of possible service locations.

In the illustration above, one example shows the service leads terminating on the wall below the roof overhang. This is a poor location and may not be acceptable to Hydro because snow sliding off the roof during the winter months could damage these lines - actually pull them out.

**Note** - Service masts which run through any part of a roof, particularly the lower part of a roof, **may** also not be acceptable to some utility companies.  Therefore, in heavy snowfall districts the entrance cap should, wherever possible, be located on the **gable end** or similar location on the house where it will not be subject to damage by snow slides.

# 9. SERVICE MAST REQUIREMENTS - Rule 6-112(4)(5)(6) & (8) and Bulletin 6- 1 - 0

The illustration below shows the minimum requirements where a service mast is needed to raise the entrance cap and service leads to the required height.

**PIPE MAST** - These must be mounted on the **outside surface** of the building, Rules 6-206(1)(e) & 6-208(1).

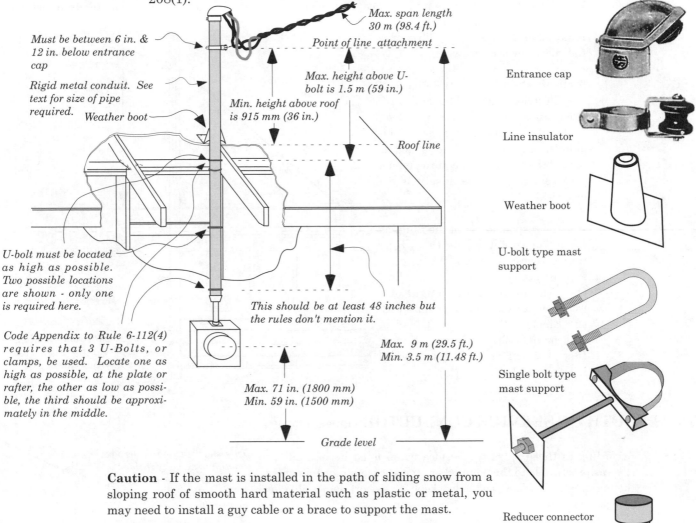

*Must be between 6 in. & 12 in. below entrance cap*

*Rigid metal conduit. See text for size of pipe required.*

*Weather boot*

*U-bolt must be located as high as possible. Two possible locations are shown - only one is required here.*

*Code Appendix to Rule 6-112(4) requires that 3 U-Bolts, or clamps, be used. Locate one as high as possible, at the plate or rafter, the other as low as possible, the third should be approximately in the middle.*

*Max. span length 30 m (98.4 ft.)*

*Point of line attachment*

*Max. height above U-bolt is 1.5 m (59 in.)*

*Min. height above roof is 915 mm (36 in.)*

*Roof line*

*This should be at least 48 inches but the rules don't mention it.*

*Max. 9 m (29.5 ft.)*
*Min. 3.5 m (11.48 ft.)*

*Max. 71 in. (1800 mm)*
*Min. 59 in. (1500 mm)*

*Grade level*

*Entrance cap*

*Line insulator*

*Weather boot*

*U-bolt type mast support*

*Single bolt type mast support*

*Reducer connector*

**Caution** - If the mast is installed in the path of sliding snow from a sloping roof of smooth hard material such as plastic or metal, you may need to install a guy cable or a brace to support the mast.

**Parts for an Acceptable Mast** - This may appear complicated but all the parts necessary for a service mast can be purchased in most building supply stores. The sales people in these stores will usually assist you in selecting the correct pieces for easy assembly of an acceptable service mast. It is not required that you use a CSA certified service mast kit; masts may be assembled from components suitable for such use.

**CSA certified electrical service mast kit** - The rule does not actually say we must use a mast kit but if you use conduit its diameter must be 2.5 inches. See also under caution below. A mast kit will usually include a length of 2 inch steel pipe (CSA refers to this as $2^{3}/_{8}$ inch but that is its outside diameter) which has been specially tested and certified for this purpose, an entrance cap and a special fitting for the lower end. It will also have the necessary U-bolts or clamps for fastening. The Appendix to this rule requires 3 U-bolts because a mast may extend as much as 59 inches above the roof. There will also be a weather boot and an insulated wireholder complete with pipe clamp so that it can be fastened to the mast as shown above.

**Caution -** **If you use a length of standard rigid metal conduit** for a service mast Rule 6-112(5) says it must be at least "2 $^{1}/_{2}$ (63) trade size". Note that the rule does not say "inches" but we can assume that is what is intended. Trade size means nominal size, which is its internal diameter. They are serious about this, we need $2^{1}/_{2}$ inch conduit.

Yes, there are probably a million 2 inch electrical conduit masts out there somewhere serving with valour but the unamended rule says that "if its conduit 2 inch pipe ain't big enough". And yes it does seem odd that the **rule** does not require a minimum length below the roof line to support this very strong 2½ inch pipe (the Bulletin requires this but the rule does not), and that it can be bolted to any 2 x 4 inch studded wall. It may also be a little difficult to find the necessary fittings for a 2½ inch pipe and therefore, you may decide to use a mast kit. It is a free country.

**Wood Mast** - Wood masts may be acceptable where, as shown in the illustration, a standard metal service mast cannot provide the required clearance for the lines on a flat roof or over a roadway.

A clarification in the 01/96 issue of the Electrical Safety Matters, a BC Government paper, says, in effect, that a wood service mast is acceptable but that it should be judged as part of the building structure and not as a service mast, because it is not electrical.

It is the responsibility of the Building Inspector to determine the size of timber required and the means of its support attachments to the building. Only the location and height of a wood service mast must comply with the Electrical Code as outlined in this book. Check first with your Inspector before installing a wood mast on any building.

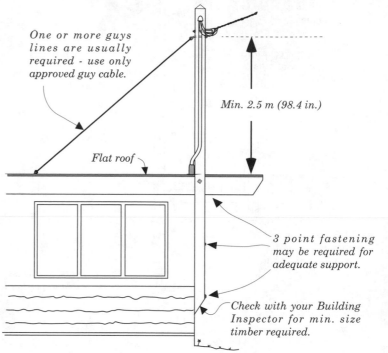

*One or more guys lines are usually required - use only approved guy cable.*

*Min. 2.5 m (98.4 in.)*

*Flat roof*

*3 point fastening may be required for adequate support.*

*Check with your Building Inspector for min. size timber required.*

## 10  LENGTH OF SERVICE CONDUCTOR - Rule 6-206(1)(e), 6-208

According to these rules the service panel must be located "as close as practicable to the point where the service conductors enter the building". That's a good rule - keep it as short as possible for two good reasons:

(1)     Because it is an unprotected conductor - only the Hydro line fuse, which is ahead of the transformer, is protecting you; and

(2)     The service run is very costly.

**(a)     Maximum length permitted OUTSIDE the building**

Where the service conductors are in a conduit or in a cable and run on the **outside surface** of the house the Code does not limit its length. It may be any reasonable length. Cost of material usually keeps this as short as possible.

**(b)     Maximum length permitted INSIDE the building**

Rule 6-206(1)(e) says the service panel must be "as close as practicable to the point where the consumer's service conductors enter the building." That means just through the wall as shown in the illustration.

*This short section of service conduit is actually inside the building but the BC guidelines say this arrangement is acceptable.*

*The service mast must be on the **outside surface** of the wall.*

*In this case the service panel is mounted opposite the meter base so that the service conductors inside the house are only about 12 inches long.*

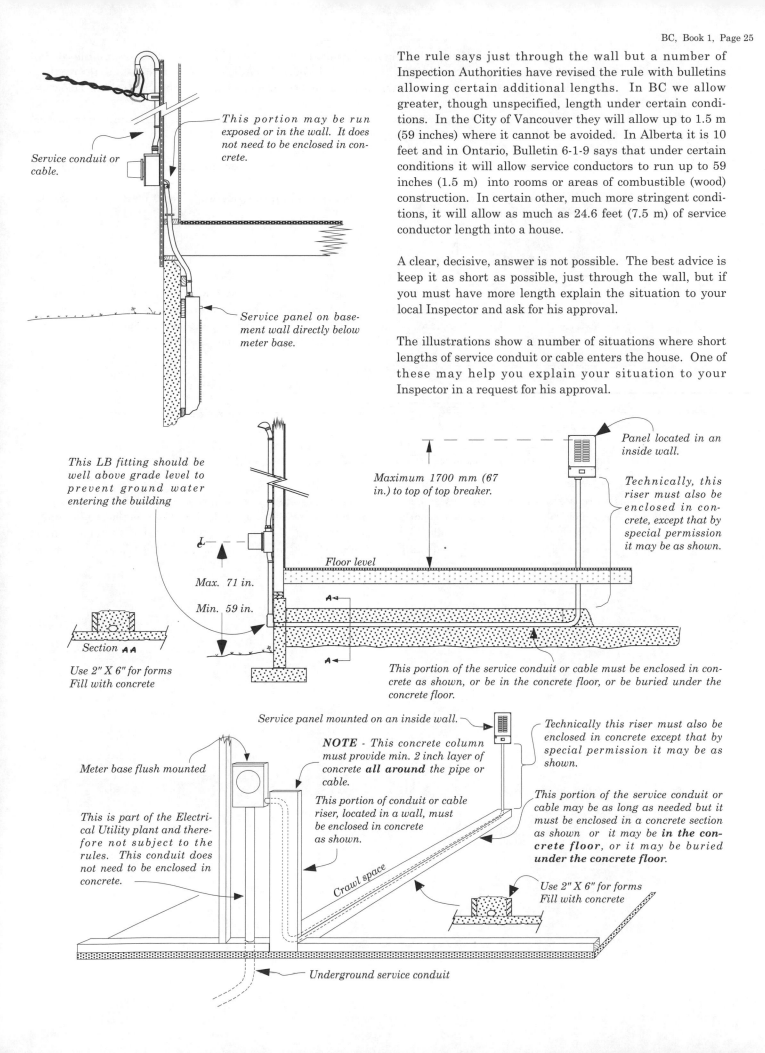

Service conduit or cable.

*This portion may be run exposed or in the wall. It does not need to be enclosed in concrete.*

*Service panel on basement wall directly below meter base.*

The rule says just through the wall but a number of Inspection Authorities have revised the rule with bulletins allowing certain additional lengths. In BC we allow greater, though unspecified, length under certain conditions. In the City of Vancouver they will allow up to 1.5 m (59 inches) where it cannot be avoided. In Alberta it is 10 feet and in Ontario, Bulletin 6-1-9 says that under certain conditions it will allow service conductors to run up to 59 inches (1.5 m) into rooms or areas of combustible (wood) construction. In certain other, much more stringent conditions, it will allow as much as 24.6 feet (7.5 m) of service conductor length into a house.

A clear, decisive, answer is not possible. The best advice is keep it as short as possible, just through the wall, but if you must have more length explain the situation to your local Inspector and ask for his approval.

The illustrations show a number of situations where short lengths of service conduit or cable enters the house. One of these may help you explain your situation to your Inspector in a request for his approval.

*This LB fitting should be well above grade level to prevent ground water entering the building*

*Max. 71 in.*

*Min. 59 in.*

Section **AA**

*Use 2" X 6" for forms*
*Fill with concrete*

*Maximum 1700 mm (67 in.) to top of top breaker.*

Floor level

*Panel located in an inside wall.*

*Technically, this riser must also be enclosed in concrete, except that by special permission it may be as shown.*

*This portion of the service conduit or cable must be enclosed in concrete as shown, or be in the concrete floor, or be buried under the concrete floor.*

Service panel mounted on an inside wall.

*Meter base flush mounted*

*NOTE - This concrete column must provide min. 2 inch layer of concrete* **all around** *the pipe or cable.*

*This portion of conduit or cable riser, located in a wall, must be enclosed in concrete as shown.*

*This is part of the Electrical Utility plant and therefore not subject to the rules. This conduit does not need to be enclosed in concrete.*

*Technically this riser must also be enclosed in concrete except that by special permission it may be as shown.*

*This portion of the service conduit or cable may be as long as needed but it must be enclosed in a concrete section as shown  or  it may be* **in the concrete floor**, *or it may be buried* **under the concrete floor.**

Crawl space

*Use 2" X 6" for forms*
*Fill with concrete*

Underground service conduit

**Note** - Where concrete encasement is required it must be at least two inches thick all around the conduit or cable. Where the conduit or cable runs inside a wall check carefully your wall thickness to insure there will be adequate space to provide for minimum all around covering as shown in the illustrations below.

It would be wonderful to have a clear workable standard all across Canada, a maximum length beyond which we could not go without first having to ask for special permission.

**Who's to blame?** - For more than 40 years we were permitted to run up to 20 feet of service conduit or cable inside a building then suddenly, with the adoption of the 1994 Code in late 1995, this length was reduced from twenty feet to less than one foot, just through the outside wall. Don't blame your Inspector for this change. It's not his fault.

**(c)    Boxed in Service Conduit or Cable**

As noted above there is no limit to the length of service conduit or cable which is run on the outside surface of the building being supplied. The condition here is that the service conduit or cable is, in fact, on the exterior; run on the outer surface of the building. Some think service conduit or cable is not a thing of beauty, that it should be covered, boxed in, that it is beautiful only when out of sight.

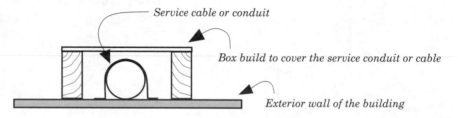

*Service cable or conduit*

*Box build to cover the service conduit or cable*

*Exterior wall of the building*

Before boxing-in exposed service conduit or cable, to hide it from view, you should check with your Inspector. The rule says service conductors must be as short as possible after they "enter the building". Since such boxing may be considered part of the building, the service conduit or cable, therefore, enters the building where it enters the boxing. Such an installation may therefore not be acceptable unless the authority enforcing the Code has agreed to accept it.

## 11   SERVICE CONDUIT or SERVICE CABLE

There are several different wiring methods permitted for service conductors.

> **(a)**     **EMT Thinwall Conduit** Method -  see this page,
> **(b)**     **Rigid PVC Conduit** Method -  see page 30,
> **(c)**     **Cable,** such as TECK 90 - see page 33.

**(a)**     **EMT - THINWALL SERVICE CONDUIT** - Rule 6-302(1)(c)

This is a thinwall conduit which cannot be threaded.  It requires very few tools for installation.

**(i)**     **Length** - See page 24 for maximum length permitted inside the building.

**(ii)**     **Couplings & Connectors** - Rule 12-1410

**Set Screw Type and Compression Type**

There are two main types of thinwall conduit couplings used today.

| Compression | Set Screw | Compression | Set Screw |
| Coupling | Coupling | Connector | Connector |

**Set Screw Type**
These may be used indoors or directly under a roof overhang or in concrete but may not be exposed to the weather.

**Compression Type** may be used in all cases wherever EMT is permitted.

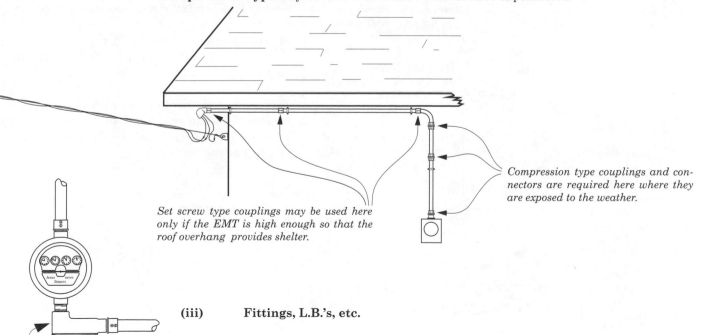

*Set screw type couplings may be used here only if the EMT is high enough so that the roof overhang provides shelter.*

*Compression type couplings and connectors are required here where they are exposed to the weather.*

*L.B. Fitting*

**(iii)**     **Fittings, L.B.'s, etc.**

**Ahead of Meter** - Power companies do not allow conduit fittings to be installed ahead of the meter base, however, on the load side of the base you may install as many as you require. Where it cannot be avoided and a fitting must be installed ahead of the base, you should seek Hydro permission first before proceeding.

**Problems using L.B. fittings** - Avoid using these fittings where service conductors are larger than #3 copper. Great care is needed when seating, or forming conductors into the fitting. Pull them into place one at a time being careful not to damage the insulation. It's okay to use a hammer to form the conductors into the fitting but do not apply directly on the insulation. Hold a smooth piece of wood against the conductors and drive that gently with a hammer.

**Double L.B. Problem** - Never use two LB fittings back to back for any conductors larger than #6. It is very difficult to force the conductors into the fitting without damaging the insulation in the process. Replace one of the fittings with a manufactured 90° bend.

*Avoid these conduit fittings if at all possible even on the load side of the meter because it can be very difficult to get the conductors to lie properly in the fitting. The conductors for 100 amp and larger services are very stiff.*

*Never use two fittings back to back as shown when the conductors are #4 or larger.*

*It is too difficult to force these conductors into this second LB fitting. Replace this second LB fitting with a quarter bend.*

*Threaded LB fittings*

**Accessible** - L.B. Fittings must be Accessible - These must be located where they will remain accessible for any maintenance work that may be required in the future.

**(iv) Bends** - Rule 12-1412 & 12-942 - The maximum permitted is the equivalent of four quarter bends (4 - 90° bends). These must be made without damage to the pipe. You can bend this pipe yourself but not on the truck bumper or around a tree. Bends must be made with a bending tool, called a hickey. You should be able to rent one from the local tool rental shop. The pipe must remain round, not oval in shape and there should not be any kinks and no, you may not heat this pipe (EMT), to bend it.

**(v) Service (Metal) Conduit Bonding** - Rule 10-604

**Locknuts and bushings** are no longer acceptable for service conduit bonding. A **grounding type bushing and a jumper**, as shown below, must be used and these must be installed where shown.

**Size of jumpers** - Use a # 8 copper jumper for any size service up to 100 amp. and a #6 copper jumper for a 101 to 200 ampere service, Code Table 41

This bonding jumper is in addition to the locknuts which connect the conduit at both ends. It may be a bit much, we haven't needed it for forty years, but now we do - it's the law.

*Bonding type bushing not required here. EMT connector threads into meter base hub.*

*Meter base is bonded with the service neutral conductor, Rule 10-516(2).*

*EMT is shown here but rigid PVC conduit is also acceptable for a service.*

*Bonding type bushing is not required here. This conduit nipple is bonded at the lower end.*

*Meter base*

*This conduit may be just a short length through the wall or it may be many feet long. In every case bonding jumpers are required only at one end.*

*Rigid metal conduit nipple. EMT or PVC could be used here instead.*

*Only one locknut is required for an EMT connector. If rigid metal conduit is used 2 locknuts and a bushing must be used.*

*Grounding jumper*

*Neutral bonding screw*

*Service grounding conductor*

*Grounding type bushing*

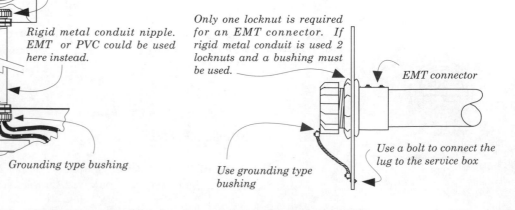

*EMT connector*

*Use grounding type bushing*

*Use a bolt to connect the lug to the service box*

The meter base must be bonded to ground with the service neutral conductor as shown.

**Note** (a) If the nipple between the meter base and the panel is rigid metal conduit, not EMT, then two locknuts are required in addition to the bonding jumper shown above.

**Note** **(b)** **Locknuts are dished**, that is they are not flat. They are designed to bite through the paint or rust and into the metal of the box. This is necessary to provide good grounding for the equipment. Make sure you install them with the sharp edges facing the panel wall where they will cut through the paint when they are tightened.

**Note** **(c)** Bushings must be grounding type and where the conductors are #8 or larger, the bushings must have an insulating ring, such as plastic or nylon, mounted in the throat to protect the service conductors.

**(vi)** **Strapping** - Rules 12-1404

Install one strap within 1 m (39 in.) of the top, (entrance cap) end, another within 1 m (39 in.) of the meter base. Install additional straps between as required so that the maximum distance between straps is not more than 2 m (approx. 6 ft.).

**(vii) Sealing** - Rule 6-312

The seal required by this rule prevents the warmer inside air from escaping through the service conduit. It has been found that the warm air, if allowed to flow, condenses to water in sufficient quantity to damage the service equipment.

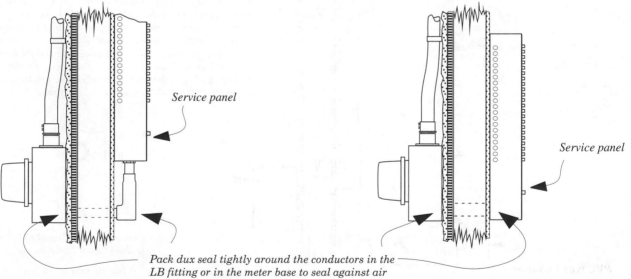

*Service panel*

*Service panel*

*Pack dux seal tightly around the conductors in the LB fitting or in the meter base to seal against air flow through the service conduit.*

This seal is usually made with a soft putty-like substance called DUX SEAL. To be most effective the DUX SEAL is placed around the conductors in the last opening, before the conduit leaves the warmer area.

**(b)    RIGID PVC CONDUIT** - Rule 6-302(1)(a)

In most cases PVC conduit is acceptable for services.  It has an advantage - very few tools are required to install it and there is no need for bonding bushings and bonding jumpers.

— Be sure to remove rough burrs from the inside edge of the pipe ends, where it has been cut. Do this with any knife.

— Be sure the pipe and fittings are clean and dry before applying solvent cement.

The illustration shows the arrangement of fittings required when installing PVC service conduit.  The female adapter and close metal conduit nipple shown above the meter base are required to prevent this conduit breaking at this point, Rule 12-1112(2).  The PVC terminal adapter used below the meter base is acceptable only where it enters an enclosure through a knock-out hole; it may not be used in a threaded hole such as the top entry into the meter base.

*PVC Entrance Cap*

*PVC service conduit*

*Cut-away view of a PVC female adapter*

*Close **Metal** Conduit Nipple*

*PVC Terminal adapter*

*PVC Conduit*

*PVC type LB fitting*

*Rule 12-1112 requires that where PVC conduit must terminate in a threaded hub, as in a meter base or in an LB fitting shown below, we must switch  from PVC pipe to a short length of metal pipe using a PVC female adapter.  Use a PVC female adapter and close metal conduit nipple shown in the exploded view.*

*The PVC terminal adapter shown entering the bottom of the meter base  is acceptable in that location because it is held with a locknut , it is not threaded into a hub . This terminal adapter may not be used to enter the top of the base, it would break too easily in a threaded hub.*

*Rule 12-1102(2) says PVC conduit must not be  enclose in  building insulation.  This means, technically, that it may not be run through an outside (insulated) wall as shown.  Converting to a short metal conduit for this part of the run may be difficult.  A simple, technical, solution is to run the pipe close to a stud or, if that is not possible, to strap it to a short section of stud material as shown below.  This prevents building insulation from "enclosing" the PVC pipe and then it becomes acceptable in this location.  (If we use the ordinary dictionary definition of  enclosed  because it is not defined in the Code, see under "Definitions" on page one of the Code.*

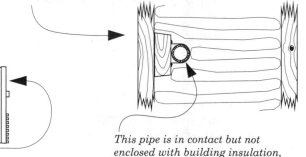

*This pipe is in contact but not enclosed with building insulation,*

*Service panel shown mounted on the surface of an outside wall.  Some provincial inspection authorities will not permit a service panel recessed **into** a wall which is required to be insulated.  See also page 40.*

The illustration also shows PVC conduit running through an external wall into the back of the panel. This external wall is required, by the Building Code, to be insulated.  Technically, therefore, it is not correct to run PVC conduit through this insulated wall.  You could get into big trouble with it because Rule 12-1102(2) says PVC conduit may not be "enclosed in thermal insulation".  Yes, it's only a short nipple and maybe no one would question it, but Rule 12-1102(2) says 'Thou shalt not'.  The rule is there and could quite correctly be enforced.  The solution suggested above is also strictly technical, but it is Code.  All that is required is to ensure that the PVC conduit is not "enclosed", (completely surrounded) with building insulation.  To do as suggested above may be a nuisance but the alternative, required by Code, is costly.

**(i)   Fittings - L.B's, L.Ls, etc.**

Power companies do not normally allow conduit fittings to be installed ahead of the meter base, however, on the load side of the base you may install as many fittings as you require. Where it cannot be avoided and a fitting must be installed ahead of the base, you should seek Hydro permission first before proceeding.

**Problems using L.B. fittings** - Avoid using these fittings where service conductors are larger than #3 copper. Great care is needed when seating, or forming conductors into the fitting. Pull them into place one at a time being careful not to damage the insulation. It's okay to use a hammer to form the conductors into the fitting but do not apply directly on the insulation. Hold a smooth piece of wood against the conductors and drive that gently with a hammer.

*PVC L.B. Fitting & pipe*

**Double L.B. Problem** - Never use two LB fittings back to back for any conductors larger than #6. It is very difficult to force the conductors into the fitting without damaging the insulation in the process. Replace one of the fittings with a 90° bend.

*Avoid these conduit fittings if at all possible even on the load side of the meter because it can be very difficult to get the conductors to lie properly in the fitting. The conductors for 100 amp and larger services are very stiff.*

*Never use two fittings back to back as shown when the conductors are #4 or larger.*

*It is too difficult to force these conductors into this second LB fitting. Replace this second LB fitting with a quarter bend.*

*PVC pipe & LB fittings*

**L.B. Fittings must be Accessible** - These must be located where they will remain accessible for any maintenance work that may be required in the future.

**(ii)   Bends** - Rules 12-1108 & 12-1112

Manufactured Bends - The maximum number of bends permitted by the rule is the equivalent of four quarter bends (4 - 90° bends or any combination of bends where the total does not exceed 360°), Rule 12-942.

**Home Made Bends** - Not Recommended - Avoid this if you can but if your installation requires a special bend you can take advantage of the fact that PVC conduit may be bent in the field. To do this the pipe must be carefully heated to 260° F at the location of the proposed bend. It is best to use a heat gun to heat the pipe. An open flame could also be used, the Code does not prohibit it, but in that case it must be done very carefully to avoid damaging the pipe. Too much heat will char the pipe or blister its smooth surface and that could be grounds for rejection. Make sure the bend section is uniformly heated all around for a distance of about 10 times the pipe diameter before you attempt to bend it. Improper heating or improper bending procedures may cause the pipe to collapse, or even worse, kink and that would very likely result in a rejection of your installation. One more thing, there is a small amount of spring back when the pipe cools. To compensate for this loss you will need to overbend it a few degrees more than is required.

*PVC pipe & couplings*

**(iii)   Strapping** - Rule 12-1114

Install one strap at the top, within 1 m (39 in.) of the entrance cap, another strap near the bottom, within 1 m (39 in.) of the meter base. Install additional straps as required so that the maximum distance between any two straps is not more than 2 m (approx 6 ft.).

Note that PVC conduit has a high coefficient of expansion. This means that it is a bit longer in the summer than in the winter. If it is exposed to direct sunlight it is even longer. For short runs, 10 ft or less, this is not a great concern but longer runs should be supported with straps that will permit the conduit to slide when it expands with temperature change.

**(iv)**     **Sealing - to stop breathing** - Rule 6-312

The seal required by this rule prevents the warmer inside air from escaping through the service conduit. It has been found that warm air, if allowed to flow through the service conduit, will condense to water in sufficient quantity to damage service equipment.

The seal is usually made with a soft putty like substance called DUX SEAL. To be most effective DUX SEAL is carefully placed to close all openings around the conductors in the last opening before the conduit leaves the inside of the house or in the first opening outside of the house. Only one seal is required. Make sure all openings around each conductor are completely sealed to prevent any air passage through the conduit.

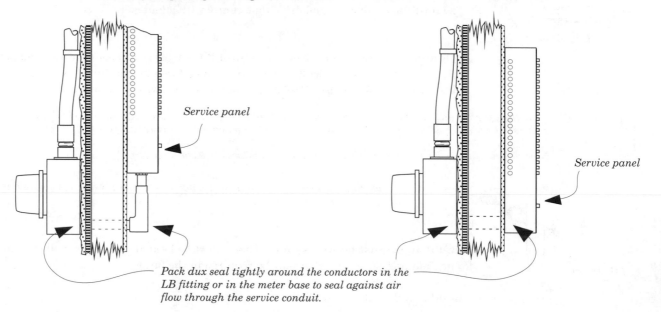

*Service panel*

*Service panel*

*Pack dux seal tightly around the conductors in the
LB fitting or in the meter base to seal against air
flow through the service conduit.*

**(v)**     **Holes in Outer Walls, floors or Roofs** - Rules 12-018 & 12-926  - These rules require that we fill in any openings around conduit or cable where these pass through an outer wall or a roof or a floor. This is not exactly electrical work but your Electrical Inspector will check this part of your installation and he is required to yell at you, or stomp his feet, if this is not properly done for the final inspection.

**(c)    SERVICE CABLE - FROM AN OVERHEAD HYDRO SUPPLY**

**(i)    Type** - Rule 6-302(1) says types ACWU75, ACWU90, AC90 or TECK90 cables may be used

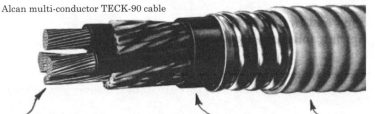

Alcan multi-conductor TECK-90 cable

*Bare Bonding Conductor*          *PVC Inner Jacket*          *PVC Outer Jacket*

Service cable is easier to install than conduit. Each of these service cables differs from the others in some way. The illustration below shows the construction of a TECK-90 cable.

**(ii)    Size** - The ampacity required for a service cable is the same as for an equivalent size conductor in conduit.   See pages 8 & 9 for sizes required.

**(iii)    Type of Entrance Cap to Use** - Rule 6-114

*Entrance cap for use on EMT*

*Entrance cap suitable for TECK cable.*

Unless you can find an entrance cap fitted with a cable connector, as shown, you really need a TECK cable connector to terminate your cable in an entrance cap which has a threaded hub.  A weatherproof connector, such as shown below, must be used where the cap is exposed to the weather.

**Entrance caps designed for EMT** are not certified for use with service cable.  They are equipped with set screws which hold the cap in place on EMT but if used on a cable could damage the cable insulation.  They are economical, fit quite well, and are often used on cable but check first with your Inspector before installing an EMT type entrance cap on a TECK cable.

*Entrance cap with threaded hub.*

*Heat shrink boot installed*

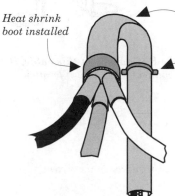

*The radius of this bend must not be less than six times the external diameter of the TECK cable*

*Strap required here*

*Rule 6-114(3) says that where we use a heat shrink boot instead of an entrance cap the cable must be bent downward as shown.  Note the additional length required to make this bend.*

**Heat Shrink Entrance cap** - This is a kind of plastic sock that slips over the top end of your service cable.  To install this sock you must remove the outer PVC jacket, the armour and the inner PVC jacket for approx 30 inches.  You should now have 30 inches of **insulated** conductors exposed for the drip loops and for connection to Hydro lines.

**Slip this sock in place,** then very carefully apply heat, as evenly as possible, with an open gas torch or heat gun, (heat lamps could also be used) as long as the heat applied is approximately 250°F.  Apply heat

*Anti-short bushing*

evenly and do not overheat the material.  When heat is applied the sock will shrink to fit snugly in place. It will seal it from rain but remember, the rule says **it must still face downward when installed**.  Be sure to allow enough length to do this.

**(iv)    Cable Connectors** - Use weatherproof connectors where the cable connects to the top of the meter base.  Be sure to use the correct size and type for the cable you are using.  Your supplier will advise you on this.

**Dry type connectors** may be used only where they are not exposed to the weather.

**Note - Anti-Short Bushings**, shown at left, must be used with dry type connectors.  This is a fibre or plastic bushing that fits into the end,

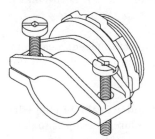

inside the armour, of the cable. It protects the conductor insulation at the point where they issue from the armour. This thing is wholly inside the connector but its presence can be easily verified through the small openings provided by the manufacturer for this detective work. It is easier to put it in place when the cable is being installed. Later, after it has been rejected, it is much more difficult to do this.

**(v)**      **Length of Service Cable Permitted** - Rule 6-206 & 6-208

**Outside of the house** - Service cable which is run along the outside surface of the house may be as long as it needs to be to get where your going. However, this cable is expensive; you will want to keep it as short as possible.

**Service cable run INSIDE the house** - The rule says service equipment, (the service panel) must be located so that the length of service cable run **inside the house** can be kept as short as practicable. See page 24 for details on maximum lengths and the exceptions permitted.

**Very Long Service Runs** - Rule 6-208 - Where the panel location is well within the building we can take advantage of another rule which permits us to install long runs of service cable inside a building if it is enclosed in at least 2 inches of solid concrete (all around covering) or if it is buried in the ground under the floor. The illustrations on page 25 show such an installation for conduit. A cable would be installed a little differently but the principle remains the same; any conduit or cable which is enclosed in at least 2 inches of concrete is considered to be outside the house and may, therefore, be as long as needed.

**(vi)**      **Strapping** - Rule 12-618 - Cable must be strapped every 59 inches (1.5 m).

**(vii)**      **Meter Connections** - Rules 10-516(2) & 10-906(3)

*Do not cut away the PVC jacket on this cable, it must run into the connector in this wet location.*

*The bare bonding wire must terminate in a separate grounding lug which is bolted to the side wall of the meter box, as shown. Do not use one of the wood screws for this purpose, Rule 10-906(3).*

*Cable neutral may be spliced in the meter base.*

*Cable neutral must be connected to this neutral terminal in the meter base.*

*Stuff dux seal around conductors at this point.*

**(viii)**      **Mechanical Damage** -.Greater care is needed when installing this cable than is required when installing conduit. This cable is more easily damaged with driven nails or where it is run on the surface of a wall.

Where the cable is run on the surface of the wall and where it may be subject to mechanical damage (in locations such as a garage or carport for example) the cable may be protected with wooden or metal guards or a short section of metal pipe may be used.

In the illustration below, the cable is shown running through the plate and over the broken edge of the foundation wall. This section of cable (where it runs through the plate) is subject to damage and must be protected. Use heavy gauge metal plates to protect the cable at these points. The side plates of metal sectional outlet boxes do this very well.

The illustration below shows TECK cable being used above the meter base to an overhead supply and from the meter base to the panel. It also shows PVC conduit from the meter base downward to an underground Hydro system. Obviously, only one of these systems will be available - either overhead supply or underground supply and therefore only the TECK cable running up or the PVC conduit running down is necessary. Both systems are shown to indicate different methods of installation.

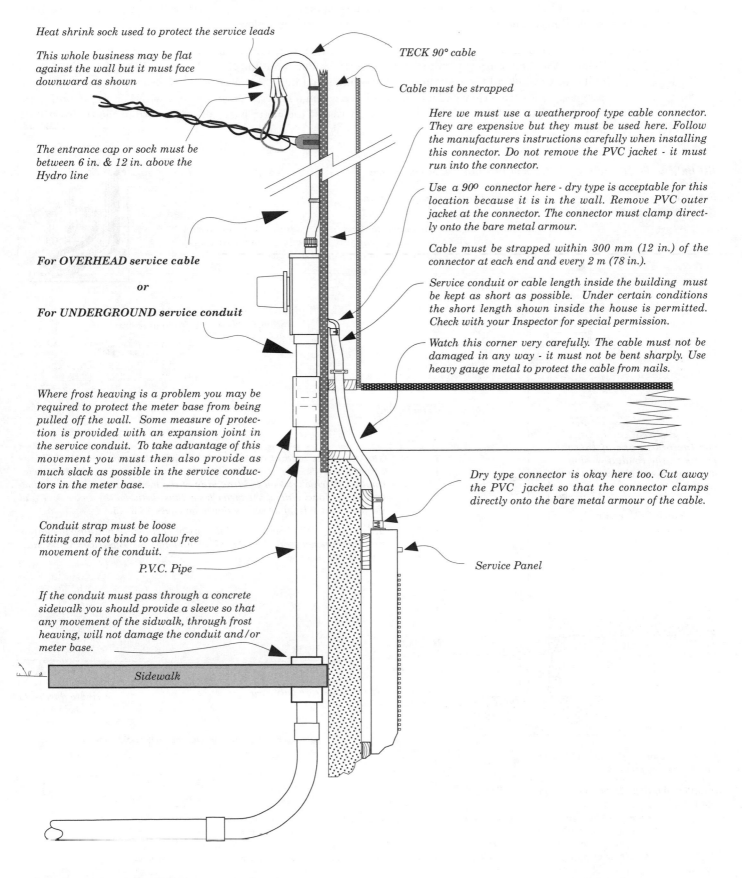

*Heat shrink sock used to protect the service leads*

*This whole business may be flat against the wall but it must face downward as shown*

*The entrance cap or sock must be between 6 in. & 12 in. above the Hydro line*

**For OVERHEAD service cable**

*or*

**For UNDERGROUND service conduit**

*Where frost heaving is a problem you may be required to protect the meter base from being pulled off the wall. Some measure of protection is provided with an expansion joint in the service conduit. To take advantage of this movement you must then also provide as much slack as possible in the service conductors in the meter base.*

*Conduit strap must be loose fitting and not bind to allow free movement of the conduit.*

*P.V.C. Pipe*

*If the conduit must pass through a concrete sidewalk you should provide a sleeve so that any movement of the sidewalk, through frost heaving, will not damage the conduit and/or meter base.*

*Sidewalk*

*TECK 90° cable*

*Cable must be strapped*

*Here we must use a weatherproof type cable connector. They are expensive but they must be used here. Follow the manufacturers instructions carefully when installing this connector. Do not remove the PVC jacket - it must run into the connector.*

*Use a 90º connector here - dry type is acceptable for this location because it is in the wall. Remove PVC outer jacket at the connector. The connector must clamp directly onto the bare metal armour.*

*Cable must be strapped within 300 mm (12 in.) of the connector at each end and every 2 m (78 in.).*

*Service conduit or cable length inside the building must be kept as short as possible. Under certain conditions the short length shown inside the house is permitted. Check with your Inspector for special permission.*

*Watch this corner very carefully. The cable must not be damaged in any way - it must not be bent sharply. Use heavy gauge metal to protect the cable from nails.*

*Dry type connector is okay here too. Cut away the PVC jacket so that the connector clamps directly onto the bare metal armour of the cable.*

*Service Panel*

## 12    SERVICE from an UNDERGROUND SUPPLY

**(a)    Hydro Connection** - Re: BC Hydro Eng.. Standards for underground service ducting - The illustration below shows a typical electrical service supplied from an underground electrical distribution system.

**(b)    Trench** - It is the owners responsibility to: prepare the needed trench, provide the required material, and install it.  Hydro stub-off duct is marked with a stake.  It is usually located 900 mm (36 in.) below grade level.  Depth of burial should be as shown in the illustration below.

**(c)    Duct** - Use 3 inch rigid DB2/ES2 PVC conduit which is readily available at local building supply stores. Remove the temporary cap on the end of the Hydro duct and find the pull cord in that pipe.   Extend this pull cord to reach all the way through the conduit and into the meter base.  Hydro want you to use 3 mm polypropylene cord.  They will use this cord to draw in a heavy rope which they will then use to pull in the service cables.  Make sure this cord is securely tied at the meter base and to the cord in the Hydro stub-off pipe.

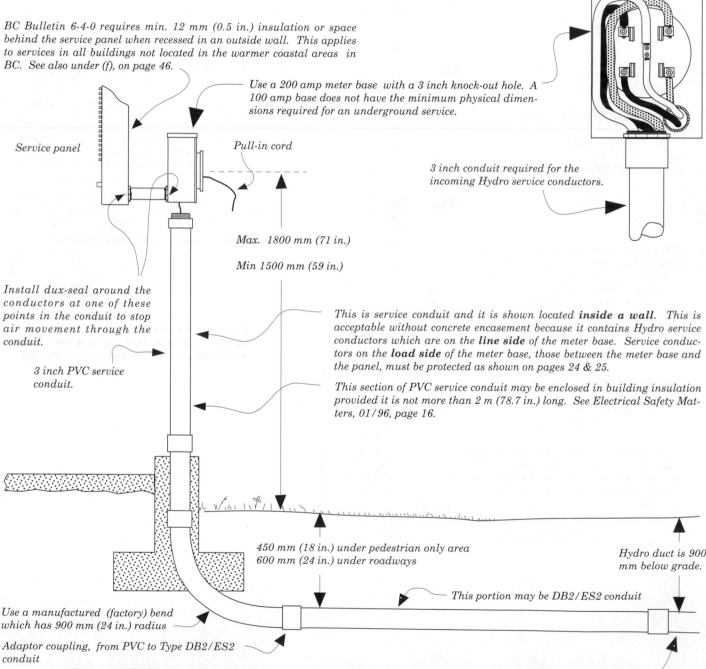

*BC Bulletin 6-4-0 requires min. 12 mm (0.5 in.) insulation or space behind the service panel when recessed in an outside wall.  This applies to services in all buildings not located in the warmer coastal areas  in BC.  See also under (f), on page 46.*

*Use a 200 amp meter base  with a 3 inch knock-out hole.  A 100 amp base does not have the minimum physical dimensions required for an underground service.*

*Service panel*

*Pull-in cord*

*3 inch conduit required for the incoming Hydro service conductors.*

*Max.  1800 mm (71 in.)*

*Min 1500 mm (59 in.)*

*Install dux-seal around the conductors at one of these points in the conduit to stop air movement through the conduit.*

*This is service conduit and it is shown located **inside a wall**.  This is acceptable without concrete encasement because it contains Hydro service conductors which are on the **line side** of the meter base.  Service conductors on the **load side** of the meter base, those between the meter base and the panel, must be protected as shown on pages 24 & 25.*

*3 inch PVC service conduit.*

*This section of PVC service conduit may be enclosed in building insulation provided it is not more than 2 m (78.7 in.) long.  See Electrical Safety Matters, 01/96, page 16.*

*450 mm (18 in.) under pedestrian only area*
*600 mm (24 in.) under roadways*

*Hydro duct is 900 mm below grade.*

*This portion may be DB2/ES2 conduit*

*Use a manufactured  (factory) bend which has 900 mm (24 in.) radius*

*Adaptor coupling,  from PVC to Type DB2/ES2 conduit*

*Hydro installs this 3 inch underground service conduit to your property line and places a temporary cap on the end of their conduit to keep it clean.  Remove the temporary cap, find the pull cord and extend it with 3 mm polypropylene cord which is long enough to reach through the meter base.  Thread this cord through each length of duct as you install it.  When completed this cord should be accessible at the meter base as shown.*

**Sand Bed** - Hydro may require a 3 inch layer of sand both below and above the duct where it is buried in very rocky earth.

**Do not cover** underground duct until the formal declaration has been submitted to Hydro. Hydro will provide the required form.

**Pull-in Cord** - Don't forget to install a 3 mm polypropylene pull cord in the pipe for the Hydro installation crew. This is a must. They will use this cord to draw in a heavy rope which they will then use to pull in the service cables.

**(d)**   **Bends** - Keep the underground conduit in as straight a line as possible. The total number of bends must not exceed 135°.

**(e)**   **Water entry** - Make sure there is adequate drainage of the underground conduit system before it enters the house. Special drainage and a seal may be required where the meter base is lower than Hydro's' underground distribution system.

**(f)**   **Meter base** - for an Underground Distribution System.

The meter base for a service from an underground supply system must be rated 200 amps. This large base is required to allow the 3 inch service conduit to enter the enclosure. The large service conductors used by Hydro for an underground service requires more physical space than is available in a standard 100 ampere meter base.

One more thing, the connector lugs inside the base must be properly rated for the size of underground service conductors used.

Check with your local power company to make sure there are no other hiccups that could cost you time and money when you finally ask them for that power connection.

**(g)**   **Length of Service Run Inside the house**

This must be kept as short as possible which means only about 8 inches through the exterior wall. The Provincial Government released guide lines in January 96 which revised the rule to allow longer runs under certain conditions. It is understood that these longer lengths, described on pages 24 & 25, will again apply under this new Code.

**(f)**   **Sealing - Rule 6-312**

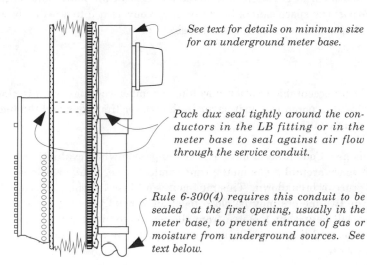

*See text for details on minimum size for an underground meter base.*

*Pack dux seal tightly around the conductors in the LB fitting or in the meter base to seal against air flow through the service conduit.*

*Rule 6-300(4) requires this conduit to be sealed at the first opening, usually in the meter base, to prevent entrance of gas or moisture from underground sources. See text below.*

The seal required by this rule prevents the warmer inside air from escaping through the service conduit. It has been found that the warm air, if allowed to flow, condenses to water in sufficient quantity to damage the service equipment.

This seal is usually made with a soft, putty-like substance called DUX SEAL. To be most effective the DUX SEAL is placed around the conductors in the last opening before the conduit leaves the warmer area.

# 13  METER BASE INSTALLATION

(a)     **Types** - In general there are two types of meter bases available, the round and the square or shoe box type. Both types are acceptable for services supplied from **overhead lines**. Make sure your base has the correct rating in amperes.

    **Note 1** For an underground service the power utility usually requires a 200 ampere meter base. This large base must be used to provide sufficient depth for the 3 inch underground service conduit entry required by Hydro and adequate working space for Hydro crew to do their work inside the base.

    **Note 2** If the knockouts provided by the manufacturer of the base are not in the correct position and new holes need to be punched out, these new holes must be totally below any live parts in the meter base. Only where a meter base is installed totally indoors, as in a service room in an apartment building, may new holes be cut above the live parts in the base.

    By the way, if you plan to use an old round type meter base which has side or back conduit entry holes, be careful. First, because some utilities do not accept them and second, only the top and bottom entries in round bases may be used where these round bases are allowed at all. One more thing, many of those old meter bases were not designed to permit splicing of the neutral in the base. This means the round base may not be suitable if you are using TECK cable for service conductors. The round base is not acceptable for an underground service.

(b)     **Locations**

Power companies usually want the meter base as close to the front of the house as possible. The illustration on page 18 shows that the preferred location of the service entrance cap and meter base is within the first 3 ft of the front of the house facing the power line.

Meter locations must be carefully chosen. Some of the things to watch for are:

(i)     **Carports**

If you plan to face your meter base into the carport you should know that there is no code rule or bulletin which specifically says you may not have it there. However, before you install it in the carport you should talk to your local Hydro people. They may not like it there.

Fact is, no matter how careful you are as a driver, when you are backing in your 50 ft. Winnebago that meter is subject to damage if it faces into the carport.

Every year there are thousands of carports closed in to make a garage or an additional bedroom. If the meter faces into the carport the space cannot be closed in to convert it into a bedroom without first relocating the meter base. This is usually a costly relocation.

(ii)     **Porch**

If it is an open porch it may be an acceptable location now but remember you may want to close it in later on in the future. A closed in porch is a heat saver in the winter time, so avoid the hassle, follow old Chinese proverb - don't do it on the porch.

(iii)     **Gas Meter Rule 2-322** - This new Code takes a more relaxed approach when evaluating a possible hazardous location. The space around a gas meter vent would not become hazardous except as a result of an accident, rupture or breakdown. This means it is a Class 1, Zone 2 location, Rule 18-006(c)(ii), and therefore the two meters may be close together if need be. Note, if your proposed electric meter location will be within 1 metre from the gas meter vent you should check with the gas supplier first. Some utilities may still insist on at least 1 m separation between the gas meter vent and the power meter.

**(c)** **Meter Base Height**

Meters must be located on an outside wall, facing out. They must be located somewhere between 59 inches (1500 mm) and 71 inches (1800 mm) above finished grade. All heights to be measured from the center of the base to permanent grade level.

**(d)** **Connections**

Rule 10-516(2) requires the neutral to be connected to the meter base as shown. All modern meter bases have provision for connecting the neutral from both the line and the load. Some of the older meter bases may not be properly equipped to make a splice in the neutral conductor. In those cases simply bare a section of the conductor where it passes the bonding terminal in the meter base - then slip it into the lug provided and tighten. Do not cut this conductor unless it is necessary to do so.

*Incoming black wires from Hydro connect to the top two terminals.*

*Load black wires connect to the lower terminals.*

*The white wire is also used to bond the meter base, Rule 10-518(2). Connect this neutral conductor to the bonding terminal in the base as shown. If you are using an older round base do not cut and splice the neutral - simply bare a section and lay it in the connector. The bonding terminal in some old meter bases were not designed for splicing .*

Incoming Service conduit

240 Volts 3-wire

**(e)** **Support**

Support the meter base with wood screws through the two or more factory drilled holes in the back of the base. Make sure it is in a reasonably accurate upright position.

**(f)** **Blank Cover** - BC Bulletin 6-5-0

In some districts the power utility will energize the electrical service but not install a meter until several days later. During this time a blank cover is required to prevent anyone coming in contact with live parts. A disk of $^1/_4$ in. plywood may also be used for this purpose.

**(g)** **Sealing Rings**

Meter sockets are equipped with either a screw type sealing ring or a spring type ring. Some Power Company's will not accept the spring clip type ring. Check with your power company.

Screw type meter ring

**(h)Fittings & LBs etc.**

**Ahead of Meter** - Some power companies do not allow fittings to be installed ahead of a meter base. This has something to do with stealing power which power company's have decided is bad for business. However, on the load side of the base you may install as many as you require. Where it cannot be avoided and a fitting must be installed ahead of the base you should seek Hydro permission before proceeding. They may be satisfied if the fitting is within sight of the meter and the fitting has been drilled to permit Hydro personnel to install a seal. See also the note on pages 28 and 31 regarding two LB fittings.

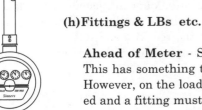
L.B. Fitting

## 14 SERVICE PANEL

**(a)**       **Type - Fuse or Breaker Panel -** Both are acceptable, however, only the circuit breaker panel is in common use today.  For this reason we will deal with circuit breaker panels only.  The illustration below shows a typical breaker panel and the cut-away in the cover shows the connections required for 3 wire cables.

**(b)**       **3-WIRE CABLES & TIE-BARS - WHEN ARE THESE REQUIRED -** Note the different uses for 3wire cables.

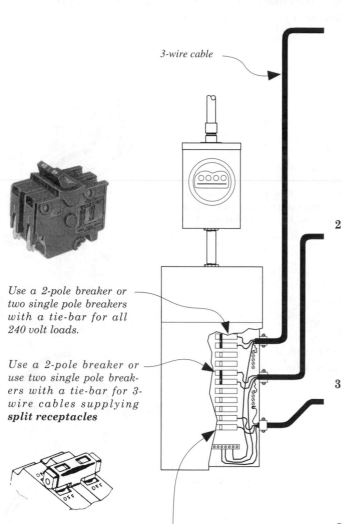

*3-wire cable*

*Use a 2-pole breaker or two single pole breakers with a tie-bar for all 240 volt loads.*

*Use a 2-pole breaker or use two single pole breakers with a tie-bar for 3-wire cables supplying* **split receptacles**

*Tie-bar not required but* **hot wires must connect to adjacent breakers** *as shown.*

**1**  **Circuit Breaker For 3-Wire Cables Supplying 240 Volt Loads -** Rule 14-010(b) is concerned with safety for anyone working on equipment such as **ranges, dryers, or electric heaters** which are supplied with 240 volts.  Two hot wires, and sometimes a neutral, are required in the supply cable to serve 240 volt equipment and both of the hot lines in this cable must be opened simultaneously whenever the supply breaker is turned off.  The best way to do this is with a two-pole circuit breaker which will open both hot lines with the operation of one handle.  However, the rule also permits two single pole breakers to be used instead, provided the operating handles are mechanically connected together with an approved tie-bar so that with one operation both circuit breakers are opened.

**2**  **Circuit Breaker For 3-Wire Cables supplying split duplex receptacles -** Kitchen counter plug outlets are required to be split duplex receptacles and these must be supplied with 3-wire cable.  These outlets supply only 120 volts but each receptacle is in fact supplied with 240 volts because both hot lines in the 3-wire supply cable are connected to it.  For this reason the rule requires either a two-pole breaker or two single-pole breakers (with a tie-bar to link their operating handles) to supply these 3-wire cables.

**3**  **Circuit Breaker For 3-Wire Cables supplying lights and ordinary duplex Plug Outlets -** Lights and convenience plug outlets (except split duplex receptacles on the kitchen counter) are connected to only one hot line and the neutral when supplied with a 3-wire cable.  Circuit breakers used to protect these 3-wire cables need not be 2-pole type nor do we need to install tie-bars when using two single pole breakers to supply these loads.

**CAUTION -** When connecting 3-wire cables in the panel make very sure that the black and the red wires are connected to two different circuit breakers which are located side-by-side, (one above the other).  The reason for this is not to install a tie-bar because, as noted above, a tie-bar is not always required by the rules.  The reason is load balance, and thus safety.  The neutral conductor in a **correctly connected** 3-wire cable carries only the **unbalance current**, usually much less than either the black or the red wire.  However, if the 3-wire cable is **incorrectly connected** the neutral wire must carry the **sum of the loads** in the black wire and the red wire and this could cause overheating of this neutral wire.  Make sure each 3-wire cable is connected to breakers located next to each other, as shown in the panel above.

**4**  **Bathroom Razor Outlet -** Rule 26-700(11) -  These must be supplied with a GFCI, (Ground Fault Circuit Interrupter) type circuit breaker or you may use a ground fault circuit interrupter type receptacle.  The old special transformer type razor outlet is no longer approved and may not be installed in new construction but may only be installed to replace a faulty unit in an existing installation.  A better alternative is to replace the old transformer type plug outlet with a special faceplate that fits over the large existing outlet box and transforms it so that a single GFI type receptacle may be installed. Note that in some older installations there may not be a bonding conductor in this bathroom outlet. Rule 26-700(8) now allows a GFCI type receptacle to be used here even when there is no bonding conductor in the outlet box.

**(c)**      **Identify Circuits** - Kinds of Loads Served - Rule 2-100(2)&(3)

Use a felt pen or some other permanent manner of marking next to the circuit breaker or fill in the circuit directory card provided by the panel manufacturer. The identification should look something like this.

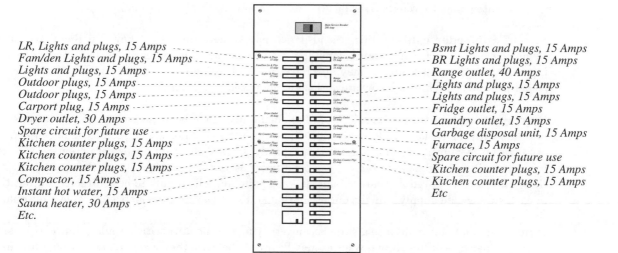

*LR, Lights and plugs, 15 Amps*
*Fam/den Lights and plugs, 15 Amps*
*Lights and plugs, 15 Amps*
*Outdoor plugs, 15 Amps*
*Outdoor plugs, 15 Amps*
*Carport plug, 15 Amps*
*Dryer outlet, 30 Amps*
*Spare circuit for future use*
*Kitchen counter plugs, 15 Amps*
*Kitchen counter plugs, 15 Amps*
*Kitchen counter plugs, 15 Amps*
*Compactor, 15 Amps*
*Instant hot water, 15 Amps*
*Sauna heater, 30 Amps*
*Etc.*

*Bsmt Lights and plugs, 15 Amps*
*BR Lights and plugs, 15 Amps*
*Range outlet, 40 Amps*
*Lights and plugs, 15 Amps*
*Lights and plugs, 15 Amps*
*Fridge outlet, 15 Amps*
*Laundry outlet, 15 Amps*
*Garbage disposal unit, 15 Amps*
*Furnace, 15 Amps*
*Spare circuit for future use*
*Kitchen counter plugs, 15 Amps*
*Kitchen counter plugs, 15 Amps*
*Etc*

**(d)**      **BASEMENT OR ATTIC SUITE PANEL** - Rule 26-400 & 26-722(a)

**IN AN EXISTING House** - Rule 26-400 was changed in the previous Code to make it less threatening and less costly to comply with. The rule says that where an existing single family house is being renovated to create one or more rental suites, all outlets in the one or more suites may be served from one panel.

Check the existing service size to insure it is adequate to supply the new suite load. In most cases, if your service is 100 amperes and heating is **not** with electricity, service size is very likely sufficient for the additional load. If there is any doubt about service ampacity calculate the total load as follows:

1      Calculate the load in the EXISTING dwelling (not the new suite load) as shown on page 15; then

2      Calculate the load in the NEW SUITE as if it were another separate house, see page 15; then
         **(Note** In this calculation for steps 1 & 2, leave out all air-conditioning and electric heating loads.)

3      Add 100% of the largest calculated load to 65% of the smaller load; then

4      Add all air conditioning loads and/or the electric heating load, whichever is greater, as shown on page 16.

5      Determine the size of service required to serve the **total load** of both suites using the table on page 12 and the List of Materials on page 8.

**If the ampacity of the existing service is NOT adequate,** (according to the above calculations) to serve the existing house load and the new suite load, then the existing service must be upgraded to supply the additional load, or another separate, (metered) service could be installed to serve only the new suite load. See also under **"Caution"** below.

**If the ampacity of the existing service is adequate** for the new suite load but there is insufficient space in the panel for the additional breakers that are needed for the new circuits, the panel only must be replaced with a larger one, or a second panel must be installed.

**Location of this second panel** - It is not required to be located in the new suite, (it may be located next to the the existing service equipment and supplied from it) nor is it required that all the circuits for the new suite be supplied from this second panel. Each of the circuits from either suite may be supplied from either panel, as convenient. If, however, your future plans call for separate metering for each suite you should separate the loads now in this renovation when it is easier to do that.

**Subfeeder to Second Panel** may be supplied with a set of breakers in the existing service. To provide space for the two subfeeder breakers you may need to reroute two circuits from the old panel to the new.

**Note - For the Student** - Rule 26-400(2) applies only when Subrule (1) requires a separate panel but if we are creating a suite in an **existing** single family dwelling Subrule (1) does not require a separate panel, therefore, Subrule (2) does not apply in the above example.

**Size of Subfeeder cable** to this second panel may be determined as shown in the above calculation. Remember, this is not just a second panel in a single occupancy; it serves a self contained suite with cooking and branch circuit loads. It may also have its own heating and hot water tank. Make sure the subfeeder is large enough to carry whatever load is connected to this panel.

**By way of explanation** - Subrule 26-722(a) should also have been revised to bring it more completely into line with the revision to Rule 26-400. These two rules could easily be seen to be in conflict. The latest revision to Subrule 26-400 was made, primarily, to ease the pain for owners creating a suite in the basement. It was intended to remove the penalty for declaring an illegal suite. Before this latest change these two rules required a separate panel in each suite and all circuits to be redirected so that the panel in each suite would supply only the outlets in that suite. It was an extremely expensive requirement

Owners did not want to declare a suite because they feared the authorities would require expensive alterations be made. As a result many suites may be unsafe because they were created without any inspection of the work. That fear was removed by the revision of Rule 26-400. We can now come clean, fess up and ease our consciences. Go ahead, say it, "I have a suite in my basement!"

**Caution** - If the separate panel noted above **is separately metered,** then all the full wrath of the rules will be applied. It is not that Hydro dislikes the extra meter but that you now have, in effect, a separately metered duplex or triplex and all the expensive electrical rules and building rules for such buildings must then be applied.

**IN A NEW HOUSE** -The major concession in the rules refers only to an **existing single family dwelling** which is being **renovated** to provide a rental unit in the basement or elsewhere. It does not apply to a new house which is constructed to include a self contained suite. In new houses each suite (if there are more than one) must be served with its own branch circuit panel which is located in the suite which it serves. In that case all the circuits in both suites must also comply with Rule 26-722(a). This subrule says branch circuits may serve only the outlets in the suite where the panel is located; there may not be any mixing of any of the loads. All this applies in a new house under construction.

**Separate metering** for each panel is not required by these rules but often is very desirable. Consider locating the suite panel so that service changes for separate metering can be made in the future with the least possible difficulty.

(e)     **How Many Circuits Do I Need?**

The number of circuits needed for a given house is determined by the minimum SERVICE AMPACITY as shown on the Service Size Table on page 12 - - - AND - - - the number of outlets installed in that house.

The table on page 12 has been designed to simplify this problem. This table specifies the required ampere rating of the service and indicates which list of materials, given on page 8, should be used for that particular house. Each list of materials also indicates the size of panel required.

There are two steps involved - proceed as follows:

**Step 1**     Determine minimum number of circuits required from the Table on page 12.

**Note**    The table on page 12 gives the minimum service ampere rating required. Next to it is a letter in brackets. This letter refers to the list of service material required on page 8. This list also indicates the minimum number of circuits required for that house.

**Step 2**    Complete the chart on page 44 to determine the actual number of circuits needed to supply the outlets you plan to install. Carefully fill in the chart to make sure you do not run short of circuits when the loads are finally being connected.

**Result**    The size of the branch circuit panel must be equal to step 1 or step 2, **whichever is greater.**

**Step 3  MINIMUM CIRCUITS REQUIRED** - Before doing this, see page 58 & 59.

**Light Outlets** ............... count all light outlets. indoor and outdoor, (do not

count switch outlets) ............................................................................ _____

**Convenience Plug Outlets** -  This refers to:

**Living room plugs** ......................................... _____

**Family room plugs** ......................................... _____

**Bedrooms plugs** ......................................... _____

**Dining room plugs** ......................................... _____

**Any Other Rooms or areas** ........................ _____

**Each Bathroom**........... Minimum 1 plug receptacle required ..................................... _____

Bathroom fan ......................................................................... _____

**Each Washroom**.......... Minimum 1 plug receptacle required ...................................... _____

**Each Hallway** .............. Minimum 1 plug receptacle required for each

hallway. See page 74 ............................................................ _____

**Each Kitchen fan**........ Counts as one outlet See page 59 & 111 ................................ _____

TOTAL **OUTLETS** REQUIRED = ......... _____

$$\text{then} = \frac{\text{Total \textbf{outlets} required}}{12} = \textbf{Circuits required} \quad \text{............................} \quad \rule{2cm}{0.4pt}$$

(12 outlets is the max. load permitted.  It is better to divide by 10, or even by 8, for fewer outlets per circuit)

**ADDITIONAL CIRCUITS REQUIRED**

**Outdoor plug outlets** .........Minimum 1 circuit required, See page 88 ........................................ _____

**Carport or Garage**..............Minimum 1 circuit required in each, See page 90 ....................... _____

**Laundry room or area**.......Minimum 1 circuit required, See page 86 .................................. _____

**Kitchen** ...............................Minimum 1 circuit for fridge.................................................... _____

Plus counter outlets, See page 78 ................................................ _____

**Larger Appliances** ........Range - 2 circuits required ............................................... _____

2nd. Range 2 circuits required ................................................ _____

Dryer - 2 circuits required .................................................... _____

Dishwasher - 1 circuit required.............................................. _____

Garburator - 1 circuit required.............................................. _____

Compactor - 1 circuit required............................................... _____

Micro~wave oven - 1 circuit required...................................... _____

Instant Hot Water Heater - 1 circuit required ......................... _____

Hydromassage Bath-tub - 1 GFCI circuit required................................ _____

Built-in vacuum Cleaner - 1 circuit required .......................... _____

Furnace (gas or oil) - 1 circuit required ................................. _____

Electric furnace - 2 circuits reqd.  See page 117 .................... _____

Electric baseboards - See page 113 to determine circuits reqd. .......... _____

Boiler - 1 circuit required....................................................... _____

Domestic Use Water Heater - 2 circuits required ..................... _____

Swimming pool - Motor Load. 1 circuit required ..................... _____

Lighting load - 1 circuit required  ............................... _____

Freezer plug (Separate circuit not required but is better)..................... _____

Sauna Heater - 2 circuits required ......................................... _____

Hot tub     Motor load - 1 circuit required ............................... _____

Electric heater - 2 circuits required ............................... _____

Domestic Water Pump - 1 circuit required (check pump rating)........... _____

Any Special plugs or lights .................................................... _____

**Plus 2 spare circuits** (Rule 8-108(2)) ................................................. _____

TOTAL CIRCUITS REQUIRED   = _____

**(f)**     **Sub-feeder to 2nd panel**

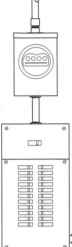

Sometimes it is an advantage to install a 2nd panel to supply the electrical loads in specific areas such as a kitchen or a garage. The kitchen requires a number of separate circuits for special loads such as the fridge, micro-wave oven, compactor etc.. The basement area directly below the kitchen is usually a good location for that second panel. Remember, the code does not require it. All the loads in the house may be served from the main service panel, however, this may require a very large service panel and a lot of costly long home runs. For this reason it may be an advantage to install a second panel - it may be a saving.

Don't forget, this second panel must be located with the same care and attention you used to locate the main service panel. All the rules regarding panel location, height, accessibility etc. as outlined below for a main service panel, must also be applied to the second panel. It may not be put just anywhere.

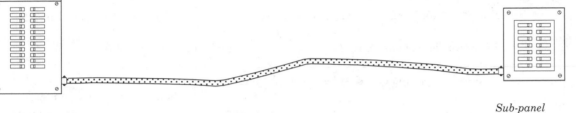

Sub-panel

Service panel

### SIZE of PANEL and FEEDER CABLE REQUIRED

Section 8 of the code has nothing to say about minimum sizes for a 2nd panel in a single family dwelling. We cannot apply Rule 8-200 to a sub-panel because that rule must be applied to the whole house, not just to a part of the load, and it sets the minimum size at 60 amps. This rule cannot, therefore, be properly applied to our sub-feeder.

However, all is not lost. We may apply a thumb rule to arrive at satisfactory sizes. The "Thumb Rule" goes like this:

For any size house up to approximately 4000 sq. ft. floor area the following is usually acceptable.

### EXAMPLE 1

**Lighting Loads Only** - If the 2nd panel will supply only lighting loads:

**Sub-feeder Size**    #10 copper loomex cable. 30 amp fuses or circuit breakers in the main panel.

**Sub-panel Size**    8 or 12 circuit panel. We may have as many as we wish. This is usually governed by the number of outlets per circuit, the area served and the bank account. Make sure your panel is large enough for the present load and for some future load additions.

### EXAMPLE 2

**Kitchen Electrical loads** - If the 2nd panel supplies lights and plugs in the kitchen area as well as other loads such as the garburator, dishwasher compactor etc. but not an electric range or dryer or any electric heating:

**Sub-feeder Size**    #8 copper loomex cable. 50 amp fuses or circuit breakers.

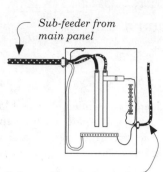

*Sub-feeder from main panel*

*Only one branch circuit shown*

**Sub-panel Size**    12 or more circuit panel is recommended. It is better to have too many circuit spaces for what you need now than to have too few spaces for your loads now and nothing for future load additions.

*Connect the black & red wires to the buses.*

*The white wire connects to the neutral bus.*

*There should be no connection between the neutral bus and the metal enclosure - if there is a bonding screw in this panel remove it and throw it away.*

*The bare wire in the supply cable connects to the enclosure at each end. This is an important connection. All grounding for all these branch circuits depends on these connections.*

**Note 1**    The range, dryer, and electric heating loads are not normally supplied from the 2nd panel. These loads are usually supplied directly from the main service panel.

**Note 2**    For a private Garage Panel - see under "Garage Wiring" on page 125.

**Note 3**    Additions & renovations to an existing house - See page 130 for more details.

**(g)**    **Location of Service Panel** - Rule 6-206 & BC Bulletins 6-3-0 & 6-4-0

The service equipment must be **inside** the building served.

The illustration shows a service panel recessed into an exterior wall. Such an installation is acceptable to Code but could result in a lot of condensation inside the panel unless there is space or building insulation behind the panel. The Electrical Code does not require this but BC Bulletin 6-4-0 suggests that there should be at least 0.5 inch (12 mm) of empty space or 0.5 inch (12 mm) of insulation behind the panel. It is best to mount the panel in a partition rather than in an exterior wall. If it cannot be located in a partition the next best location is on the surface of an outside wall.

*This conduit is considered inside the house and must therefore be kept as short as possible, see page 24 & 25.*

*This service panel is shown recessed in an outside wall - this may not be acceptable without building insulation behind the panel, see text.*

**Accessible** - The service panel should be mounted in a free wall space where it will remain accessible. It should not be located above freezers, washers, dryers, tubs, counter space, etc. It should not be on the back wall of a storage room where access may become difficult due to stored items, nor should it be in bathrooms, clothes closets, stairwells, kitchen cabinets or similar places, Rules 6-206, 2-308(1) & 26-402.

*Empty space or insulation required behind the panel in all areas except those installations:*

*In Vancouver Island districts*
*All lower Mainland districts*
*Chilliwack district*
*Prince Rupert district*
*Powell River and Squamish district*
*The Gulf Islands, UBC, Howe Sound & Bella Coola sub-districts*
*Terrace district*

Service panel in a shallow enclosure

Where such equipment is flush mounted in a wall, a covering door may be installed over the equipment for appearance sake. This cabinet would be very shallow, providing no storage space for other items. Sometimes a calender or large picture is hung over the panel. This always provides a certain amount of excitement when a fuse blows, all the lights go out and you cant remember whether the panel is under that old picture of uncle George, who knew nothing about electricity, or the Mona Lisa, who seems to think it funny you cant find the panel.

**(h)** **Height of Service Panel**- Rules 6-206(1)(b) & 26-402(2)

**Minimum height above floor** - The code no longer specifies a minimum height for the panel. The revised rule now simply says the panel must always be placed **as high as possible** but never more than **1.7 m (67 in) to the top of the top breaker** in the panel.

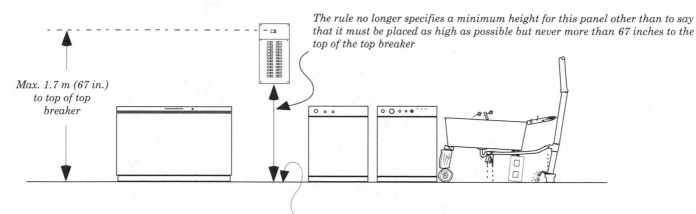

*Max. 1.7 m (67 in.) to top of top breaker*

*The rule no longer specifies a minimum height for this panel other than to say that it must be placed as high as possible but never more than 67 inches to the top of the top breaker*

*This floor area, 1 m. (39.4 in.) in front of the panel, must be kept clear. The service panel may not be located above any appliances or counters or similar objects.*

**(i)** **Which end is up?**

Service circuit breaker panelboards should be mounted in a vertical position although there is no rule that actually says so, (circuit breakers will function in either the horizontal or vertical position). There is, however, the question of - - of - well, - professionalism. Panels mounted in a vertical position do look more handsome, don't you think?.

**Please note** - Most fused service switches may not be mounted upside down or on their side, Rule 14-502.

**(j)** **Arrangement of conductors** - Rule 6-212, 12-3034

Inside your service panel is a barrier that divides the space into two separate sections. The main service breaker is (usually) in the top section and the branch circuit breakers are (normally) in the lower section although there is nothing wrong with installing it with the mains section at the bottom.

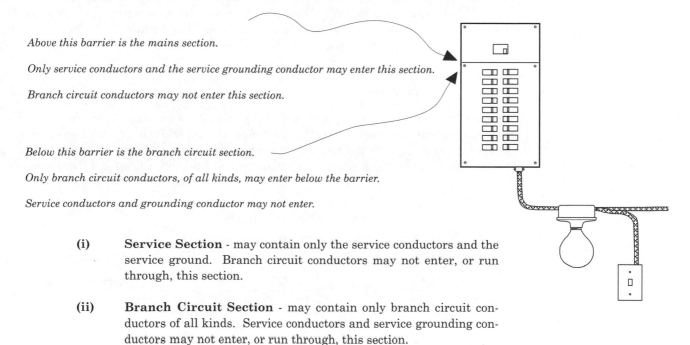

*Above this barrier is the mains section.*

*Only service conductors and the service grounding conductor may enter this section.*

*Branch circuit conductors may not enter this section.*

*Below this barrier is the branch circuit section.*

*Only branch circuit conductors, of all kinds, may enter below the barrier.*

*Service conductors and grounding conductor may not enter.*

**(i)** **Service Section** - may contain only the service conductors and the service ground. Branch circuit conductors may not enter, or run through, this section.

**(ii)** **Branch Circuit Section** - may contain only branch circuit conductors of all kinds. Service conductors and service grounding conductors may not enter, or run through, this section.

**(k)** **Grounding Connections in Service Panel**- Rule 10-204

The service grounding conductor must inter the service box at the correct location in the service section of the box, and be correctly connected to the neutral pad as shown below.

**COMBINATION PANELBOARD**

**FUSED SERVICE SWITCH**
**and breaker PANEL**

Neutral bus usually has provision for three connections and a bonding screw or jumper strap to
the enclosure. Do not forget this connection.

The two hot conductors from the
**service fuses** to the panel are not
shown to avoid confusion.

Switch neutral connected to enclosure with a bonding screw or jumper as shown

Bare bonding wire in the branch circuit cable connects to the bonding terminals on the enclosure not
the neutral bus.

Ground clamps on water service pipe

Neutral pads

**White wire** connects to the neutral bus.
**Red or black wire** connects to the breaker.
**Bare wire** connects to the bonding terminals
in the enclosure.

**(l)** **Grounding Electrodes** - Rule 10-002, 10-106, 10-700 & 10-702

**(i)** **The object of grounding** the electrical wiring and equipment in your house is to reduce the possibility of electrical shock and fire damage. This is a very important part of your installation. Good grounding depends on good grounding electrodes. The rules permit the following different kinds to be used:

    **1**   **Buried Metal Water Pipe** - See below.
    **2**   **Metal Water Well Casing** - See page 49.
    **3**   **Just Plain old Ground Rods** - See page 49.
    **4**   **Concrete encased grounding electrode** - See page 50.

**Interconnection Required** - Rule 10-700(2) says that where both #1 & #2 type electrodes, listed above, are available we must connect them together with a copper conductor the **same size** as
for the **main service ground**. For **artificial grounding electrodes**, types #3 & #4 listed
above, we must connect them together with a **#6 copper conductor**. If you have more than one
electrode use the wiring methods and the means of connection to each electrode as described
below.

**(ii)** **Metal Water piping System**

Rule 10-700 says that whenever we have at least 10 ft. (3 m) of continuously conductive metal
water piping system that is located underground at least 600 mm (24 in.) below finished grade
level entering a single family house we must use that metal pipe as the service grounding electrode. This arrangement is acceptable without any additional artificial grounding electrodes.

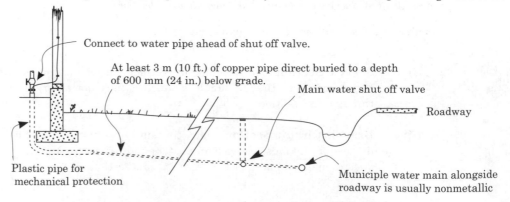

Connect to water pipe ahead of shut off valve.

At least 3 m (10 ft.) of copper pipe direct buried to a depth
of 600 mm (24 in.) below grade.

Main water shut off valve

Roadway

Plastic pipe for
mechanical protection

Municiple water main alongside
roadway is usually nonmetallic

**(iii)** **Metal well Casing** - Rule 10-700(1)(b) permits a metal water well casing to be used as the service grounding electrode. Note that the casing must be at least 75 mm (Approx. 3 in.) in diameter and must be at least 15m (approx. 50 ft.) deep.

If the well casing is smaller, or shorter, or both, it may not be used as the principle service grounding electrode, we must find a grounding electrode that will satisfy the rules.

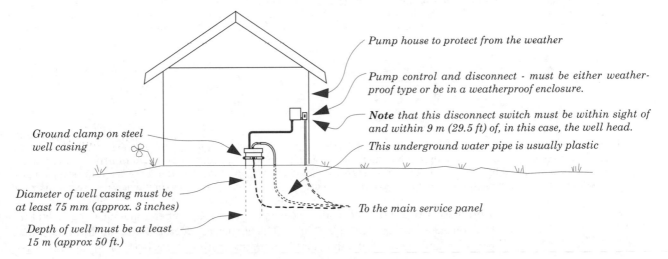

*Pump house to protect from the weather*

*Pump control and disconnect - must be either weatherproof type or be in a weatherproof enclosure.*

***Note** that this disconnect switch must be within sight of and within 9 m (29.5 ft) of, in this case, the well head.*

*This underground water pipe is usually plastic*

*Ground clamp on steel well casing*

*Diameter of well casing must be at least 75 mm (approx. 3 inches)*

*Depth of well must be at least 15 m (approx 50 ft.)*

*To the main service panel*

**(iv)** **Ground Rods** - Where there is no continuously conductive metal water piping system available we may use ground rods. The following picky points must be remembered when installing ground rods.

**Minimum Size -** ⁵/₈ inch in diameter by 3 m (10 ft.) long if of galvanized iron; or
¹/₂ inch in diameter by 3 m (10 ft.) long if of copper or is copper clad.

**How Many Rods?** - Rule 10-702(3) says we must have **at least two rods in every case** but we may actually need more in some special cases in order to provide an adequate ground return path for fault currents. Your Inspector will advise you if more than two rods are required.

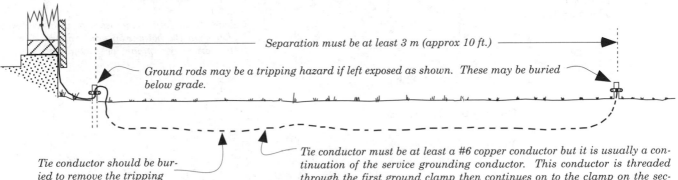

*Separation must be at least 3 m (approx 10 ft.)*

*Ground rods may be a tripping hazard if left exposed as shown. These may be buried below grade.*

*Tie conductor should be buried to remove the tripping hazard.*

*Tie conductor must be at least a #6 copper conductor but it is usually a continuation of the service grounding conductor. This conductor is threaded through the first ground clamp then continues on to the clamp on the second ground rod.*

**Depth** - Ground rods must be driven into the ground their full length plus one inch as shown above.

**Spacing** - Ground rods must be spaced at least 3 m (10 ft.) apart.

**Tie Conductor** - The rods must be connected together with a #6 or larger, copper bonding conductor. Normally, this tie conductor is a continuation of the service grounding conductor.

**Ground Clamps** - must be of copper or bronze. Dry type connectors may be used only indoors in dry locations.

**Tripping Hazard** - In the illustration above the ground clamp connections to the rods are buried at least 1 inch below grade level. This is required by Rule 10-702(3)(d) to remove the tripping hazard.

**Rock Bottom** - Can't drive that thing into the ground? There will be locations where the ground cover is less than 3 m (10 ft.) and the ground rods can not be driven in the usual way. The rules allow the following labour intensive solutions. Choose one that best fits your situation.

Where ground cover is less than 1.2 m (48 in.) deep the rule says we must bury the ground rods at least 600 mm (24 in.) below finished grade in a horizontal trench. Where the ground cover is less than 600 mm, you , are in deep trouble. The solution is to find a location with sufficient ground cover to use one of these arrangements shown then run your grounding conductor to that location. This grounding conductor will need to be adequately buried to protect it. Where this cable must run across bare rock you will need to chip out a trench at least 150 mm (6 in.) deep. Rule 12-012(7) says the ground cable must then be laid in this trench and grouted with concrete to the level of the rock surface.

Rock bottom

The rule requires that where rock is encountered at a depth of 1.2 m (48 in.) the ground rod is to be driven to rock bottom then the remainder bent over and placed in a horizontal trench at least 600 mm (24 in.) below grade. This is more difficult but it is according to code.

This ground rod is driven into the ground at an angle. The problem with this method is not knowing what angle to drive the rod to get maximum depth. If it is driven at too steep an angle it will not be at maximum depth as required by code.

**(v)**   **Concrete Encased Electrode** - consists of a single copper conductor, #4 or larger, encased in the concrete footings of the building. The copper conductor is thus in intimate contact with the concrete and thence with the earth under the footings. Properly installed these electrodes are very effective. Herein lies the key - to ensure an acceptable installation your Inspector may want to see it before he will permit it to be covered. Check with your Inspector.

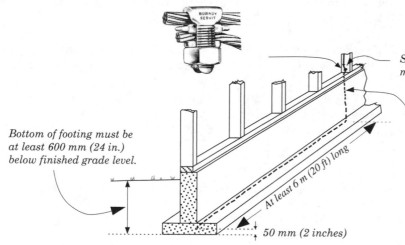

*Bottom of footing must be at least 600 mm (24 in.) below finished grade level.*

*At least 6 m (20 ft) long*

*50 mm (2 inches)*

*Servit type, thermit weld or compression type connectors may be used to make this connection.*

*The cable must be in the footing of a load bearing wall. It must be within the bottom 50 mm (approx. 2 in.) of the footing as shown.*

*Cables placed in a grade beam or in a grade slab or higher than the bottom 50 mm (approx. 2 in.) of the footing are not acceptable for grounding.*

**Conductor Required**

**Type** - must be copper.
  - must be bare.

**Length**   Must be at least 6 m (approx. 20 ft.) but may be much longer. This is the minimum horizontal length of conductor along the base of the footing.

In addition to the 6 m length of conductor run horizontally along the bottom 50 mm (approx. 2 in.) of the footing, you will require enough length to run up to the top of the foundation wall. Allow an additional 6 in.(approx. 150 mm) or so for connection to the service grounding conductor. See illustration above.

**Size-**   Note the following grounding conductor sizes for both the portion which is concrete encased and the part above the concrete, the home run to the panel. This cable may be spliced above the concrete foundation level as shown in the illustration above.

| Service Size | Concrete encased portion | Home run to panel |
|---|---|---|
| 0 to 125 amps | #4 copper | #6 copper |
| 126 to 165 amps | #4 copper | #4 copper |
| 166 to 200 amps | #3 copper | #3 copper |
| 201 to 260 amps | #2 copper | #2 copper |

**Position**  This grounding conductor must be in the bottom 2 inches ( 50 mm) of the footing.  It is not correct to place it in the floor slab or under it even if it is encased in concrete.  The effectiveness of this electrode depends, in part, on the weight of the building to maintain intimate contact with earth under the footing.

**Connection**  It is best to use one continuous conductor and run it all the way back to the service panel but there is nothing wrong with a splice as shown in the illustration.  Use a split bolt type connector to make the splice.

**(m)**    **Plastic Water Service Pipe** - Rule 10-406(2) & 10-702(3)

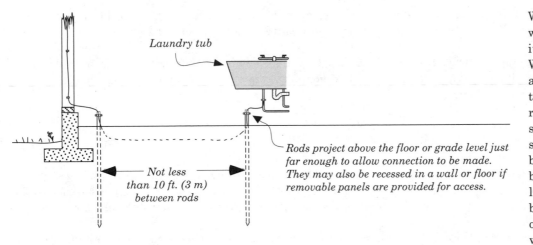

*Laundry tub*

*Rods project above the floor or grade level just far enough to allow connection to be made. They may also be recessed in a wall or floor if removable panels are provided for access.*

Not less than 10 ft. (3 m) between rods

Whenever the water service is with plastic pipe we cannot use it as our grounding electrode. We must in those cases install an artificial grounding electrode. Don't forget the bonding requirement. Even if the water service is plastic pipe, the piping system inside the building may be metallic. If it is, it must be bonded to the ground rods, Rule 10-406(2). This connection may be made at any convenient point on the cold water pipe where it will remain accessible.

**(n)**    **Ground Cable** - Home runs from the electrode to the service panel, Rule 10-806

**Use a #6 Insulated or Bare ground cable** for any service up to 125 amperes.

This cable may be used where it is not subject to mechanical injury.  Wood moulding or plastic pipe, as shown below, may be used to protect those portions which are subject to mechanical injury.

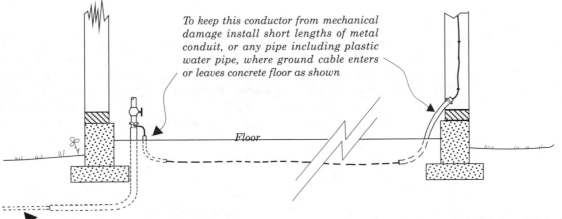

*To keep this conductor from mechanical damage install short lengths of metal conduit, or any pipe including plastic water pipe, where ground cable enters or leaves concrete floor as shown*

*Floor*

*Minimum 3 m (10 ft.) of bare copper water pipe direct buried 600 mm (24 in.) below finished grade level.*

**#4 Insulated or Bare ground cable**

If not exposed to severe mechanical injury, may be used for grounding any size service up to 165 amp.

**(n)**      Accessibility - Rules 10-902(2) & 10-904(2)

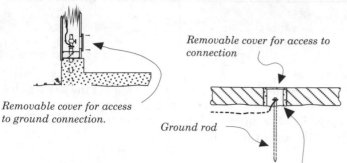

*Removable cover for access to ground connection.*

*Removable cover for access to connection*

*Ground rod*

*Wood frame or short section of pipe set flush with surface of sidewalk or grade.*

Rule 10-902(2) says that if the electrical service is grounded to the incoming water service pipe, as described above, the connection must remain accessible wherever possible. Rule 10-904(2) says the same thing about connections to ground rods. This means just what it says - leave it accessible - if it is practical to do so. If the rods or the water pipe are located in a wall, provide an access panel as shown. Ground rods are considered a tripping hazard therefore they must be recessed into the ground or in the concrete floor as shown or directly buried in the ground. See also below under "Ground Clamps".

**(o)**      Ground Clamps - Rule 10-908

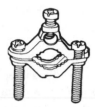

Make sure that the ground clamps you install are not only CSA certified but also that they are of copper, bronze or brass. The dry type connectors will not be approved in any outdoor location.

Where the ground clamps are in a consistently dry location, such as in a dry crawl space or basement or located in a wall, as shown under "Accessibility" above, the dry type clamp may be used. It's easy to get caught on this one - watch it.

**(p)**      Bonding

**(i)**      Service Switch - Rule 10-204 - All service equipment is provided with a brass bonding screw, or a bonding jumper, which must be installed to connect the neutral bus in the mains section to the metal enclosure. See sketch under "(j) Grounding Connections in a Service Panel" on page 48.

**(ii)**      Gas Line - Rule l0-406(4) - This rule requires metal gas lines to be bonded to the service grounding electrode. Yes, most of these gas burning devices are also connected to the electrical system and are bonded to ground with a bonding conductor in their supply cable but the rule still says bond it again. This may not make a whole lot of sense but that is what the rule says.

The gas piping system is normally bonded to ground at only one point as described for water pipe bonding on page 51 . The service grounding conductor may continue on from the grounding electrode to pick up the cold water piping system, the gas piping system and, if in an old house with cast iron plumbing, a waste piping system. Do not cut the grounding conductor at the connectors, simply run through it and on to the next bonding clamp as shown for a furnace on page 110

*Use 2 bolts - do not try to do this with one bolt.*

*This strap may be used for bonding gas tubing to the service ground.*

**CAUTION** - the standard ground clamp shown, above left, may damage soft copper tubing used in some gas distribution systems. Where the gas lines are of soft copper, Rule 10-616(2) permits the use of a copper strap wrapped around the pipe and clamped tightly with a bolt as shown. A #6 copper grounding conductor is then connected to this strap with a connector lug bolted (with another separate bolt) to the strap. The other end of this #6 copper conductor is then connected to the nearest grounded metal cold water pipe. This grounding conductor must be installed with the same care and attention you would use in installing a service grounding conductor.

# 15 BRANCH CIRCUIT WIRING

**(a)** **Overcurrent Protection**

**(ii)** **Light and Plug Outlets** Rules 30-104, 14-600 - The maximum rating of fuse or breakers supplying branch circuits for lighting or plug outlets, in a dwelling unit, is 15 amp except as noted below for kitchen appliance plugs under Item (ii).

**(iii)** **Bedroom plug outlets only** must be supplied with a special circuit breaker called an arc-fault circuit interrupter. This is described on page 73.

**(iv)** **Kitchen Appliance Plug Outlets** - Rule 14-600 - The maximum rating of fuses or breakers supplying appliance plug outlets in kitchens and utility rooms is 15 amp. Throw away that 20 amp fuse or breaker - you need more circuits, not bigger fuses. Except that subrule, Rule 26-710(b), allows T-slot receptacles rated for 20 amperes. See page 83 for details.

**(v)** **Range and Dryer Plug Outlets** - Rule 26-744 requires plug outlets for these heavy appliances. See also page 106 under "Heavy appliances".

**(vi)** **How Many Circuits** - Rules 8-108, 12-3000 & 26-722 - Each circuit breaker or fuse may supply only one circuit. It is not correct to connect two or more wires to a circuit breaker or fuse, Rules 6-212 & 12-3034. A sufficient number of breaker or fuse spaces should be provided in the service panel to comply with this requirement. See also page 44 under "Minimum Circuits Required".

**(vii)** **Fuses** - Rule 14-204 - Where fuse type panels are used it is difficult, if not impossible, to control the size of branch circuit fuses used. It is too easy to replace a blown fuse with one of a higher rating. To avoid this, the Code requires that all plug fuse holders must be equipped with a rejection feature that will make it impossible to replace a fuse with one of a higher rating. The illustration on the left shows a fuse and a rejection washer. The washer is inserted into the fuse socket. Each washer has a different size opening which will prevent a fuse of higher rating from making contact. Do not remove these washers.

**(b)** **Size of Cable**

Use only #14 wire unless your runs are unusually long, say more than 40 m (approx. 130 ft.) long. Exception, Kitchen plugs rated for 20 amps must be wired with #12 copper wire. The #12 wire is stiff; it can cause excessive strain on the switch and receptacle terminals and may require larger outlet boxes.

3-Wire Cable can save time and money - you are running two circuits in each cable. Rule 14-010(b) now says that we do not need tie bars or two pole circuit breakers for 3-wire cables except where these cables supply 240 volt loads, such as a range or dryer etc. or 120 volt SPLIT receptacles. This means that two single pole circuit breakers, without a tie-bar are acceptable for a 3-wire cable which supplies only lighting or plug outlets each of which is connected to the neutral and one hot conductor.

**EXCEPTION -** 3-wire cables used to supply any split receptacles, such as are used on the kitchen counter, must be protected with either a two pole circuit breaker or with two single pole breakers which have their operating handles connected together with a tie-bar. This is to ensure that both circuits are de-energized for safety for anyone working on these special outlets. If you are using a fuse panel you will need a special fuse block and fuse pull for these special circuits. See also page 40 for details on 2-pole breakers and tie-bars.

For heavy appliance wiring, look under specific type.

**(c)** **Cables Bundled together** - Rule 4-004(10)

This rule says that where cables are "in contact with each other for distances exceeding 600 mm (24 in.) the ampacity of the conductors must be corrected by applying the factors of Table 5C."

**Table 5C** - page 280 in the Code

1 to 3 conductors may carry ............................ 100.% load.
4 to 6 conductors may carry ........................... 80.% load.
7 to 24 conductors may carry ......................... 70.% load.
25 to 42 conductors may carry ........................ 60.% load.
43 or more conductors may carry ................... 50.% load.

A #14 loomex cable is normally permitted to carry 15 amperes but when it is run bundled together with other cables it may have to be derated to 80% or even 70% depending on the number of conductors, (not cables) in the bunch.

**Logic** - Before the days of super insulated and super sealed houses cables could be bundled together without concern. There was usually sufficient air movement in the walls and the ceiling to prevent dangerous temperature rise in the bundle due to mutual heating. Today we build fully sealed sardine cans which are highly insulated against heat loss. (The BTUs your furnace produced in the fall cannot escape until you open the doors in the spring.) Under these conditions cables bundled together could overheat unless they are derated so that each conductor carries a smaller load.

The rule is aimed at cables which supply electric heat, range, dryer, water heater and any other heavy loads such as an A/C unit. The concern is not with cables supplying general residential lighting and ordinary plug outlets although the rule could be applied to these cables as well.

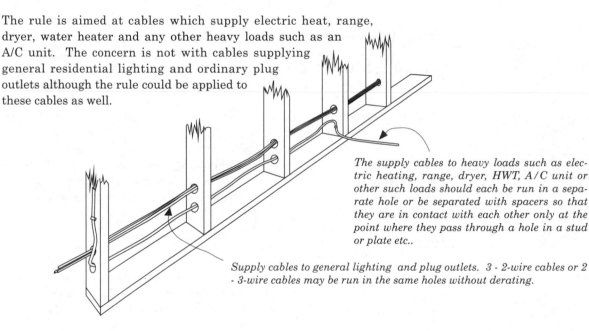

*The supply cables to heavy loads such as electric heating, range, dryer, HWT, A/C unit or other such loads should each be run in a separate hole or be separated with spacers so that they are in contact with each other only at the point where they pass through a hole in a stud or plate etc..*

*Supply cables to general lighting and plug outlets. 3 - 2-wire cables or 2 - 3-wire cables may be run in the same holes without derating.*

**Solution**

Cables supplying general lighting and plug outlets have always been derated to 80% by Rule 12-3000 and Table 5C permits 6 conductors bundled together with this 20% reduction in current carrying capacity. Therefore, cables supplying these outlets may be bundled as follows:

3 - 2-conductor cables may be run in contact without further derate, or

2 - 3-conductor cables may be run in contact without further derate

All other cables should be run in separate holes to insure separation.

**Note 1**  The bare bonding wire in the cables is not counted in this application.

**Note 2**  The derating applies only where cables are in **continuous contact** with each other for distances greater than 24 inches. Where the contact is less than 24 inches the derating does not apply. This means you could have many cables running through a hole in a stud without derating provided that the cables then fan out in different directions so that they are not in physical contact for more than 24 inches at any one point.

**Caution**  If you fail to observe this rule your inspector may need to ask you to restring the cables in different holes, or worse, replace them with larger cables.

The simplest solution is to force a bit of insulation or a wood chip between the cables to provide the required separation. Even though the cables are in contact with each other where they pass through holes the continuous contact in each case would then be less than 24 inches.

**(d)**      **Type of Cable** - Rules 2-126 & 30-408

     **FT1 Cable marking** - All loomex cables used in any wiring in any building must have at least an FT1 marking. This mark shows the cable insulation has been properly tested for burn-out. That is, in the event of a fire the cable insulation will not be the means by which the fire can travel from one part of the house to another. Your local building supply store will not likely have unmarked cable but you may have some left over from that last bit of wiring you did. Check that old cable. If the FT1 marking is not shown the cable is usable only for non-electrical applications such as fencing wire, or as a clothes line, etc..

     **90° Insulation on loomex Cable** - All ceiling outlet boxes **on which it is intended to mount a light fixture,** ( not junction boxes) must be wired with 90°C conductors such as NMD90 loomex cable. This sounds threatening, but the truth is it would be difficult to find any loomex cable intended for dry locations with a rating less than 90°C. There is one exception. NMW and NMWU cable has only a 60°C rating. NMW cable is intended for wet locations such as barns etc. NMWU cable is intended for use underground. In these damp or wet locations the rule permits these 60°C cables to enter a ceiling light outlet box which is also located in the damp or wet location..

     **Cold Regions** - Rule 12-102, - Thermoplastic insulated cables such as NMD-90 cable can be seriously damaged if it is flexed at temperatures lower than -10 degrees C (14 degrees F). Do not install cables in cold temperatures unless the cable is specifically approved for use at that temperature. Failure to observe this requirement may result in a seriously compromised installation. It's no fun doing this work in cold weather anyhow. This work should be done in warm weather when it can be fully enjoyed.

**(e)**      **Cable Strapping** - Rule 12-510

     Loomex cable should be strapped within 300 mm (12 in.) of the outlet box and approximately every 1.5 m (59 in.) throughout the run.

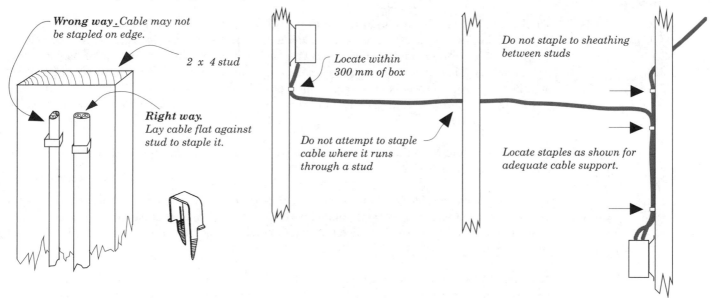

**Caution**

1 - **Do not staple 2 wire cable on edge** - they must lie flat. See Rule 12-506(5). This applies to two wire cables only.

2 - **Do not overdrive the staples.** Drive staples only until they contact the cable sheath - don't squish the cable. Because the cables are scantily dressed (insulated) the installers must be more careful when handling and strapping it.

**3 - Rule 2-108 - Be sure to use the correct size staple** or strap for each size cable. It is not correct to use a 2-wire cable strap on a 3-wire cable unless the staple or strap is specifically approved for both sizes, nor is it correct to put two cables under a single strap or staple. (You may get away with two cables under a strap if they are very carefully installed).

**4 - Where cables are run along studs** or joists they should be kept at least 1¼ in. from the nailing edge. Between staples the cable is free to move aside should a dry-wallers nail miss the stud but at the point of the staple the cable is held captive. If the cable has been stapled too close to the edge of a stud or joist it really needs protection. There is no code rule which specifically requires this protection except that Rule 2-108 says poor workmanship will not be accepted by the inspection department. It is best to run your cables along the middle, or as near the middle, of the stud or joist wherever possible and provide additional protection where it is not possible to run it there.

**(f)      Cable Protection** - Rule 12-516

(i)      Where the cable is run through holes in studs, plates or joists, these holes must be at least 32 mm (1¼ in.) from the edge of the wood member.

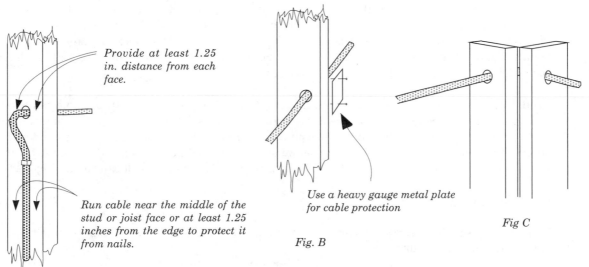

*Provide at least 1.25 in. distance from each face.*

*Run cable near the middle of the stud or joist face or at least 1.25 inches from the edge to protect it from nails.*

*Fig. A*

*Use a heavy gauge metal plate for cable protection*

*Fig. B*

*Fig C*

(ii)      **In the case of small dimension members** such as may be used in partitions, the cable hole should be located so that there is 32 mm (1¼ in.) clearance on one side. Fig.B. To protect the other side use a minimum #16 MSG steel plate (the side of a metal sectional outlet box does this job very well). This must be done in every case where the 32 mm (1¼ in.) clearance cannot otherwise be obtained. In corners of rooms, as in Fig.C., the holes may need to be drilled at an angle providing less than the minimum distance - here too, use heavy metal plates to protect the cable from dry-wallers nails.

Holes may contain more than one cable but must be large enough to prevent damage to the cable sheath during installation.

**Caution** - Bundled cables could be a serious problem. Where a number of cables are run in contact with each other you may be in conflict with Rule 4-004(10) depending somewhat on the type of loads served by those cables. See under (c) Cables Bundled together on page 53 for detailed information.

**Kitchen Cabinets** - Kitchen cabinets, or other similar cabinets, are often supported with long screws or nails that penetrate more than 1.25 inches into the studs. For this reason all cables not directly required in this wall space, (where cabinets may be mounted) should be kept out of this wall area or be protected with #16 MSG metal plates. The rules do not specifically require this but it may keep you out of a lot of trouble later.

Obviously some cables will need to be run in this wall space to supply the counter plugs, dishwasher, garburator, hood fan etc. but all other cables should be kept out of this wall space. Where possible, cables which must run in this wall space should be run in a vertical direction, not horizontally. Where it must be run horizontally through a stud, use heavy (#16 gauge) steel plates or the equivalent, or keep the cable at least 2 in from the nailing edge of the studs. Remember, this is not a Code rule, but it may save trouble later.

**(iii)**     **Attic Spaces** - Rule 12-514(a) says cables may be run on the upper faces of joists or lower faces of rafters, as shown below, provided the head clearance, joist to rafter, is 1 m (39.4 in) or less. Where the head room is greater than 1 m the cables must be run through holes.

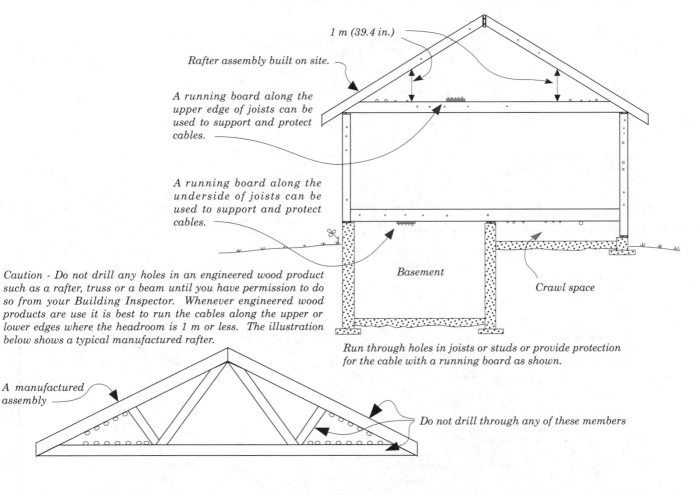

*1 m (39.4 in.)*

*Rafter assembly built on site.*

*A running board along the upper edge of joists can be used to support and protect cables.*

*A running board along the underside of joists can be used to support and protect cables.*

*Caution - Do not drill any holes in an engineered wood product such as a rafter, truss or a beam until you have permission to do so from your Building Inspector. Whenever engineered wood products are use it is best to run the cables along the upper or lower edges where the headroom is 1 m or less. The illustration below shows a typical manufactured rafter.*

*Basement*

*Crawl space*

*Run through holes in joists or studs or provide protection for the cable with a running board as shown.*

*A manufactured assembly*

*Do not drill through any of these members*

**(iv)**     **Basements and crawl spaces** - Rule 12-514(b) says cables may be run on the lower face of basement or crawl space joists provided the cables are suitably protected. A running board nailed to the underside of the joists may be an acceptable protection - check with your Inspector.

It is best to protect the cables by running them through holes drilled in the joists. This allows the basement to be finished without having to re-run cables to get them out of the way.

**(v)**     **Exposed Cable** - Rule 12-518 - Where loomex cable is run on the surface of the wall and within 1.5 m (59 in.) from the floor, as is often the case in buildings of solid wall construction, the cable must be protected from mechanical damage with wood or similar moulding.

**(vi)**     **Hot Air Ducts or Hot Water Pipes** - Rule 12-506(4) requires loomex cable to be kept at least 25 mm (1 in.) away from all hot air heating ducts and hot water piping. A chunk of building insulation may be placed between the cable and the duct or pipe, as shown.

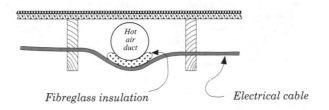

*Hot air duct*

*Fibreglass insulation*

*Electrical cable*

# 16    CHART of BRANCH CIRCUITS

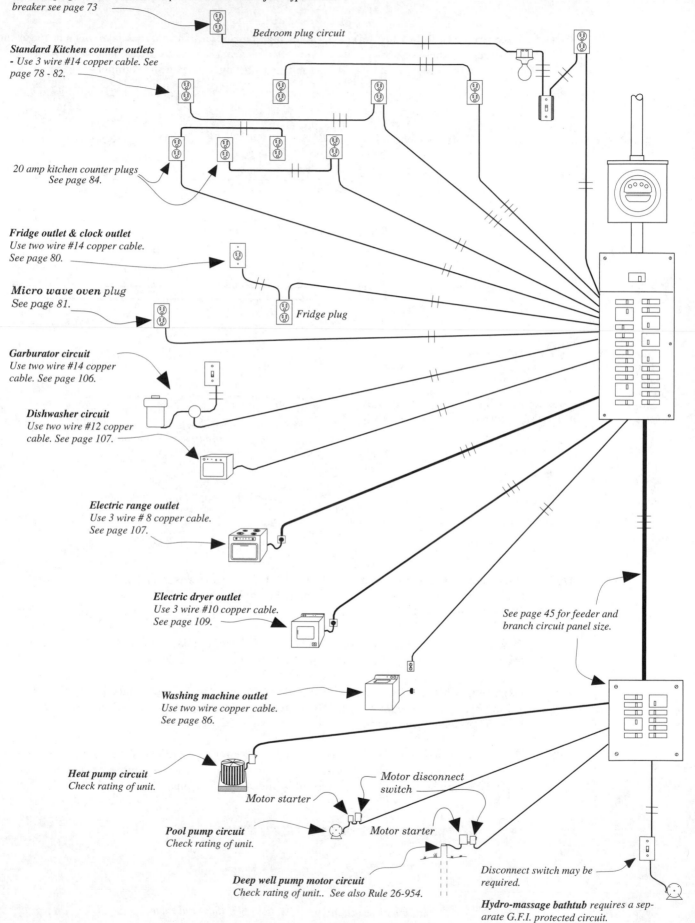

**Bedroom plugs -** *These must now be protected with an* **arc-fault type** *circuit breaker see page 73*

Bedroom plug circuit

**Standard Kitchen counter outlets**
*- Use 3 wire #14 copper cable. See page 78 - 82.*

*20 amp kitchen counter plugs*
*See page 84.*

**Fridge outlet & clock outlet**
*Use two wire #14 copper cable.*
*See page 80.*

**Micro wave oven** *plug*
*See page 81.*

*Fridge plug*

**Garburator circuit**
*Use two wire #14 copper cable. See page 106.*

**Dishwasher circuit**
*Use two wire #12 copper cable. See page 107.*

**Electric range outlet**
*Use 3 wire # 8 copper cable. See page 107.*

**Electric dryer outlet**
*Use 3 wire #10 copper cable. See page 109.*

*See page 45 for feeder and branch circuit panel size.*

**Washing machine outlet**
*Use two wire copper cable. See page 86.*

**Heat pump circuit**
*Check rating of unit.*

*Motor disconnect switch*

*Motor starter*

**Pool pump circuit**
*Check rating of unit.*

*Motor starter*

**Deep well pump motor circuit**
*Check rating of unit.. See also Rule 26-954.*

*Disconnect switch may be required.*

**Hydro-massage bathtub** *requires a separate G.F.I. protected circuit.*

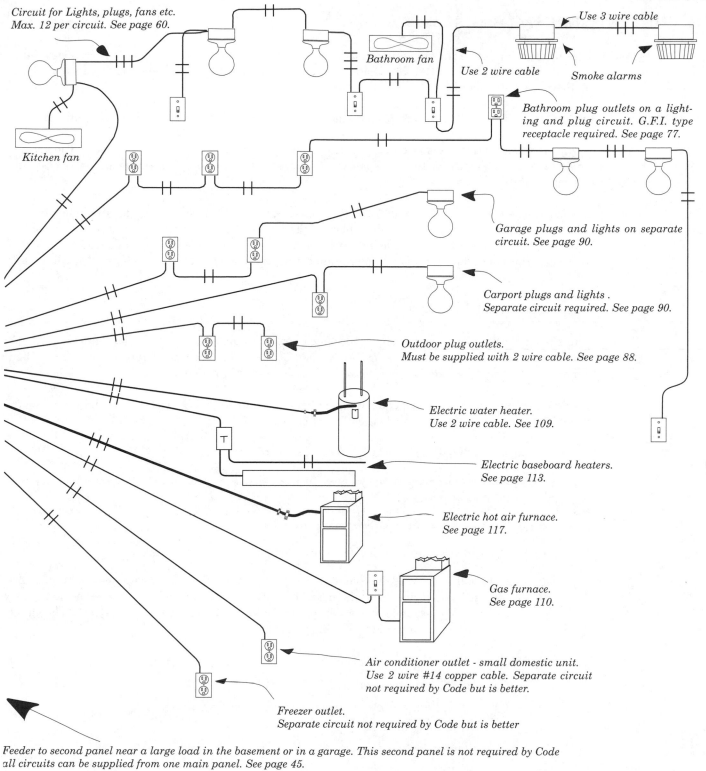

Circuit for Lights, plugs, fans etc.
Max. 12 per circuit. See page 60.

Use 3 wire cable

Bathroom fan

Use 2 wire cable

Smoke alarms

Kitchen fan

Bathroom plug outlets on a lighting and plug circuit. G.F.I. type receptacle required. See page 77.

Garage plugs and lights on separate circuit. See page 90.

Carport plugs and lights .
Separate circuit required. See page 90.

Outdoor plug outlets.
Must be supplied with 2 wire cable. See page 88.

Electric water heater.
Use 2 wire cable. See 109.

Electric baseboard heaters.
See page 113.

Electric hot air furnace.
See page 117.

Gas furnace.
See page 110.

Air conditioner outlet - small domestic unit.
Use 2 wire #14 copper cable. Separate circuit
not required by Code but is better.

Freezer outlet.
Separate circuit not required by Code but is better

Feeder to second panel near a large load in the basement or in a garage. This second panel is not required by Code all circuits can be supplied from one main panel. See page 45.

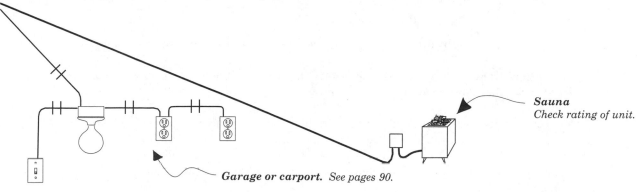

**Sauna**
Check rating of unit.

**Garage or carport.**  See pages 90.

## 17. OUTLET BOXES - for Lights, Smoke Alarm & Fans

**(a)**      **Vapour Barrier for Light Outlet Boxes -** - The Building Code requires boxes to be surrounded with a moisture resistant barrier if they are located in a wall or ceiling which is required to have a vapour barrier. See page 66 for details.

**(b)**      **Light Outlet Boxes** - Rule 30-302(6) says rigid PVC boxes shall not be used to support lighting fixtures unless the boxes are marked to show they are suitable for that purpose. It is not clear if this refers to all plastic type light outlet boxes or only to those boxes identified and marked as PVC boxes. The problem seems to be the weakness of the material when it is subjected to the operating temperature of certain lighting fixtures.

This is not a new subrule, it was Rule 12-1110 in the old Code book. To my knowledge this rule has never been enforced. It may suggest that the problem, if there is one, is probably not very serious. You should be aware that the Code Committee has flagged this rule and that it may now be enforced. Check with your local Inspector before you install any **nonmetal light outlet boxes** which are not marked for such use.

**(c)**      **Outlets Per Circuit** - Rule 12-3000

A maximum of 12 outlets may be connected to a circuit. This may consist of 12 light outlets or 12 plug outlets (not appliance plugs, see page 78 for "Kitchen Counter Plug Outlets") or any combination of light and plug outlets mixed, as long as their total number does not exceed 12 outlets.

It is better to have the load consist of a mixture of lights and plugs. This gives better load diversity on the circuit and less chance of a complete blackout in case of circuit failure.

To avoid confusion and costly duplication proceed as follows:

    (i)      Make a floor plan of your house. If more than one floor, draw a separate plan for each floor.

    (ii)      Show each outlet using the symbols given below.

    (iii)      Determine the best location for service equipment.

    (iv)      Draw a line showing the course each cable run will take. Start with one circuit and complete it before going on to the next. Identify each circuit and each outlet for quick, easy location. For example, the outlets on the first circuit would be A1, A2, A3 etc. The outlets on the next circuit would be B1, B2, B3 etc.

**Symbols** usually used are:

| Symbol | Description |
|---|---|
| ⊸◯⊸ | Light outlet on ceiling |
| ⊸◯ | Wall light outlet such as over a bathroom vanity |
| $ | Wall switch |
| $3 | Three way switch |
| $4 | Four way switch |
| ⏀ | Duplex plug receptacle |
| ⏀ | Split duplex receptacle used above kitchen counter see page 70 |

**(d)**      **Light Outlets Required** - Rule 2-314 & 30-502 - The Electrical Code now requires at least one lighting outlet at, or in, the following locations:

| | |
|---|---|
| Front door | An exterior light fixture controlled by a wall switch located inside the house. |
| Kitchen | A light fixture, controlled by a wall switch |
| Bedrooms | A light fixture controlled by a wall switch or a wall receptacle controlled by a wall switch. |
| Living rooms | A light fixture controlled by a wall switch or a wall receptacle controlled by a wall switch. |

| | |
|---|---|
| Utility rooms | A light fixture controlled by a wall switch |
| Dining room | A light fixture controlled by a wall switch |
| Bathrooms | A light fixture controlled by a wall switch |
| Washrooms | A light fixture controlled by a wall switch |
| Vestibules | A light fixture controlled by a wall switch |
| Hallways | A light fixture controlled by a wall switch |

Electrical Service Panel - One light fixture for operation and maintenance of that equipment.

**Stairway Lighting** - Rule 30-504. All stairways must have illumination - there is no exception to this Rule.

**Stairway lighting Control Switches** - Rule 30-504. These rules say that it must be possible to control stairway lights from both the head and foot of the stairway. There is an exception. Where the stairway has only three or fewer risers, or in the case of a basement stairway leading to a dungeon like space which has no finished area and no egress other then the one stairway leading into it, one switch at the head of the stairway is acceptable.

Note - The light outlet nearest the stairway must be **wall switched** at the **head of the stairs.**

**Watch this one!** The Rule says you must be able to control that stairway light from either the top or bottom of the stairway. In the case of an open stairway leading to a living room, or other such area on a different level, the normal switch locations for general lighting in that area may not also meet the requirements for stairway lighting. Additional switching may need to be installed or separate lighting and control may need to be installed for the stairway. Note that illumination is required at all stairways but the special switching requirement applies only in cases where the stairway consists of four or more steps.

**Unfinished Basement Lighting** - Rule 30-506 says that "A lighting outlet with fixture shall be provided for each 30 m$^2$ (323 sq.ft.) or fraction thereof of floor area in unfinished basements". Note that the rule does not say there must be a lighting fixture "in" each 30 m$^2$ (323 sq.ft.) area in the basement. Compute the total floor area of the basement then divide by 30 or by 323 to determine the minimum number of light outlets required by this rule. These light outlets must be spaced to provide reasonably uniform light distribution over the whole floor area.

**Storage rooms** - Rule 30-508 - This rule requires a lighting outlet with fixture in each storage room. The rule does not require this light outlet to be wall switched but that is best.

**Garages and Carports** - Rule 30-510 This rule requires a light outlet with fixture in each garage and carport. If the fixture is mounted above the car parking space it must be wall switched. If it mounted off to the side it may be a switched lampholder type.

Note - In the case where the entranceway lighting fixture provides light for the carport area the rule says we do not need to install any additional lighting in the carport.

**Simple Light Outlet** - The standard light outlet consists of a loomex cable run into an octagon or round outlet box set flush with the ceiling finish.

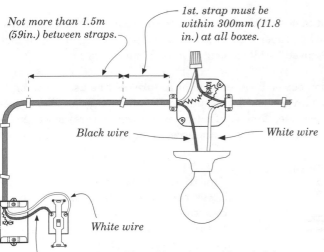

*Not more than 1.5m (59in.) between straps.*

*1st. strap must be within 300mm (11.8 in.) at all boxes.*

*Black wire*

*White wire*

*White wire*

*Black wire*

*Note - The **white** wire at this switch is HOT. This is the standard connection method.*

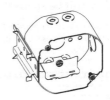

**(e)** **Recessed Light Outlet** - Rules 30-900, 30-910 - The wide variety of recessed light fixtures available today makes it difficult to be specific on installation instructions. The best advice, as always, is follow the manufacturer's instructions. Some IC and non IC fixtures are similar in appearance therefore check each fixture to be certain you are installing the correct fixtures. Do not deviate from the manufacturer's instructions. Basically there are three different types of recessed light fixtures available:

**(1)** **IC type** - This recessed light fixture is certified for direct contact (blanketing), with building insulation and may be in contact with wood support members, Rule 30-906.

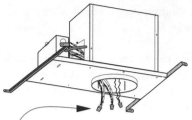

*All connection leads must be long enough to reach drown through the fixture opening for future maintenance*

This is a specially designed, thermally protected, recessed light fixture which is totally enclosed in a metal box. This fixture may be covered with building insulation.

**Lamp Wattage Rating** - At present fixtures certified for covering with building insulation are limited to 75 watt lamps with appropriate trim. In some cases a simple change in fixture trim will alter the permitted lamp rating - check with your supplier.

As noted above, this fixture is equipped with a built-in thermostat to shut itself off in case it overheats. Some homeowners have installed 150 watt lamps in these 75 watt fixtures. It works fine, for a few minutes until the higher wattage lamp overheats the fixture. At this point the thermostat shuts it off. When it cools it turns itself back on again. Obviously, it could not do this for very long. The thermostat is not designed for repeated on off switching, it would very soon fail. Make sure you use the correct size lamp in your fixture.

**(2)** **IC inherently protected recessed light fixture.** This means it's construction and the special lamps used in this fixture are designed to limit the heat generated so that it does not require a thermal protective device normally found in the IC type fixture noted in item (1) above. These are generally low output fixtures intended for special effects. This fixture may be in contact with building insulation, Rule 30-906.

**(3)** **Non IC type** - This is the standard recessed light fixture approved for locations where there is no building insulation.

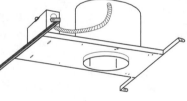

**(f)** **Fire Hazard - Improperly Installed Recessed Light Fixtures**

A number of fires have been caused by incorrectly installed recessed light fixtures. There are two problem areas to watch out for when installing recessed light fixtures. First, make sure you have provided all the minimum clearance required in the manufacturer's instructions. Second, make sure all recessed light **fixtures installed in insulated areas** are properly certified for blanketing with building insulation. Look for the manufacturers label which clearly states the fixture is acceptable for blanketing with building insulation. Without this label the fixture should be rejected for that location. The Inspector is working to make your home safe. Because these fixtures can be a fire hazard you really want him to be very careful.

The insulation does exactly what it is supposed to do - it traps the heat in the fixture. When the fixture reaches the combustion temperature of the wood or paper next to it the result is charring and sometimes fire. Use only fixtures certified and marked approved for blanketing with building insulation.

**Connection or Terminal Box** - The connection box on a recessed light fixture may be used only for the supply conductors to this one light fixture. You may not use it as a junction box for any other loads unless the fixture connection box is approved for that purpose. You will find many of these fixtures are equipped with boxes which are certified for use as a junction box. If they are acceptable for use as a junction box they will be so marked.

*This box must be marked approved for use as a junction box, Rule 30-408(6), because the cable continues on to the next light.*

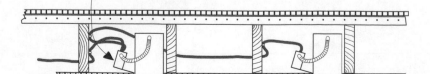

The illustration shows a second floor above the recessed light fixture. In this case there is no requirement for building insulation and therefore, standard recessed light fixtures may be used. However, these fixture can still be a fire hazard if the minimum ¹/₂ in. clearance from wood is not maintained all around and on top of the fixture. The only points where the $^1/_2$ in. clearance is not required is where the ceiling finish material butts up against the fixture and at the support points around the lower edge.

**Combination Heat Lamp and Fan Fixture** - Unless the fixture is **marked certified for blanketing with building insulation** it should be regarded as not approved for covering.

**Personal Opinion** - If these fixtures are not CSA certified for direct covering with building insulation it may be dangerous to cover them. This particular fixture is usually equipped with a 250 watt heat lamp which generates a great deal of heat. As long as the fan continues to operate it will tend to keep the internal temperature of the fixture to a safe level. In the event the fan fails to operate, for whatever reason, fixture temperature may rise above the safe level. The ducting from this fan to outdoors will provide some natural ventilation provided there is no automatically operated flapper valve in this duct which is closed when the fan is not operating. It would also be necessary for the ducting to be adequately inclined to provide a chimney effect for heated air to move away from the fixture. Finally the Building Code requirements for very well sealed houses may stifle air movement to a point where you would have a 250 watt heater in the ceiling covered with R40 insulation. If the fan fails . . . . . . . who knows how long it would take start a fire.

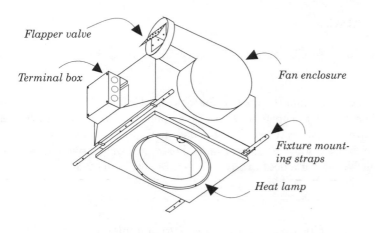

*Flapper valve*

*Terminal box*

*Fan enclosure*

*Fixture mounting straps*

*Heat lamp*

**(g)    Fluorescent Light Outlets** - Rules 12-506(1), 12-3002(6), 30-310(3)

Loomex cable may be run directly into a fluorescent light fixture as shown. Where fluorescent fixtures are mounted end to end as in valance or cornice lighting, the loomex cable should enter only the first fixture. The interconnecting wires between fixtures must be R90 or better.

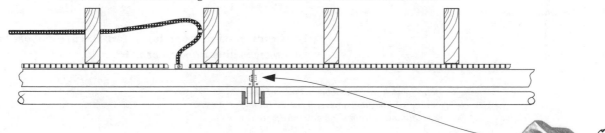

*Where fixture ends are close together as shown use the fixture coupling devices, if the fixtures are equipped with them, or use a chase nipple such as shown. Make sure the bonding conductor in the supply cable is securely connected to the first fixture and that there is a secured mechanical connection to the second fixture to insure a good ground return path.*

That threaded thing with a locknut next to it, in the illustration, is called a chase bushing. Punch out the knockout holes in the end of the fixtures where they join. The fixtures are then fastened to the ceiling with their ends as close together as possible. The chase nipple is now inserted through the two knockouts and the locknut is used to bring the two fixture end plates together for grounding. This chase bushing also provides a smooth throat to protect the fixture supply conductors.

**Outlet Box Not Required**

As shown, the loomex cable is run directly into the fixture. An outlet box is not required provided the cable used is NMD7 or NMD90 and not more than two cables enter any fixture.

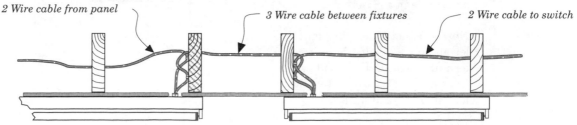

*2 Wire cable from panel*          *3 Wire cable between fixtures*          *2 Wire cable to switch*

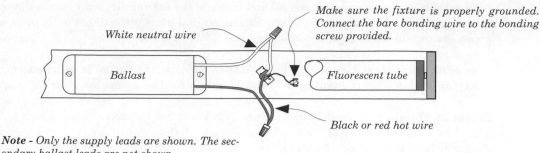

*White neutral wire*

*Make sure the fixture is properly grounded.*
*Connect the bare bonding wire to the bonding*
*screw provided.*

*Ballast*

*Fluorescent tube*

*Black or red hot wire*

**Note** - *Only the supply leads are shown. The secondary ballast leads are not shown.*

**(h)** **Bathroom Light Outlets** - Rule 62-110(1)(b)

Heat Lamps - Like any other recessed light fixture, heat lamps can be a very real fire hazard if improperly installed. Care should be taken to:

**(i)** **Locate the Heat Lamp fixture** away from the door so that it cannot radiate heat directly onto the upper edge of the door when it is in the open position. This applies to the shower stall doors or curtain rod as well as the bathroom entry door. The rule does not specify a distance but some Inspection Authorities require at least 12 inches, (300 mm), horizontal measurement, between the edge of the fixture and a shower rod or a door in any position, BC Bulletin 62-1-0.

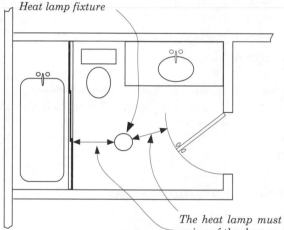

*Heat lamp fixture*

*The heat lamp must be outside of the swing of the door and at least 12 inches (300 mm) from shower curtain rod.*

**The reason** for all this is to eliminate a possible fire hazard. The upper edge of the door may be too close to the fixture and could become overheated if the lamp was inadvertently left on for a long time; it is, after all, a heat lamp. The shower rod could be used to hang towels and clothing. These could become overheated if they were directly under the heat lamp.

**(ii)** **Combination heat lamp/fan fixture** for use in a bathroom is illustrated on page 63.

**Swag Lamps in a Bathroom** - Rule 10-514(2) - Be sure to use the correct fixture - it must have a ground conductor to each chain hung lamp holder. Do not depend on the chain to provide adequate grounding.

**(i)** **Clothes Closet Light Outlets** -

Light outlet boxes in closets may be in the ceiling or on the front wall above the door, Rule 30-204(l).

**Note** - The Rule now requires an enclosed light fixture. A bare lamp type fixture is no longer acceptable in a closet

**Note** - Do not locate this light outlet above the shelf where it could be a fire hazard. Use great care in locating this fixture. It could be left on for days at a time.

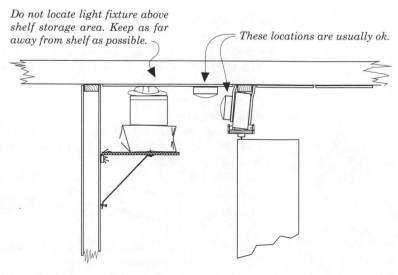

*Do not locate light fixture above shelf storage area. Keep as far away from shelf as possible.*

*These locations are usually ok.*

**(j)**     **Smoke Alarms** - Rule 32-110

The National Building Code requires smoke alarm devices in each residential dwelling unit.

**(i)     How Many Required** - The rule says they "shall be installed between each sleeping area and the remainder of the dwelling unit; and where the sleeping areas are served by hallways, the smoke alarms shall be installed in the hallway". All the bedrooms facing onto a common hallway could be served with one device, however, bedrooms on another floor or in the basement are in another "area" and would therefore require another device. The number of smoke alarm units required for your house, and the location of these devices is controlled by the local Building Inspector or Fire Officer, make sure he is satisfied.

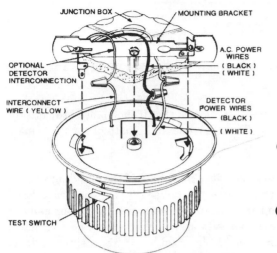

**(ii)     Outlet Box Required** - Use a standard light outlet box mounted as for a light outlet. This box may also be used as a junction box to serve other loads, it need not be at the end of a run.

**(iii)    Position** - The rule says the smoke alarm shall be installed "on or near the ceiling" depending on the installation instructions that come with the device.

**Circuit Required** - May be supplied with any general lighting circuit or plug outlet circuit (except those circuits which are G.F.I. protected or which supply kitchen plug outlets, laundry or outdoor plug outlets).

**Note** -    Do not switch this outlet. It must not be possible to turn this thing off except with the breaker in the panel.

**(iv)     2 or More Smoke Alarms** - Where two or more smoke alarms are installed the Building Code says they must all operate together - that is, if one alarm is activated to sound an alarm the others must all be connected together so that they all automatically sound the alarm together.

Units designed for line voltage (120 volts) require a 2-wire #14 supply cable to the first unit, then 3-wire from there to all the other units. The third conductor in these cables is for the signal circuit so that all units can sound the alarm together, the other two conductors are required to supply power to the second and third units. This type is in common use today.

**(k)     Overhead Rotary Fans**

These fans are becoming more and more popular. They not only look smart they also serve a useful purpose by moving the heated air downward to the floor level. - **Some things to watch for:**

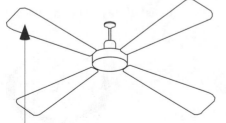

*Minimum elevation above floor level is 8 ft.; except that in some cases it may be as low as 7 ft.*

*Floor level*

**(1)  Look for a** certification label. Never purchase any electrical appliance unless it is clearly marked with a CSA or one of the other certification labels described on page 2. This is your protection and assurance that the device has been checked against a good standard.

**(2)  Look for mounting instructions.** - Each fan has a caution marking which gives the minimum mounting height above floor required for that particular fan. This marking will look something like this;

    **Caution:**     Mount with the lowest mounting parts at least 8 ft. above floor or grade level.

**(3)  Use a special mounting box** to support the fan.

Some fans will not turn as fast at maximum speed or the fan blades are designed so they are less hazardous to anyone coming in accidental contact with the blades. These fans will also have caution markings similar to the words given above except that in this case the minimum mounting height will be 7 ft. instead of 8 ft. In this case the fan blades may be as low as 7 ft. above the floor.

**Near Stairways, Balconies and such like.**

The fan blades may not be within reach of a person standing on a stairway, a landing or a balcony. If the blades are within reach the minimum height given on the caution notice must be measured from the level the person is standing on. Check this detail carefully in the rough wiring stage - it is very difficult to change the location of the supply outlet later.

**Circuit required**

This fan may be supplied with any lighting circuit which has only 11 or fewer outlets. The fan outlet, though it is a small load, counts as one outlet.

**Caution;** CSA has issued a caution regarding these fans. It warned that if the blades are not properly installed they may work loose and fall to the floor. Anyone in the path of such a flying blade could be seriously hurt.

**(l)** **Vapour Barrier** - This is not an Electrical Code requirement, it is now part of the Building Code. This means that the Electrical Inspector does not ask for these boxes but he is still very concerned how they are installed. Where the Building Code requires a vapour barrier on a wall or ceiling, (normally this is required only on insulated walls or ceilings) all electrical boxes located in that wall or ceiling must then also be enclosed in a vapour barrier. The vapour barrier for an electrical box is like a shroud. It consist of a separate plastic or fiberglass box which has a wide gasketted flange to allow contact, and seal with, the vapour barrier sheet which is normally fixed to the joists or studs. The electrical outlet box is placed inside this shroud, then together, they are fixed to a stud. Some box manufacturers produce what they call "airtight boxes". These are equipped with a wide flange and seals where cables must enter the box. Whichever kind of vapour barrier you use, the Building Code rules require it at:

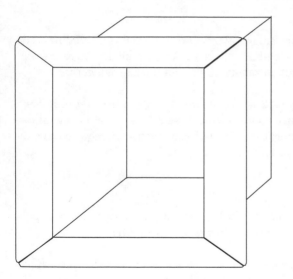

Each light outlet box; and
Each light fixture if it is recessed into the wall or ceiling; and
Each switch outlet box; and
Each plug outlet box; and
Each outlet box for other purposes such as a smoke alarm J-box etc..

One more thing; don't forget to apply a sealing compound around each cable entering the outlet box. The whole idea is to make the house fully air tight. There must not be any unauthorized fresh air entering the house.

A recessed light fixture located in an insulated ceiling must also be equipped with a vapour barrier. These must enclose the whole fixture thus requiring a rather large box as shown at left.

Don't forget this detail; it's easier to install these to begin with then later, after the rejection.

There is a rumor that says this whole exercise is designed to make our houses air tight so that the stale air inside cannot get out to pollute the atmosphere, it's probably true.

# 18   Switch Outlet Boxes

**(a)**   **Vapour Barrier for a Switch Outlet Box** - The Building Code requires boxes to be surrounded with a moisture resistant barrier if they are located in a wall or ceiling which is required to have a vapour barrier.  See page 66 for details.

**(b)**   **Height of Switches** - The rules do not specify a required height for wall mounted light switches.  They may be located at any convenient height - usually they are set at approximately 1.2 m (approx. 48 in.) to the lower edge of the box.

**(c)**   **Bathroom Light Switch** - Rule 30-322(3) says the light switch must not be located within reach of a person in a shower or bathtub.  Appendix B for Rule 30-322(3), page 395 in the Code, defines out of reach as 39.4in. (1m).  This means that switches controlling these loads may be inside the bathroom provided they are at least 39.4in. from the a bathtub or shower stall.

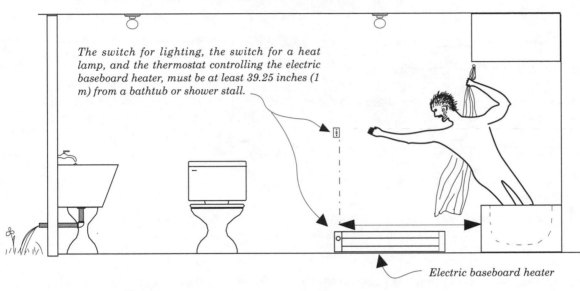

*The switch for lighting, the switch for a heat lamp, and the thermostat controlling the electric baseboard heater, must be at least 39.25 inches (1 m) from a bathtub or shower stall.*

*Electric baseboard heater*

**Note**   **1 - Horizontal Measurement** - The Code does not specifically say so but it is best to understand this is a horizontal measurement from the switch to the nearest outside face of a shower stall, or tub, as illustrated above.

**2 - Other Switches & Controls Located in a Bathroom** - The Code does not specifically say all controls and switches located in a bathroom must be 1 m (39.4 in.) from a bath tub or shower stall but they are all equally dangerous if they operate at the same voltage.

**Heat Lamp Control Switch** - The switch for the infra-red heat lamp should, not must, be at least 39.4 inches (1 m) from the bath tub or shower stall.

**Thermostat Control** - Thermostats located on a wall or on a heating unit should, not must, be at least 39.4 inches (1 m) horizontal distance from the outside face of a tub or shower stall.

**Bathroom Fan Switch** - This switch is just as dangerous as the others listed above and should also be located at least 39.4 inches (1 m) from the outside face of a tub or shower stall.

**3   Hydromassage bath tub Control** - See page 111 for details.

**(d)**   **Stairway Lighting Control Switches** - Rule 30-328 requires illumination at all stairwells - there is no exception.  Control switches for these light outlets are required at both head and foot of each stairway in all cases except where the basement is a dungeon like space which has no finished area and no egress other than the one stairway leading into it.

**Watch this one!**  The Rule says you must be able to turn off that stairway light from either the top or bottom of the stairway.  This may not be possible with the area lighting switch in the case of open stairways leading into lower level rooms or areas.  See page 61 for more details.

**(e)**    **Connection of Switches** - Rules 4-034(2), 30-602 - Switch connections shall be made so that there is a white wire and a black wire to the fixture. To do this the connection should be made as follows: The white wire in the supply cable shall connect directly to the screw shell (the silver terminal) in the lamp holder. The black wire from the switch connects to the center (gold) terminal in the lamp holder. In this way the fixture has a black and a white wire supplying it. It also has the black wire connected so that the screw base of the bulb cannot become energized. This is very important,

The following drawings illustrate acceptable connection arrangements in switch and light outlet boxes.

**Simplest Switching Arrangement** — Power entering light outlet box first.

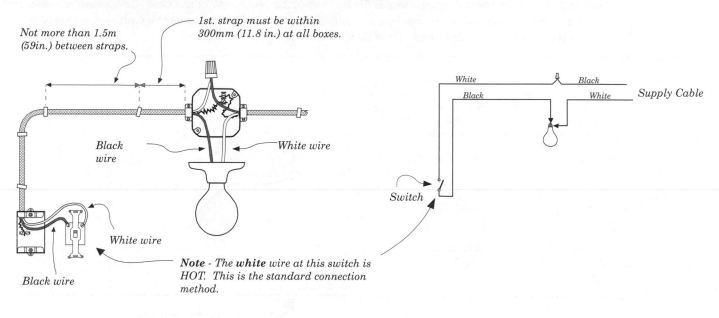

Make sure that you always connect the neutral wire, the white wire, to the screw shell in the fixture. Your life could depend on this detail.

### Power Entering Switch Outlet Box First

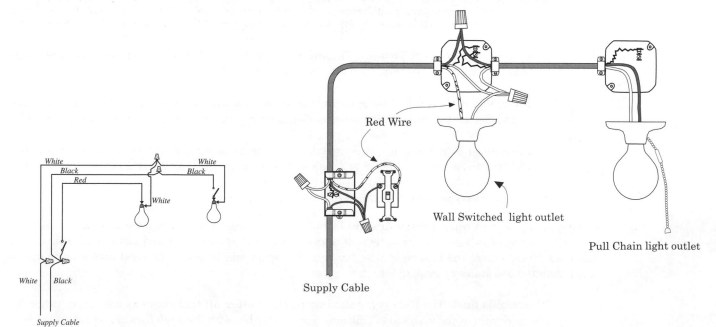

## Power Feeding through Switch Box to a Plug Outlet

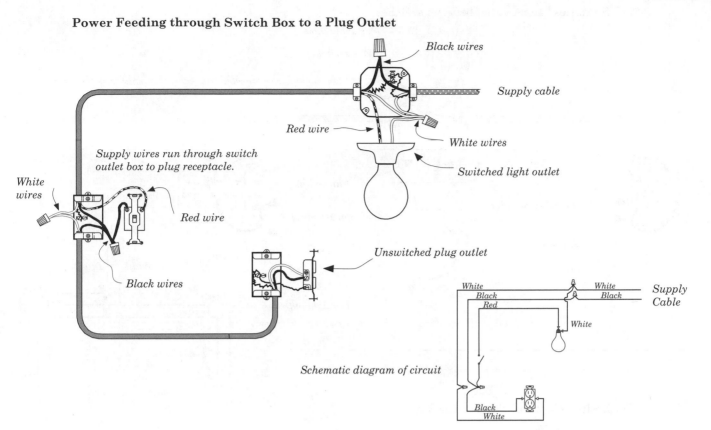

*Black wires*

*Supply cable*

*Red wire*

*White wires*

*Switched light outlet*

*Supply wires run through switch outlet box to plug receptacle.*

*White wires*

*Red wire*

*Black wires*

*Unswitched plug outlet*

*White* *White* *Supply Cable*
*Black* *Black*
*Red*
*White*

*Schematic diagram of circuit*

*Black*
*White*

## 3-Way Switches, First, Simple arrangement - Both switches on the same side of the light.

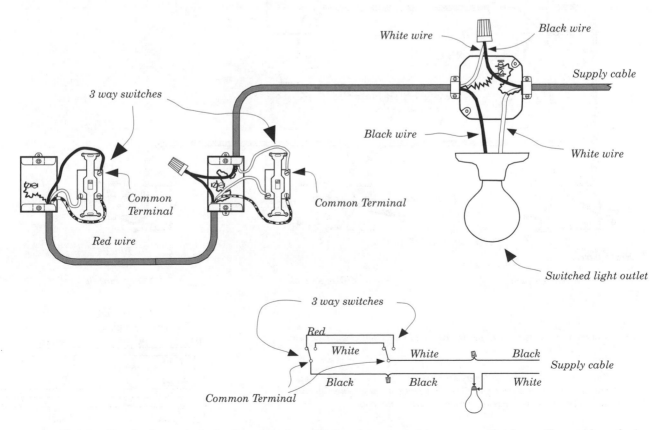

*White wire*

*Black wire*

*Supply cable*

*3 way switches*

*Black wire*

*White wire*

*Common Terminal*

*Common Terminal*

*Red wire*

*Switched light outlet*

*3 way switches*

*Red*

*White*

*White*

*Black*

*Supply cable*

*Common Terminal*

*Black*

*Black*

*White*

**Note** Bond wires must also be properly spliced and connected in every outlet box. To avoid confusion these bond wire connections are not always shown.

**3-Way Switches** - Light outlet between switches

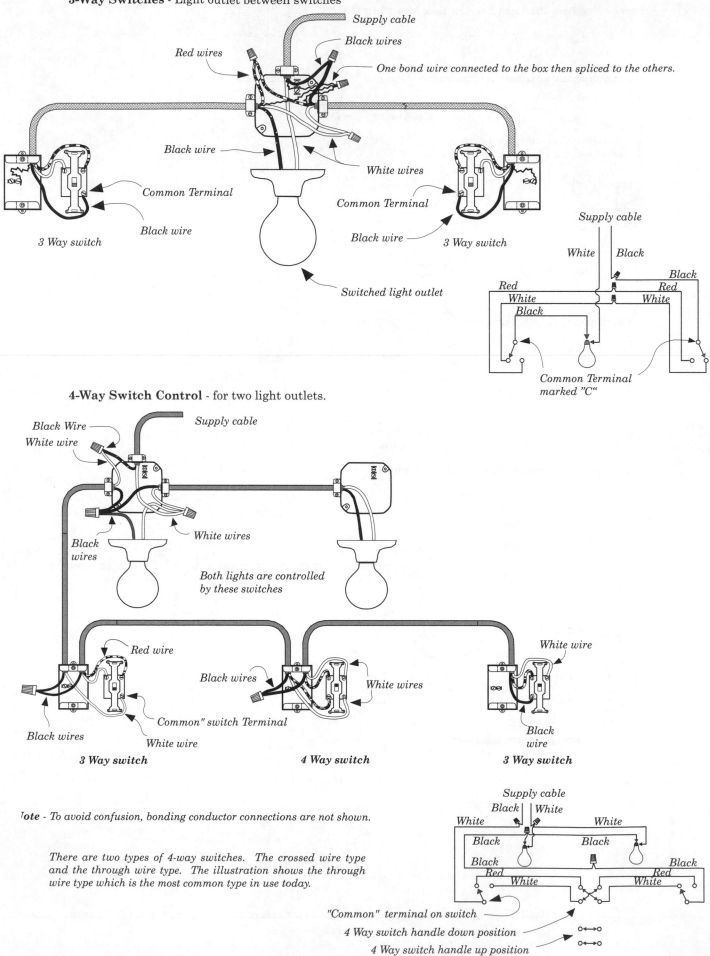

Supply cable

Black wires

Red wires

One bond wire connected to the box then spliced to the others.

Black wire

White wires

Common Terminal

Common Terminal

Black wire

Black wire

3 Way switch

3 Way switch

Switched light outlet

Supply cable

White    Black

Red

White        Red

Black        White

Black

Common Terminal
marked "C"

**4-Way Switch Control** - for two light outlets.

Black Wire

White wire

Supply cable

Black
wires

White wires

Both lights are controlled
by these switches

Red wire

Black wires

White wire

White wires

Common" switch Terminal

Black wires

White wire

Black
wire

3 Way switch

4 Way switch

3 Way switch

Note - To avoid confusion, bonding conductor connections are not shown.

There are two types of 4-way switches. The crossed wire type
and the through wire type. The illustration shows the through
wire type which is the most common type in use today.

Supply cable

Black    White

White                                    White

Black            Black

Black                                         Black

Red      White                    Red      White

"Common" terminal on switch

4 Way switch handle down position

4 Way switch handle up position

## 2-Gang Switch Box With Two Switched Plugs

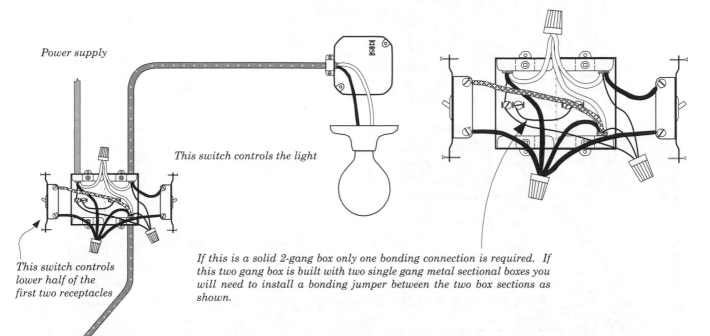

*Power supply*

*This switch controls the light*

*This switch controls lower half of the first two receptacles*

If this is a solid 2-gang box only one bonding connection is required. If this two gang box is built with two single gang metal sectional boxes you will need to install a bonding jumper between the two box sections as shown.

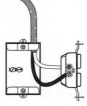

*This duplex receptacle is not switched. Both upper and lower are always hot.*

The lower half of these plug outlets are controlled by the wall switch above. The **upper half** of each outlet is not switched - it is always hot.

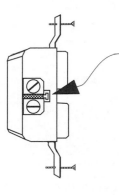

**Note** - These small break away tabs on the hot side of the two receptacles shown in the illustration above must be removed. If this is not done the above switch will not work and both halves of the duplex receptacle will always be hot at the same time.

Note - Bond wires must also be properly spliced and connected in every outlet box. To avoid confusion these bond wire connections are not always shown. See page 100 for examples of these connections required by Code.

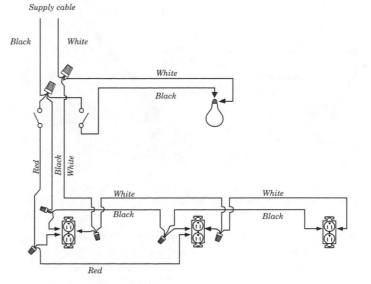

Supply cable

Black    White

White

Black

Red

Black

White

White

Black

White

Black

Red

**Some typical branch circuits.**

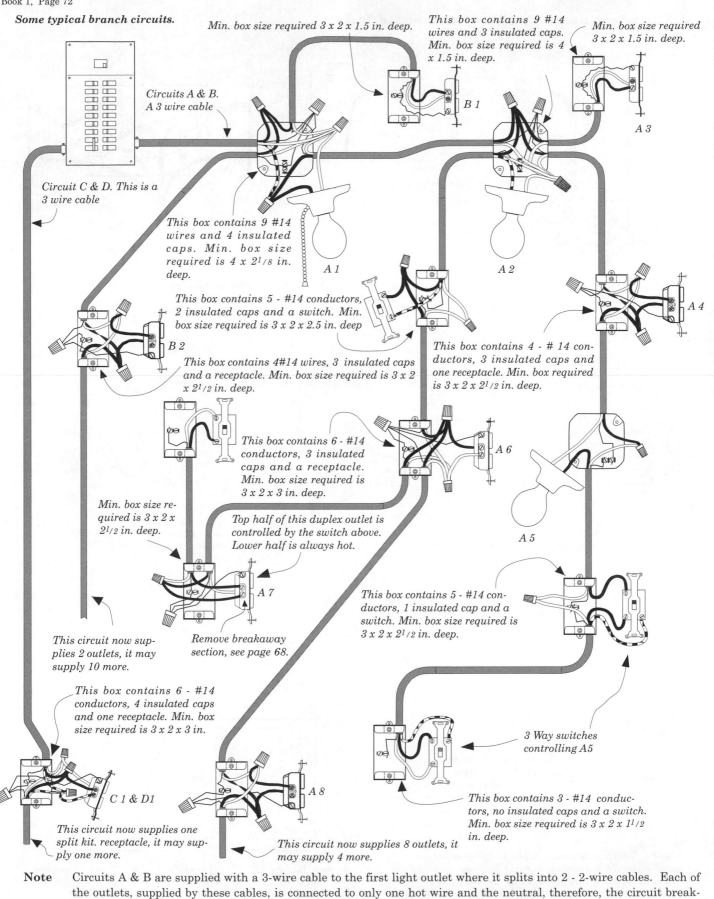

Min. box size required 3 x 2 x 1.5 in. deep.

This box contains 9 #14 wires and 3 insulated caps. Min. box size required is 4 x 1.5 in. deep.

Min. box size required 3 x 2 x 1.5 in. deep.

Circuits A & B. A 3 wire cable

B 1

A 3

Circuit C & D. This is a 3 wire cable

This box contains 9 #14 wires and 4 insulated caps. Min. box size required is 4 x 2¹/8 in. deep.

A 1

A 2

This box contains 5 - #14 conductors, 2 insulated caps and a switch. Min. box size required is 3 x 2 x 2.5 in. deep

A 4

B 2

This box contains 4#14 wires, 3 insulated caps and a receptacle. Min. box size required is 3 x 2 x 2¹/2 in. deep.

This box contains 4 - # 14 conductors, 3 insulated caps and one receptacle. Min. box required is 3 x 2 x 2¹/2 in. deep.

This box contains 6 - #14 conductors, 3 insulated caps and a receptacle. Min. box size required is 3 x 2 x 3 in. deep.

A 6

A 5

Min. box size required is 3 x 2 x 2¹/2 in. deep.

Top half of this duplex outlet is controlled by the switch above. Lower half is always hot.

A 7

This box contains 5 - #14 conductors, 1 insulated cap and a switch. Min. box size required is 3 x 2 x 2¹/2 in. deep.

This circuit now supplies 2 outlets, it may supply 10 more.

Remove breakaway section, see page 68.

This box contains 6 - #14 conductors, 4 insulated caps and one receptacle. Min. box size required is 3 x 2 x 3 in.

3 Way switches controlling A5

C 1 & D1

A 8

This circuit now supplies one split kit. receptacle, it may supply one more.

This circuit now supplies 8 outlets, it may supply 4 more.

This box contains 3 - #14 conductors, no insulated caps and a switch. Min. box size required is 3 x 2 x 1¹/2 in. deep.

**Note** Circuits A & B are supplied with a 3-wire cable to the first light outlet where it splits into 2 - 2-wire cables. Each of the outlets, supplied by these cables, is connected to only one hot wire and the neutral, therefore, the circuit breakers supplying this 3-wire cable do not need to be equipped with a tie-bar. The 3-wire cable on the left supplies kitchen counter outlets. Each of these is connected to both hot wires and the neutral, therefore, this cable must be supplied with either a two pole circuit breaker or two single pole breakers with their operating handles tied together with a tie-bar. See page 40 for very important details on 3-wire cable connections to breakers in the panel.

# 19  Plug Outlets - Rules 26-700 & 26-702

**(a)**   **Vapour Barrier for a Plug Outlet Box** - The Building Code requires boxes to be surrounded with a moisture resistant barrier if they are located in a wall or ceiling which is required to have a vapour barrier. See page 66 for details.

**(b)**   **Height** - The rules do not specify any definite height for plug outlets. They may be at any convenient height. Usually they are placed at approximately 300 mm (approx. 12 in.) to lower edge of the outlet box in the living room, dining room, bedrooms and hallways etc.

**Horizontal or Vertical** - may be either way but if you want a professional looking job, install them all in the vertical plane.

**Outdoor plug outlets** - If these are mounted in a horizontal plane (the Code does not require these to be so mounted) there is a greater possibility of nuisance tripping due to moisture gathering and remaining around the upper terminals. To prevent nuisance tripping (GFI breakers trip with only 5 ma leakage to ground,) horizontal receptacles should be mounted with the **live terminals** facing down. Outdoor outlets must be supplied with GFI breakers.

**(c)**   **Bedroom Plug Outlets - Rule 26-722(f)(g)** now require special protection for the circuits which supply plug outlets in the "sleeping facilities of a dwelling unit." These are called "arc-fault circuit interrupters". Every circuit which supplies one or more plug outlets in a bedroom must be protected with a circuit breaker which can distinguish between a normal heavy load and an arcing short circuit. The reason for this new requirement is that a standard circuit breaker could fail to open the circuit under certain short circuit conditions. A short circuit with massive current flow will normally trip a standard circuit breaker very quickly but a short circuit in which certain technical features limit the current that can flow, may not be recognized by such a circuit breaker. It may continue to feed the fault until enough heat is generated to ignite the surrounding combustibles such as wood or paper. Remember this is not a G.F.C.I. breaker and it cannot protect as a GFCI breaker,

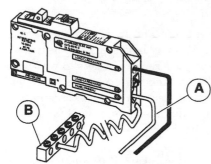

Arc-D-Tect Circuit Breaker by Square D

The illustration above shows an arc-fault circuit breaker manufactured by Square D Company. Its connection is similar to that of a G.F.C.I. breaker in that the lead from the breaker must terminate in the neutral bus as shown at (B) and both the black and the white conductor in the loomex cable must connect to the breaker as shown at (A).

Every plug outlet in any room where there are "sleeping facilities" must be protected with this special kind of circuit breaker. **Note** - This breaker cannot be used with three wire cables, only two supply wire cables may be used.

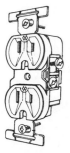

**(d)**                    **How Many Plugs and Where Required**

Living room
Family room
Rec. room
Bedroom
Den
Study

Rule 26-702(2)(3)(4)(5) & (6) require plug outlets in these rooms to be located so that it is not possible for an electrical appliance to be more than 1.8 m (approx. 6 ft.) from a plug outlet when it is located anywhere along the wall.

**Note** - This measurement is not a radius - you must measure into corners as shown in the illustration. This is the strict interpretation of Subrule (3).

**Notes**   Wall space less than 900 mm (approx. 36 in.) wide is not required to have an outlet.

Rule 26-712(c) & BC Bulletin 26-1-0 both say, do not count spaces occupied by:

**(I)  Doorways**, and the area occupied by the door when fully open.

**(2)  Window** - The space occupied by windows that extend to the floor need not be counted.

**(3)  Fireplaces**

**(4)  Other permanently fixed installations** which limit the use of wall space.

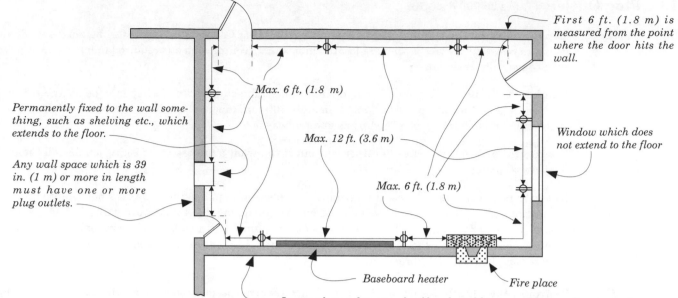

*First 6 ft. (1.8 m) is measured from the point where the door hits the wall.*

*Max. 6 ft, (1.8 m)*

*Permanently fixed to the wall something, such as shelving etc., which extends to the floor.*

*Max. 12 ft. (3.6 m)*

*Window which does not extend to the floor*

*Any wall space which is 39 in. (1 m) or more in length must have one or more plug outlets.*

*Max. 6 ft. (1.8 m)*

*Baseboard heater*

*Fire place*

*Locate plug outlets at ends of baseboard heaters so that appliance supply cords need not pass over a heater where it would be roasted.*

**Electric & Other Types of Baseboard Heaters** - are a permanent unit and they do limit the use of that wall space to some extent, however, appliances such as radios, T.V., swag lamps, etc. can be placed in that wall space and each of these requires power. The rule therefore, does require outlets in wall spaces occupied by baseboard heaters. These outlets should not be located above the heaters unless it cannot be avoided. Usually they can be located at the ends of the heaters so that electrical supply cords need not run over the heater and be roasted every time the heater comes on. See also Appendix B for Rule 26-712(a) on page 390 in the Electrical Code for confirmation of this requirement.

**(e)**   **Entrance (Foyer)** - Rule 26-712(a) - If this is a room, treat it as a living room. If it is like a hallway, apply the rule for hallways. If it is something in between - well - just put in the extra outlets and be done with it  - don't quibble over little things.

**(f)**   **Hallways**- Rule 26-712(f) - Locate the plug outlet so that no point on the hallway floor is more than 4.5 m (15 ft) from a plug outlet without having to to go through a doorway fitted with a door.

**Note**   A short open type hallway (such as between a living room and kitchen where there are no doors) does not require a plug outlet at all, provided that no point in the hallway is more than 4.5 m (approx. 15 ft.) from a plug outlet in either of the rooms at the ends of the hallway.

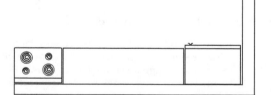

*Short open hallway. No point in the hall- way is more than 4.5 m (177 inches) from an outlet.*

**(g)**   **Basement Wiring** - Rules 26-710(a)(b) & (e); 26-712(a)(b)(c)

**Finished Basement** - The rules require the same number of outlets along the walls of a basement as for similar rooms upstairs. The walls of basement bedrooms, hallways, family rooms etc. which are finished must be wired as similar rooms on the main floor.

**Unfinished Basement**

**First A Definition of Unfinished** - Rule 26-710(a)

This Rule defines an unfinished basement as follows:

**(1)**      **If the wall finish material** does not extend fully to the floor, ie. if the lower 450 mm (17.7 in.) of the wall is not finished with any kind of finishing material that wall is considered to be unfinished. Such a wall is required to have only minimum wiring as described below. Building insulation and vapour barrier may be installed in all walls and it may extend to the floor. Building insulation is not finishing material.

**(2)**      **Each wall or partition** is considered separately. Full wiring is required in all walls and partitions which are finished completely. If only the outside walls of the basement are finished to the floor then only those walls require full wiring as similar rooms on the main floor. Any wall of any basement room where the wall finish stops 450 mm (17.7 in.) above the floor need not be wired except as noted below under "Minimum Basement Plug Outlets Required".

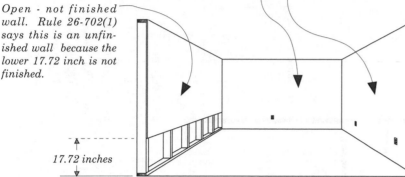

*Open - not finished wall. Rule 26-702(1) says this is an unfinished wall because the lower 17.72 inch is not finished.*

*These walls are finished therefore full wiring is required.*

*17.72 inches*

**Minimum Basement Plug Outlets Required** - Rule 26-710(e)(iv) - requires only one plug outlet in an unfinished basement. If there are no walls to divide the basement into two or more rooms or areas the rule is satisfied with just one duplex plug outlet in the whole basement. See also below under "Laundry Plug in Basement".

**Note -**    **Basement partitions** - unfinished - studs only

If there are no partitions to divide the basement into two or more areas AND the lower portion of the basement outside walls are not finished except as described above AND there is no laundry facility in the basement, this rule is satisfied with just one duplex plug outlet in the whole basement.

**Caution** - Rule 26-710(e)(iv) refers to an "area" not to a room. The rule says "at least one duplex receptacle shall be provided in any unfinished basement area." Unfinished partitions consisting of studs only, can and do divide the total basement floor space into two or more areas and each of these areas is required to have at least one duplex plug outlet. Note too that Rule 26-712(a) also refers to a "room or area" and says that both must be treated equally. There may be differences of opinion on this interpretation, therefore you should check with your local inspector before proceeding.

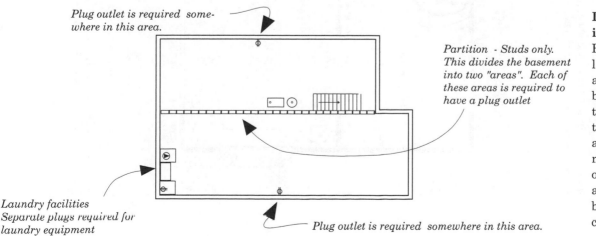

*Plug outlet is required somewhere in this area.*

*Partition - Studs only. This divides the basement into two "areas". Each of these areas is required to have a plug outlet*

*Laundry facilities Separate plugs required for laundry equipment*

*Plug outlet is required somewhere in this area.*

**Laundry Plug in Basement**. - Rule 26-720(b) - If laundry facilities are located in the basement then the plug outlet for the washer is in addition to the minimum plug outlets described above and it must be on its own circuit.

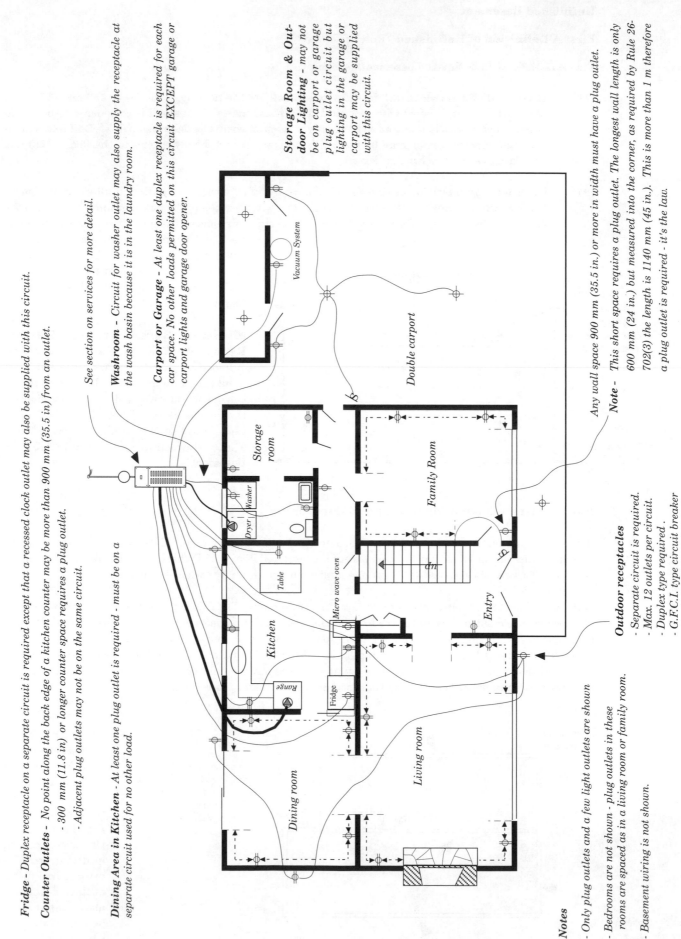

**Fridge** - Duplex receptacle on a separate circuit is required except that a recessed clock outlet may also be supplied with this circuit.

**Counter Outlets** - No point along the back edge of a kitchen counter may be more than 900 mm (35.5 in) from an outlet.
- 300 mm (11.8 in) or longer counter space requires a plug outlet.
- Adjacent plug outlets may not be on the same circuit.

**Dining Area in Kitchen** - At least one plug outlet is required - must be on a separate circuit used for no other load.

See section on services for more detail.

**Washroom** - Circuit for washer outlet may also supply the receptacle at the wash basin because it is in the laundry room.

**Carport or Garage** - At least one duplex receptacle is required for each car space. No other loads permitted on this circuit EXCEPT garage or carport lights and garage door opener.

**Storage Room & Outdoor Lighting** - may not be on carport or garage plug outlet circuit but lighting in the garage or carport may be supplied with this circuit.

Any wall space 900 mm (35.5 in.) or more in width must have a plug outlet.

**Note** - This short space requires a plug outlet. The longest wall length is only 600 mm (24 in.) but measured into the corner, as required by Rule 26-702(3) the length is 1140 mm (45 in.). This is more than 1 m therefore a plug outlet is required - it's the law.

**Outdoor receptacles**
- Separate circuit is required.
- Max. 12 outlets per circuit.
- Duplex type required.
- G.F.C.I. type circuit breaker or receptacle must be used.

**Notes**
- Only plug outlets and a few light outlets are shown
- Bedrooms are not shown - plug outlets in these rooms are spaced as in a living room or family room.
- Basement wiring is not shown.

**(h)**    **Bathroom Plug Outlet** - Rule 26-710(f)(g) requires at least 1 plug outlet in each bathroom.  To comply with the rules this outlet must:

A    **Be at least 1 m** (39 in.) away from the bathtub or shower stall.  This is a horizontal distance between the outlet and a shower stall or bath tub as shown below; and

**Note** - Rule 26-710(g) has been revised.  Where it is not possible, (the subrule says "practicable",) to locate the bathroom plug at least 1 m from the tub or shower it can be at a lesser distance but it may not be closer than 500 mm (19.7 inches).  This shorter distance is allowed only in the very small bathrooms where the 1 m distance is simply not possible.

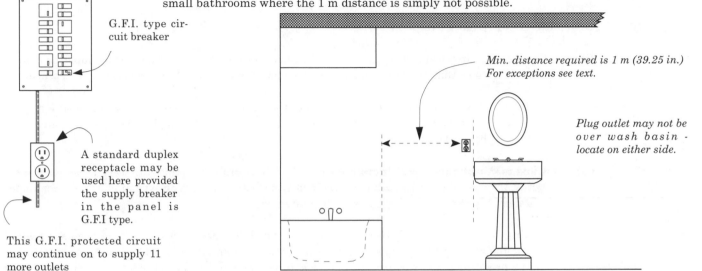

G.F.I. type circuit breaker

*Min. distance required is 1 m (39.25 in.) For exceptions see text.*

*Plug outlet may not be over wash basin - locate on either side.*

A standard duplex receptacle may be used here provided the supply breaker in the panel is G.F.I type.

This G.F.I. protected circuit may continue on to supply 11 more outlets

B    **Be adjacent** to the wash basin.  The rule requires that this outlet be not above the basin but on either side of it; and

C    **Be GFI protected** - Rule 26-700(11) This subrule requires GFI protection for plug outlets in **all bathrooms and washrooms.**  It may be either a G.F.I. type plug receptacle; or it may be an ordinary duplex plug receptacle which is supplied from a special type circuit breaker (G.F.C.I.) in the service panel.  This circuit breaker is called a Class A Ground Fault Circuit Interrupter.  These breakers mount in the service panel as ordinary breakers.  If you are using an older type circuit breaker panel make sure they are available for the particular service panel you are using.

This subrule is very broad in its scope when applied according to the definition for bathroom and washroom.  Those definitions do not really refer to a bathroom or to a washroom but to rooms which contain a tub or a shower or a washbasin.  The room **contains** this appliance.  It could be any room in the house.  For example, a large bedroom with a tub is included in this definition.  The fact that there is also a bed in the same room is irrelevant.  This means that bathroom rules will apply wherever any appliances, such as a tub or shower are being installed.  Washroom rules apply wherever there is a washbasin; any room will do.  Any plug outlets within 3 m (118 in.) of a bathtub, shower stall or washbasin must be GFI protected; and may

D    **Be Supplied** with any nearby lighting circuit which has 11 or fewer outlets.

Note    **Bathroom / Laundry Room Combination** - Rule 26-710(h) - This is an important detail.  See under 'Laundry in Bathroom', page 87.

**(i)**    **Washroom Plug Outlet**

The definition, on page 11 in your Code book, says a "Washroom means a room containing a wash basin(s) and may contain a water closet(s) but without bathing or showering facilities"

(i)    **Plug outlet Required** - Rule 26-702(13) requires at least one duplex plug outlet adjacent to, ie. next to, but not above, the wash basin.

**(ii)**     **Circuit Required** - The rules do not require a separate circuit. This outlet may be connected to any nearby lighting circuit.

**(iii)**     **G.F.I Protection Required** - Yes, this outlet must be GFI protected. Rule 26-700(11) requires GFI protection for all plug outlets within 3 m (118 in.) of a washbasin no matter where the washbasin is located. You may use a GFI circuit breaker in the panel or you may use a GFI type receptacle. In either case the rule permits other plug outlets and lights in other washrooms and bathrooms, bedrooms, hallways etc. to be protected with the same GFI protective device. The maximum number of outlets must not exceed 12. See also above under bathroom plug outlets.

**(j)**     **Other Rooms or Areas - Plug Outlets**

**(i)**     **Storage Rooms** - Rule 26-712(a) - Every finished room, including storage rooms, must have minimum wiring so that no point along the wall is more than 1.8 m (71 in.) from a plug receptacle.

    Note     Storage spaces such as areas under the stairways, attics or crawl spaces do not require a plug outlet. In fact it is safer without one, so that appliances must be unplugged before being stored.

**(ii)**     **Closets, Cupboards, Cabinets etc.**- Rule 26-710(i) prohibits plug outlets in these enclosures except for special cavities built for specific heating and non-heating type appliances. See under "Kitchen Appliance Garages" on page 85 for details.

**(iii)**     **Dining Room** - Rule 26-712(a) - Dining rooms which are **not part of a kitchen** must be wired as a living room so that no part along the wall is more than 1.8 m (71 in.) from a plug outlet. For dining or eating areas **forming part of a kitchen**, see under "Eating Area in Kitchen" on page 80.

**(k)**     **Kitchen Counter Plug Outlets**

**(i)**     **Types Required** - Rule 26-710(b) according to the definitions on page 9 in the Code.

    **Receptacle** - "means one or more female contact devices on the same yoke".

    **Duplex Receptacle** - Means "two female contact devices on the same yoke" See illustration.

    **SPLIT Receptacle** - "Means a duplex receptacle" which is equipped with a break-away tab as shown below. Rule 26-722(b) refers to "split receptacles"which means that we must use duplex receptacles for the counter plug outlets.

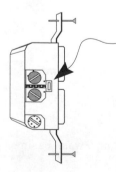

    A split duplex receptacle is a standard duplex receptacle, except that it has a small break-away section of metal on the hot (brass colored) side terminal block as shown below. When this section of metal is broken off it disconnects the two halves of the duplex receptacle from each other so that each half can be connected to a different circuit. They share a common neutral (white) wire.

*This small tab connects the two halves of the receptacle together. Normally this tab is left in place but for split receptacles on kitchen counters this gold coloured tab must be removed.*

This type of receptacle must be used for all appliance outlets above the kitchen counter work space. Remember, the Code permits two duplex receptacles on one 3-wire circuit. The upper half of each duplex receptacle is on one circuit and the lower half of each receptacle is on the other circuit in the 3-wire supply cable.

**(ii)**     **Height** - The rules do not specify any height for these outlets except that they not be on the counter work surface facing up, Rule 26-710(c). They must be located on the wall above the normal splash level of the counter work surface.

**(iii)**     **Behind & In front of the Kitchen Sink** - Rule 26-712(e) - Plug receptacles must be located on the wall behind the counter and on either side of the kitchen sink but not behind it. It must not be necessary for appliance supply cords to pass over the sink. Just as important, plug outlets must not be located anywhere directly in front of the sink. Anyone in contact with a plug outlet while working in the sink could suddenly become damaged goods.

**(iv)**     **Adjacent Plug Outlets** - It has been determined, we are not told how, that the average home-maker in an average home is much more likely to use two adjacent receptacles at the same time than two receptacles spaced a bit farther apart. That is why adjacent outlets are not permitted to be supplied with the same 3-wire circuit. The illustration below shows a simple arrangement where three plug outlets are connected to two 3-wire circuits in such a way that adjacent outlets are on different 3-wire circuits as required by the rules.

Watch this very carefully, it's easy to get caught on this one and sometimes a bit costly to correct.

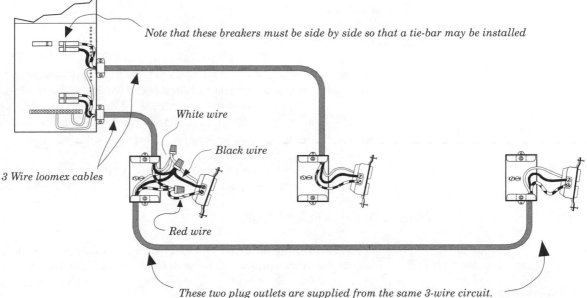

*Note that these breakers must be side by side so that a tie-bar may be installed*

*White wire*

*Black wire*

*3 Wire loomex cables*

*Red wire*

*These two plug outlets are supplied from the same 3-wire circuit.*

*Adjacent counter plug outlets may not be supplied with the same circuit. The third outlet supplied from a different circuit and placed between these two outlets is required to comply with the Rules.*

**(v)**     **Kitchen Counter Plug Outlets** - The cabinet layout shown below may not be the ideal for a modern kitchen but it shows the normal circuit arrangements for kitchen counter plug outlets required by Code.

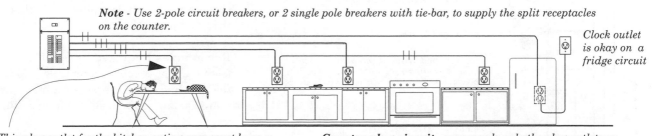

*Note - Use 2-pole circuit breakers, or 2 single pole breakers with tie-bar, to supply the split receptacles on the counter.*

*Clock outlet is okay on a fridge circuit*

*This plug outlet for the kitchen eating area must be on a separate circuit used for no other load.*

*Counter plug circuit - may supply only the plug outlets on the counter - it may not supply any other outlets.*

**Notes**   **(I)**     **As shown above**, the two split duplex receptacles on the counter (to the left of the range) are on different 3-wire circuits. The outlets on each side of the range are also on different 3-wire circuits. This is to comply with Rule 26-722(b) which says that "adjacent receptacles shall not be connected to the same multi-wire branch circuit".

    **(2)**     **Where circuit breakers are used** to supply split receptacles, you need either 2-pole type circuit breakers or two single pole breakers with tie-bar; either one is acceptable; Rule 14-010, 14-302(b). See also page 40 for clarification.

**Where fuses are used** Rule 14-010(b) requires that both fuses can be removed simultaneously. A "fuse pull" similar to that required for a range or dryer, is required. Where the existing fuse panel is not equipped with this feature, check with your Inspector for permission to install separate 2-pole fused disconnect switches for these circuits.

**(3)**   **Polarization** - This is an important detail. You will notice the receptacle has a brass terminal screw and the chrome plated terminal screw. Be sure to connect the black, or sometimes the red wire, to the brass terminal screw and the white neutral conductor to the chrome plated terminal screw. The Inspector has a little tester he uses to check this connection without removing any cover etc. If you have connected incorrectly, he will very likely find it.

**(vi)**   **Kitchen Plugs in General** - According to Rule 26-712 & 26-722 kitchen plug outlets are required as follows:

**Fridge Outlet -** Rule 26-720(a)

A receptacle must be installed for each fridge. It may be a single receptacle. It could be a **split** duplex receptacle but then both circuits of the 3-wire supply circuit would have to end there. One of these circuits would never be used because the receptacle is usually behind the fridge and not readily accessible for other loads. It's best to run a separate 2-wire cable to this location and install a duplex receptacle.

**Note** - The circuit supplying a fridge outlet may continue on to supply a clock outlet as shown above but it **may not be used** to supply the kitchen hood fan or any other load.

**Counter Outlets** - Rule 26-712(d)(iii)

A sufficient number of receptacles must be installed so that no point along the wall line on the work surface will be more than 900 mm (35.4 in.) from a receptacle. This is measured from the receptacle along the back edge of the counter, as shown below.

**Work Surface** does not include area of sink, range, fridge or similar appliance.

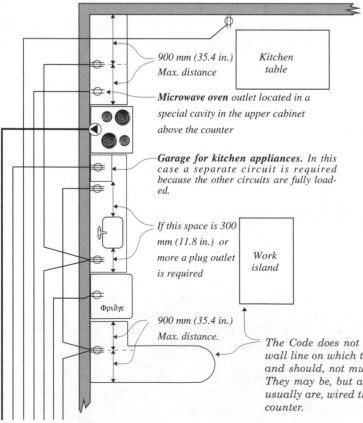

*900 mm (35.4 in.) Max. distance*

Kitchen table

**Microwave oven** *outlet located in a special cavity in the upper cabinet above the counter*

**Garage for kitchen appliances.** *In this case a separate circuit is required because the other circuits are fully loaded.*

*If this space is 300 mm (11.8 in.) or more a plug outlet is required*

Work island

Φριδγε

*900 mm (35.4 in.) Max. distance.*

**Eating Area in Kitchen** - Rule 26-712(d)(iv)
It there is an eating area in the kitchen Rule 26-702(7)(d) requires a duplex plug outlet in that area and Rule 26-722(e) says this plug outlet must be supplied with a circuit used for no other purpose. Except that a plug outlet for the gas range may also be supplied with this circuit as shown on page 83.

**Receptacles Required** - Each of these work surfaces must have a plug receptacle. No point along the wall line above the work counter may be more than 900 mm (approx. 36 in.) from a plug receptacle.

**Note**   Any counter space which is 300 mm (approx. 12 in.) long must be provided with one or more outlets. Any counter space less than 300 mm long is not required to have an outlet.

*The Code does not require plug outlets for these work spaces because there is no wall line on which to mount the outlets, however they are definitely needed here too and should, not must, be installed. They may be installed below the counter level. They may be, but are not required to be, split type receptacles. They may be, and usually are, wired the same as and in the same circuits with, the plug outlets on the counter.*

**Receptacle on Range** - Rule 26-710(k) - Plug outlets on the range or those located in cabinets or cupboards are not acceptable as alternatives for wall outlets. See illustrations.

**Note 1  Built-in Microwave Oven** - Rule 26-720(d)

A separate circuit is required for a built-in microwave oven. The plug outlet for this oven should be located in the same special cavity in the kitchen cabinet. Make sure there is adequate ventilation provided for this oven.

If it is not a built-in microwave oven, i.e., if it stands on the kitchen counter, this rule does not apply. In that case one of the counter outlets may be used to supply this oven.

**Note 2  Work Surface** - Rule 26-712(d)(iv)

As shown above, the counter work space is often divided into several isolated sections. Each of these isolated sections must be considered separately and each must have a split duplex receptacle if it is 300 mm (11.8 in.) or longer. This measurement is along the back wall of the counter space. The reason for this requirement is to make all counter work surfaces properly accessible to appliance receptacles without the supply lines having to cross over sinks, ranges, etc.. Make sure you have a sufficient number of outlets along the counter before covering. It is difficult to add more later after the finish material is in place.

**Rule 26-710(c) says** plug outlets may not be mounted facing up in the work surfaces or counters in the kitchen or dining area. The concern is spillage and clean up with a wet cloth. Plug outlets must be mounted on a vertical plane above the level of the work surface so that any spillage on the work surface cannot enter the outlet.

**Note 3  Work Island** - Rule 26-712(d) does not refer to this work space.

There is no back splash on a work island, therefore, the rules do not require a plug outlet at this location. If plug outlets are installed on the work island they are not required to be wired as counter plugs, but really, they should be wired the same way.

**Note 4  The Peninsula** - The one outlet on the back splash of the peninsula is usually acceptable as shown in the illustrations.

**Note 5  Appliance Storage Garage** - Rules 26-710(i) & 26-710(j)

Some modern kitchen cabinets provide space, (special cavities) inside the cabinets to store appliances normally left standing on the kitchen counter. The rules now permit us to install a plug outlet in that enclosure and to leave the appliance plugged into that receptacle when it is stored in that enclosure. There is nothing wrong with this provided the plug outlet, and therefore the appliance, is automatically de-energized when the enclosure door is not fully open. The Electrical Code Committees are very concerned with safety from electrical shock and from fire. Rule 26-710(i) & 26-710(j) sets minimum standards necessary for a safe installation of an appliance garage. See page 85 for detailed description of those minimum requirements.

**Note 6  Disabled Persons** - have difficulty using counter plug outlets when they are located along the wall behind the counter. Rule 26-710(d) allows additional split plug outlets to be installed along the front or end wall of the lower cabinet to provide better access for the disabled. It should be noted that the rule does not require these outlets, it simply allows them in addition to the normal outlets. The two subrules that deal with these special plugs are:

A        **Rule 26-710(d)** says that these special counter plug outlets are in addition to those shown in the illustration above, **they are not a substitute** for the plug outlets normally required along the counter; and

B        **Rule 26-722(d)** permits these additional outlets to be supplied from the 3-wire circuits used to supply the outlets along the wall behind the counter. Actually this rule refers to only one additional split receptacle. The intent, it seems, is to allow one additional split plug on each 3-wire circuit supplying counter plugs as shown below.

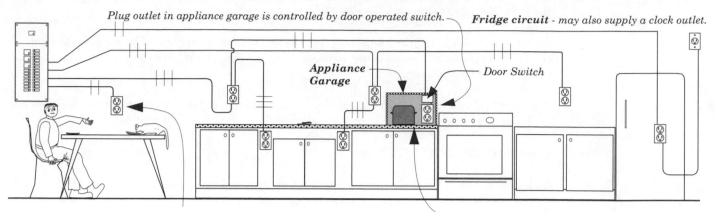

*Plug outlet in appliance garage is controlled by door operated switch.* **Fridge circuit** - *may also supply a clock outlet.*

*Appliance Garage*

*Door Switch*

*This plug outlet for the kitchen eating area must be on a separate circuit used for no other load.*

**Appliance garage** *must be factory built and certified by CSA or one of the other certification agencies. For clarity the garage is shown with the door removed .*

**Note 7   Split Duplex Receptacles** - Rule 26-712(d)(iii) all receptacles along counter work surfaces must be split duplex type.

— Single receptacles may not be used.
— Only two such split duplex receptacles may be supplied from a 3-wire circuit except for special outlets, as noted above, under "Disabled Persons" on page 81..
— This 3-wire circuit may not supply any other load.

**Short counter** - Limited workspace - only one split receptacle is required, Rule 26-722(c).

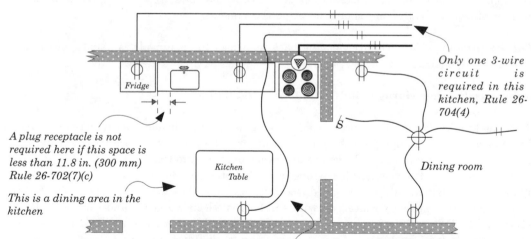

*Fridge*

*Only one 3-wire circuit is required in this kitchen, Rule 26-704(4)*

*A plug receptacle is not required here if this space is less than 11.8 in. (300 mm) Rule 26-702(7)(c)*

*This is a dining area in the kitchen*

*Kitchen Table*

*Dining room*

*Separate circuit required for this eating area plug*

**Note** that Rule 26-722(c) applies only when using the 15 amp 3-wire plug circuits. If you are using 20amp plug circuits you must install two receptacles in this short counter space and each must then be supplied with a separate 2-wire 20 amp circuit.

**Where the counter is longer** there will be more usable work spaces and therefore more receptacles are required. In the illustration below we had to add one more receptacle for the additional work space. Even though we are permitted to connect two split receptacles to a 3-wire circuit we could not connect this additional outlet to the 3-wire cable supplying the plug outlet on the right side of the sink. The rules will not allow this because these plugs are adjacent to each other. We need to run a new 3-wire 15 amp supply cable for this one additional split counter plug.

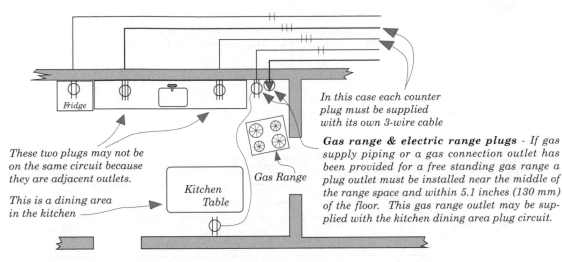

*In this case each counter plug must be supplied with its own 3-wire cable*

**Gas range & electric range plugs** *- If gas supply piping or a gas connection outlet has been provided for a free standing gas range a plug outlet must be installed near the middle of the range space and within 5.1 inches (130 mm) of the floor. This gas range outlet may be supplied with the kitchen dining area plug circuit.*

*These two plugs may not be on the same circuit because they are adjacent outlets.*

*This is a dining area in the kitchen*

*Gas Range*

**Note 8 Gas Range power Supply** - Rule 26-712(d) This subrule is illustrated above. It requires that where gas supply piping or a gas connection outlet is provided for a free standing gas range, we must also provide a standard 15 amp plug receptacle for the control voltage in that gas range. Rule 26-722(e) says this plug outlet may be supplied by the kitchen eating area plug circuit. The subrule does not say so but it is probably safe to assume this gas range plug could be supplied from any nearby lighting circuit as well. This plug outlet must be:

1 Installed in or on the surface of the wall behind the intended range location.

2 Located near the midpoint measured horizontally along the back wall of the cavity.

3 Not more than 130 mm (5.1 inches) above the finished floor level.

**Caution** - Rule 26-744(4)(11)(12) & Bulletin 26-14-0 say that in every dwelling unit, in a quadplex, triplex, duplex, or detached single family house, **where the range is not a built-in type, a** plug outlet for an electric range must be installed, (See Definition of "single dwelling"). Please note, this applies even where gas piping is provided for a free standing gas range. The rule requires a plug outlet for an electric range as well so that a new owner of the house, (should it be sold,) could bring in and connect a standard free standing electric range.

**Note 9 20 Ampere Kitchen Plugs** - Rule 26-710(b) & 26-726

This rule allows 20 amp plug outlets on the kitchen counter. This is an option, not a requirement. We can choose to install 15 amp plugs in the normal way using split receptacles, as described above, or we can choose to install 20 amp circuits and 20 amp non-split receptacles as described below.

If we choose to install 20 amp receptacles on the kitchen counter there are a few things we must keep in mind. These are:

1 We must use #12 copper supply cable

2 We must use a 20 amp fuse or breaker.

3 We must use the type of 20 amp T-slot receptacle shown at left. Officially it is called a CSA Configuration 5-20RA receptacle.

4 We can still supply two of these plugs with each circuit but if we do that we would actually reduce the total load capacity available at those two outlets. You see, with that arrangement there would be only one 20 amp breaker supplying two duplex outlets compared with two 15 amp breakers supplying the same two duplex outlets with the old arrangement.

5 Adjacent plugs **must not be** supplied with the same circuit

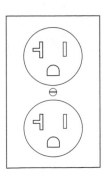

*T-Slot Receptacle*

6    The only way to gain an advantage with this new arrangement is by installing a separate circuit for each outlet. 3-wire #12 cable could be run to the first outlet then continue with two wire #12 cable to the second outlet. Watch your box size when installing #12 cable.

7    The number and placement of plugs is the same as for the 15 amp circuits described above.

*Note* - *20 amp single pole breakers may be used to supply the counter plugs shown. Two conductor #12 copper cable is shown but the two circuits supplying counter plugs could be supplied with one three conductor cable.*

*The circuit for the eating area plug outlet, the fridge plug outlet, the clock outlet may all be 20 amp. In that case you must use 20 amp plug receptacles, 20 amp wiring and 20 amp breakers.*

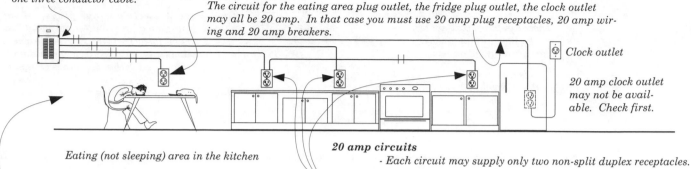

*Clock outlet*

*20 amp clock outlet may not be available. Check first.*

*Eating (not sleeping) area in the kitchen*

**20 amp circuits**

*If there is an **eating area** in the **kitchen** the rules require at least one duplex plug outlet for use in that area. All the plug outlets **in the kitchen eating area** may be supplied with the same (2-wire) circuit. Do not use this circuit for any other outlets in any other location in the kitchen or in any other part of the house. **There is one exception**, the plug outlet required for a gas range may also be supplied from this circuit, Rule 26-704(6).*

- *Each circuit may supply only two non-split duplex receptacles.*
- *Duplex receptacle must be configuration 5-20RA as shown,*
- *These circuits may supply only plugs but not any light outlets.*
- *Adjacent plugs may not be supplied with the same circuit.*
- *At least two 20 amp branch circuits are required. More circuits may be required because these plugs are located and spaced as with 15 amp split duplex counter plugs.*

**At least two 20 amp circuits** are required in every case. Two 20 amp receptacles and two 20 amp circuits are required even on the short kitchen counters.

**Yes,** these are 20 amp receptacles protected with a 20 amp breaker or fuse, and yes. these receptacles will accept a standard parallel blade 15 amp attachment cap. It will not be necessary to change the attachment caps on the appliances we now use in our kitchens. We will have various small kitchen appliances, with very small cords and which were designed and approved for use on 15 amp circuits, but will now be operating on 20 amp circuits. The fact that this arrangement has been used successfully for many years in The United States should convince us this is a safe and acceptable practice.

**One more thing** - Rule 26-710(b) makes it clear that all plug circuits in the house could be wired with #12 copper cable and supplied with 20 amp breakers. But remember, this rule refers to plug outlets only, it does not mention lighting outlets. Rule 30-104(a) says that all lighting circuits in a dwelling unit must be protected by 15 amp fuses or breakers, not 20 amp. Most circuits in a residence supply a mixture of plugs and lighting to give better load diversity, and because it is more economical to do so. For this reason 20 amp circuits should only be used for special plug outlets.

**Special circuits** supplying only plug outlets, such as shop outlets could be wired with #12 copper cable, a 20 amp T-slot receptacle, and supplied with a 20 amp breaker.

Note 10      **KITCHEN APPLIANCE GARAGES** - Rules 26-710(i) & 26-710(j)

Some modern kitchen cabinets provide space inside the cabinets to store the appliances normally left standing on the kitchen counter. There is nothing wrong with this provided the appliances cannot be left plugged in when they are stored in that cavity. This means that there may not be any plug outlets inside that enclosure except as noted below.

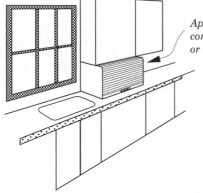

*Appliance garage must be factory assembled complete with door operated switch and one or more plug outlets.*

**Subrules 26-710(i)(i)(ii)(iii) & 26-710(j)** permit plug outlets inside of an appliance garage under certain conditions. Following is a breakdown of these subrules.

Subrule (i)      This Subrule says receptacles may be installed in an enclosure provided that "The receptacle is an integral part of a factory-built enclosure." This means that an appliance garage, complete with one or more plug outlets, must be a factory built assembly, not one built on site. The garage must also be properly certified and labeled by CSA or by one of the other certification agencies.

This arrangement involves a door operated switch to control the plug receptacle located inside the enclosure. In order to insure the correct and dependable operation of the door operated switch the subrule requires the garage assembly to be factory built and properly certified by CSA or one of the other certification agencies.

Subrule (ii)    This Subrule says the receptacle in the enclosure is "intended for use within the enclosure". Obviously this subrule is not referring to an appliance garage located on the kitchen counter top. An appliance garage is only a storage space for appliances which might otherwise be left standing on the counter. It is not large enough for normal functioning of any kitchen appliances. This subrule really describes an enclosure for appliances such as a microwave oven, a compactor, an in-line water heater etc which are "intended for use within the enclosure" but in most cases do not require a door operated switch.

Other appliances, such as mixers, are sometimes mounted on a base that can move the appliance out of sight into a cavity below the counter level when not in use. The plug outlet would be located in the cavity and the appliance could remain plugged into that receptacle when in the stow-away position. Subrule 26-710(j) requires the receptacle to be de-energized whenever the access door to the appliance is not fully open. This is a very important detail. A door operated switch must be installed and connected to insure power is disconnected from the receptacle as soon as the door is not fully open.

This Subrule does not specifically require this arrangement to be certified and labeled but it is understood that the mechanism required makes it necessarily a factory built item and therefore subject to certification and a label.

**Subrule (iii)** This Subrule says "The receptacle is intended for use with a microwave oven."

This is usually an open cavity above the kitchen counter, it is rarely fitted with a door. Two things to watch out for: the microwave oven must be certified for use in a cavity. The concern is adequate ventilation for the oven. The other detail is the receptacle. It may be, in fact should be, located in that cavity. It does not need a switch to shut it off when not in use, but it does require a separate circuit, Rule 26-720(d).

**Note 11** Dining Areas

**Kitchen Dining Area** - Rule 26-712(d)

If there is an eating area in the kitchen Rule 26-712(d)(iv) requires a duplex plug outlet in that area and Rule 26-722(e) says this outlet must be supplied with a separate circuit used for no other purpose. The rule does not require a split receptacle in this location, therefore, the supply cable need be only a 2 wire cable with bond.

**Dining Room** - Rule 26-712(a)

A dining room which is a separate room and not part of the kitchen must be wired similar to the living room, i.e. no point along the floor line of the walls may be more than 1.8 m (71 in.) from a plug outlet. These outlets may be supplied with any lighting circuit.

**(l)** **Laundry Room or Area** - Rules 26-710(e)(i), 26-720(b)

At least one appliance plug outlet must be installed in the laundry room or area.

This laundry room plug outlet:

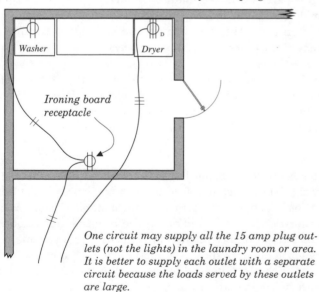

*One circuit may supply all the 15 amp plug outlets (not the lights) in the laundry room or area. It is better to supply each outlet with a separate circuit because the loads served by these outlets are large.*

- Must be duplex type - a single receptacle is not acceptable in the laundry room. It may be, but does not need to be, a split receptacle.

- May be at any convenient height in the laundry room.

- Must be supplied by a circuit used for no other purpose than to supply the one or more duplex appliance plug receptacles in the laundry room or area.

**Note** - The rule says we must provide "at least one branch circuit for receptacles" in the laundry room. According to this rule, two or more receptacles in the laundry area could be supplied by one circuit. It is better to install more circuits - one for each outlet. If there is sufficient space to do the ironing in this room you should, the rule does not say must, install a separate circuit for the iron.

**(m)** **Utility Room or Area.** - Rules 26-710(c), 26-720(c)

These rules require at least one duplex plug outlet in "each utility room". The term "utility room" is not defined in the Electrical Code. It is not referring to the laundry room because that room or area is dealt with separately under another subrule. It is not referring to the porch, or mud room, because those are covered under Rule 26-712(a)&(b), see below for details on porch wiring. It could be the furnace and water heater room but then what on earth would we do with a plug outlet in that room. It would serve no obvious purpose there.

Since there is no definition of the term "utility room" then obviously no one can be sure when he is in that room. Such rooms are difficult to wire properly, but then, it would be just as difficult to prove it was not wired properly.

If the Inspector finds you with a "utility room" - - which has not been properly wired, you could be in serious trouble - - - I suppose. See also under "Freezer Outlet" below.

**(n)**      **Laundry in Bathroom** - Rule 26-710(h)

Laundry equipment may be located in a bathroom provided the plug outlets for that equipment are properly located.

**(1)**      **Locate** the washer plug outlet **behind** the washer.

**(2)** **This washing machine outlet** must not be more than 23.6 in. (600 m) above the floor. The intent here is to make this outlet inaccessible for use with any other electrical appliances which may be used in that room.

**(3)** **If there is an ironing plug,** locate it at least 39.4 inches (1 m) from the tub and/or shower stall. This receptacle must be GFI type or be protected with a GFI type circuit breaker in the panel and it should, (not must) be on it's own circuit.

*Rule 26-702(11) requires at least one plug outlet adjacent to the washbasin and Rule 26-702(12) says this plug must be located at least 39.4 inches (1 m ) from the tub and/or shower stall.*

*Plug outlets for the laundry equipment must be located behind the equipment and not more than 24 in above the floor. Because this is also a bathroom the outlets must not be readily accessible for use with any other device.*

**(o)**      **Dryer Receptacles** - see under ``Heavy Appliances", page 106.

**(p)**      **Freezer Outlet** - The rules do not demand a separate circuit for the freezer but it is a good idea. We are still allowed to think of this one ourselves. The possible loss of a freezer full of meat because someone tripped the circuit breaker and forgot to reset it, makes this a good investment. Rule 26-704(8) requires a separate circuit for a plug outlet in the utility room. It may be this utility room outlet is intended for a freezer.

**(q)**      **Balcony outlet** - Rule 26-702(4) Yes, the Code requires a plug outlet on each balcony which is 'enclosed'. The Building Code refers to balconies with 'guards around' and others which are 'enclosed'. Enclosed balconies may well become an added living space with activity requiring electric power. The outlet may be supplied with any lighting circuit - maximum 12 outlets per circuit.

**(r)**      **Porch** - Rule 26-712(b) - The lowly porch, it was discovered a few years ago and with its discovery came the requirement for a plug outlet. A plug outlet is required only if the thing is closed in. The Rule does not require the walls to be finished, just enclosed. This outlet may be supplied with any lighting circuit, - maximum 12 outlets per circuit.

**(s)**     **Outdoor Plug Outlets** - Rules 26-714(a); 26-714(b) & 26-724(a)

> **Basic requirement** - Rule 26-702(18) - The rules require at least one plug outlet which is "readily accessible from ground or grade level for the use of appliances which, of necessity, are used outdoors".

> These outlets must:

> - **Be duplex type** - single outlet is not acceptable.

> - **Be readily accessible**, which means it must not be necessary to use chairs or ladders to reach the plug outlet. See definition on page 9 in the Code.

> - **Be supplied** with a circuit used solely for this one or more outdoor plug outlets.

> - **Be a G.F.I. type** receptacle or be supplied with a Class A ground fault circuit interrupter in the panel.

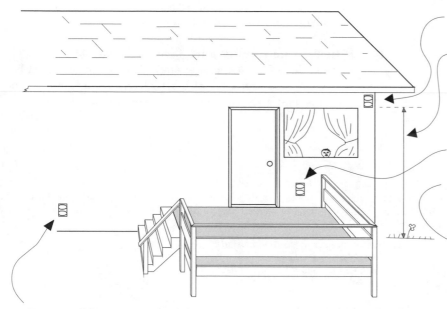

*This outlet is for decorative lighting*

*This outlet may be any height. If it is more than 2.5 m (98.5 in.) above grade it may be supplied by any lighting circuit inside the building. If it is less than 2.5 m (98.5 in.) above grade the outlet must be GFCI type or be supplied with a GFCI type circuit breaker. This outlet may be supplied by the same circuit used for other outdoor plug outlets.*

*This outlet must be GFCI type or be supplied with a GFCI type circuit breaker.*

*Other outdoor plug outlets for special garden may also be supplied with the same GFCI protected circuit used to supply this outlet.*

*Plug outlet for special garden lighting*

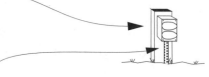

- *This is the preferred location for the required outdoor plug outlet.*
- *It must be a GFCI type receptacle or be supplied with a GFCI type circuit breaker.*
- *Other outdoor plug outlets may also be supplied with this GFCI protected circuit.*

*Use rigid metal or PVC conduit to protect the cable at this point.*

### NOTES and BEWARES.

> **(1) Sundeck Plug Outlets** - Rule 26-714(a) & (b) - If the deck is low and the plug outlets are within 98.5 in. of ground or grade level the plug outlets must be G.F.I. protected with either a circuit breaker in the panel or a G.F.I. type receptacle. These outlets must be supplied with a separate circuit used for no other purpose or with the circuit which supplies the other outdoor plug outlets.

> **(2) Higher Sundecks** - Rule 26-714(b) - Where the outlet on the sundeck is more than 98.5 in. (2.5 m) above ground or grade level, it may still be supplied with the same G.F.I. circuit breaker as noted above, but it is not required to be on this circuit. It could be supplied with any nearby lighting circuit.

> **(3) Other Outdoor Plugs** - Rules 26-714(b) & 26-724(a) & Bulletin 26-1-0 - The Bulletin says that all receptacles installed outdoors of single dwellings and located within 2.5 m of ground or grade level shall be protected by a ground fault circuit interrupter of the Class A Type." This means that plug outlets in a garden and outlets on an unattached garage or on other out-buildings on the same property must be either GFCI type or be protected with GFCI type circuit breaker.

**(4) G.F.C.I. Protected Plug Circuits Required** - The Rules require **separate** G.F.I. protection for the following:

A    **All plug outlets** - within 118 in. (3 m) of a bathtub or shower stall, (except washing machine and dryer plugs in a combined bath and laundry room), Rule 26-700(11); and

B    **All plug outlets** - within 118 in. (3 m) of a wash basin, (except washing machine and dryer plugs in a combined washroom and laundry room), Rule 26-700(11),; and

C    **All carport plugs** - See explanation below, under "Carport only Plug Outlets".

D    **All outdoor plugs** - which are ON the outside of a single family dwelling or an attached garage and which are within 98.5 in. (2.5 m) of grade, Rule 26-714(b).

Things do get complicated don't they?

**(5) Decorative Lighting Outlets (Christmas Lighting)** - These plug outlets need not be G.F.I. protected if they are at least 98.5 in. (2.5 m) above ground or grade level. If they are 98.5 in. or less above grade level they must be wired as described for any other outdoor plug outlet, Rule 26-714(b).

**(6) Two Wire Cable** - Use only 2-wire cable for this circuit. The G.F.I. circuit breaker will not work if wired with 3-wire cable.

**(7) Maximum Circuit load** - The rule requires at least one circuit for outdoor plug outlets. Where there are two or more outdoor plug outlets these may all be supplied with one circuit provided the total number does not exceed 12 outlets.

### WHAT'S A G.F.C.I. FOR? WHAT'S IT D0? - - - - it saves lives.

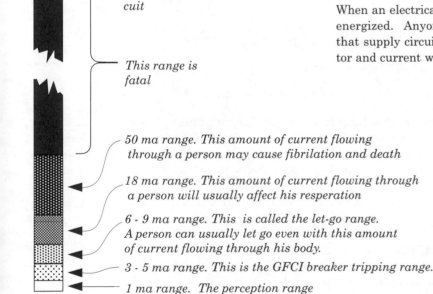

*15 amp circuit*

*This range is fatal*

*50 ma range. This amount of current flowing through a person may cause fibrilation and death*

*18 ma range. This amount of current flowing through a person will usually affect his resperation*

*6 - 9 ma range. This is called the let-go range. A person can usually let go even with this amount of current flowing through his body.*

*3 - 5 ma range. This is the GFCI breaker tripping range.*

*1 ma range. The perception range*

When an electrical appliance is faulty the appliance itself may become energized. Anyone holding such an appliance could become part of that supply circuit to ground. He would become an electrical conductor and current would flow through the person to ground. Only a very small current is needed to kill a human being. The graph indicates the enormous difference between the small amount needed to kill a person and the large amount available in every 15 amp. circuit in the house.

The graph also indicates the very low current that a G.F.C.I. will pass to ground. It is designed to trip at a maximum 5 m.a. which is only 0.005 ampere. This means that a person holding a faulty electrical appliance, such as an electric lawn mower or an electric drill, could become an electrical conductor to ground and he could get an electrical shock but the G.F.I. type circuit breaker would open the circuit before the current reached a dangerous level.

It would be very expensive to protect all the circuits in the house with these special circuit breakers. What's more, it is not necessary. The code requires only certain outlets to be protected with this special breaker. As indicated above, outdoor plug outlets are among those outlets which must be protected with this special circuit breaker.

**Test record** - The test procedure and chart that comes with a GFCI circuit breaker is important. Attach this to the panel cover where it will serve as a reminder to test the circuit breaker each month and to record the test. If at any time this breaker fails a test it should be turned off until it can be replaced; do not allow it to be used.

**(t)**     **Carport only Plug Outlets** - Rules 26-714(b) & (c), 26-724(b)

At least one plug outlet must be installed for each car space in the carport.

This outlet must:-     **Be duplex type** - single outlet is not acceptable.

**Be installed**, one in each car space. (The rule does not say 'in' each car space it says 'for' each car space. However, the intent of the rule seems to be that there should be a plug outlet **in** each car space.)

**Be supplied** with a circuit used solely for these outlets located in a carport except that the carport lighting may also be supplied with this circuit.

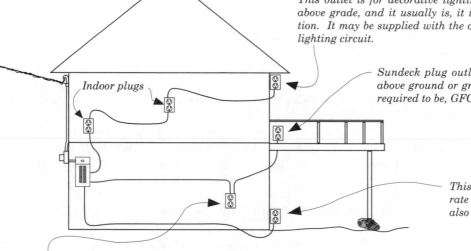

*This outlet is for decorative lighting. If it is more than 98.5 in (2.5 m) above grade, and it usually is, it is not required to have G.F.C.I. protection. It may be supplied with the outdoor plug circuit or with any nearby lighting circuit.*

*Sundeck plug outlet - if it is more than 98.5 in. (2.5m) above ground or grade level this outlet may be, but is not required to be, GFCI protected.*

*Indoor plugs*

*This carport plug outlet must be on a separate circuit except that carport lighting may also be supplied with this circuit.*

*This outdoor plug outlet must be accessible from grade and must be supplied with a separate circuit used for no other load except that there may be as many as 12 **outdoor plug outlets** supplied with this circuit.*

*Use a GFCI type circuit breaker in the panel or use GFCI type receptacles.*

*Sundeck plug outlet may be supplied with this circuit but need not be if it is more than 98.5 in. above grade level.*

**Notes**     **(1) Is G.F.I. Protection Required for the Carport Plug?** - Yes it is. - well, sort of. Although this is a carport plug outlet it is in fact facing outdoors just as any other outdoor plug does, and could be used as any other outdoor plug outlet. Therefore, Rule 26-714(b) must be applied. BC Bulletin 26-1-0 confirms this by saying that plug outlets on the outside of buildings, receptacles in carports or other covered areas on grade, and receptacles installed in other outdoor locations on the same property must be GFI protected.

**(2) Separate Circuit Required** - Rule 26-724(b) says carport plug outlets must be supplied with a circuit used for no other purpose except that the carport lights may also be supplied with this circuit.

**(u)**     **Garage Plug Outlets** - Rules 26-714(c) & 26-724(b)

At least one appliance plug outlet must be installed in each car space in a garage.

This outlet must:

-     **Be duplex type** - single receptacle is not acceptable.

-     **Be installed** so that there is a plug outlet in each car space. To be truthful, the rule does not say "in" each car space, it says "for" each car space. However, the intent seems to be that each plug outlet should be located in its own car space.

- **Be supplied** with a circuit used solely for the plug outlets located in the garage except that garage light outlets and garage door openers may also be connected to this circuit.

Note     **G.F.I. protection** - The garage plug outlets are not required to be protected with a G.F.l. type circuit breaker.

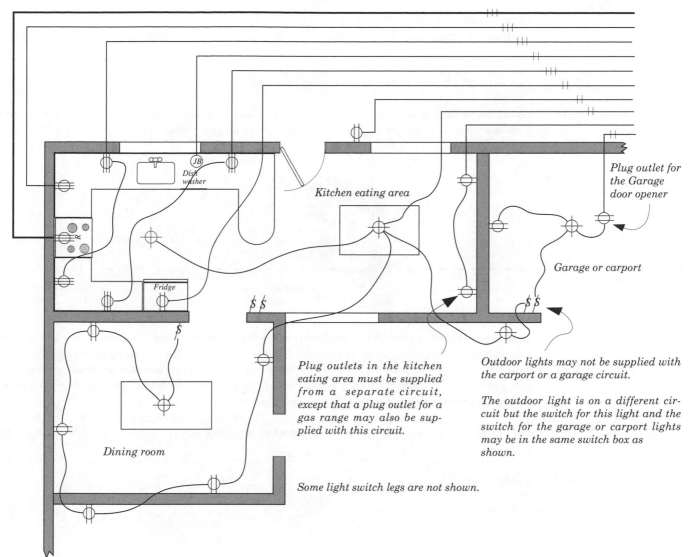

*Plug outlet for the Garage door opener*

*Kitchen eating area*

*Dish washer*

*Garage or carport*

*Fridge*

*Plug outlets in the kitchen eating area must be supplied from a separate circuit, except that a plug outlet for a gas range may also be supplied with this circuit.*

*Outdoor lights may not be supplied with the carport or a garage circuit.*

*The outdoor light is on a different circuit but the switch for this light and the switch for the garage or carport lights may be in the same switch box as shown.*

*Dining room*

*Some light switch legs are not shown.*

**(u)**     **Junction Boxes**

**(i)**     **Accessibility** - Rules 12-3016(1), 12-112(3) - Junction boxes must remain accessible. This means they may not be concealed in a wall or ceiling or similar location.

**(ii)**     **Head Clearance** - Rule 12-3016(2) - Where junction boxes are installed in an attic or crawl space, there shall be at least 900 mm (35.4 in). vertical space to provide access.

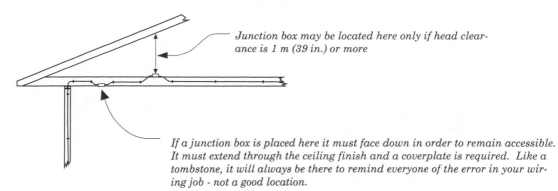

*Junction box may be located here only if head clearance is 1 m (39 in.) or more*

*If a junction box is placed here it must face down in order to remain accessible. It must extend through the ceiling finish and a coverplate is required. Like a tombstone, it will always be there to remind everyone of the error in your wiring job - not a good location.*

**(iii)** **Where to use** - Use junction boxes very sparingly, only where you absolutely have to. Usually all the joints are made in light, switch and plug outlet boxes

**(v)** **Door Bell Transformer** Rule 16-200, 16-204

**(i)** **Type** - Must be a CSA certified Class II transformer. This is usually die stamped somewhere on the transformer. This Class II label, is very important. It means the transformer is designed so that it will not be a fire hazard even if improperly wired.

**(ii)** **Circuit** - may be connected to any lighting circuit.

**(iii)** **Location** — Watch this one. This transformer must be located where it will remain accessible. This means it may not be inside a finished wall or ceiling where there is no access for maintenance or replacement later.

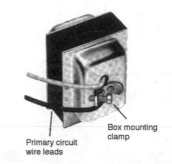

Box mounting clamp

Primary circuit wire leads

**Caution** - Do not mount this transformer inside the service panel. It may be nippled into the side of the branch circuit panel provided the wall finish is kept back to keep it exposed and accessible. If you locate it here it must then be supplied with a circuit breaker used for no other load. It is not correct to connect two wires to a breaker or to splice the transformer primary leads onto another circuit conductor in the panel, Rule 12-3034(1).

The furnace room or basement workshop area light outlet box is usually a good location for this transformer.

**(iv)** **Cable** - Type LVT cable may be used.

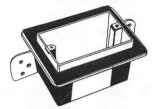

## 20  TYPE OF BOXES - **Don't forget**, some of these boxes must be in a Vapour Barrier enclosure.  See page 66 for details.

**(a)Type** - There are many types of boxes available but only a few are in common use today.

*These boxes do not require the additional outer vapour barrier box.*

*Sectional metal box. This box can be dismantled.*

*Fixed Metal 3-gang switch box*

*Light outlet box*

*Knockout filler. Use these to close any open & unused knockout holes.*

*Blank cover Make sure all junction boxes are covered.*

*Handy box for surface work*

*Switch or plug box for additional wiring after the wall finish is in place.*

*Rigid metal box*

*Extension ring*

**Caution** - For bonding metal gang boxes see also under "Bonding of Boxes" on page 96.

**(i)  Internal Cable Clamp**

Use the clamp properly.  Where the cable enters the back or top knockout, as shown, it must emerge at the lower edge.  It is not correct to double it back over the sharp edge, as shown.

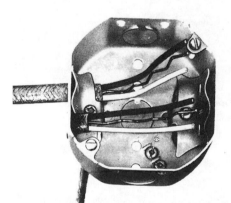

*Wrong way! Cable can be damaged by clamping it against the sharp edge of the knock out hole.*

*Right way! If the cable enters the back wall of the outlet box it must emerge along the side wall inside the box as shown.*

**(ii)  Saucer Boxes** - The restrictions on the use of this box have been removed.  This box may be used anywhere that similar deeper boxes are permitted.

**Caution**  Do not use the center KO hole in this box unless the fixture you plan to connect to this outlet is the simple lamp-holder type shown.

Most light fixtures use a mounting strap to hold the fixture in place.  There is usually a long hollow bolt which runs through the center of the fixture base and into the mounting strap.  It's this long hollow bolt that may cause trouble if it extends too far into the shallow box because it is directly in line with the center KO hole in the box.  If your supply cable enters the center KO hole it could be seriously damaged with this fixture mounting bolt.  For this reason you should never enter a shallow box through the center KO hole.  Always use one of the off center KO holes for cable entry.  That center KO was not intended for cable entry but for special box mounting and heavy fixture support with a special box supporting bar.

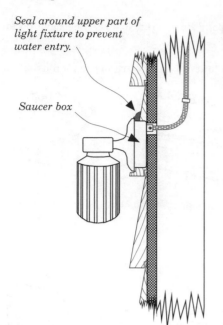

*Seal around upper part of light fixture to prevent water entry.*

*Saucer box*

These shallow boxes are often used at front and back doors when the outside wall finish is not smooth. As shown, the box is fastened directly to the outside rough sheathing. Because it is so shallow it need not be recessed into the sheathing. When the finish siding is installed the box may be shifted to match the boards so that it is fully recessed into the outer finish sheathing material. This eliminates the possibility of the outlet box being somewhere on the joint, between two boards, where it is difficult to fit the fixture properly and to seal (weatherproof) the opening around the fixture.

**Note - Box Loading** - saucer boxes are very shallow, approximately $1/2$ in. deep, and therefore may be used only at the end of a cable run. Only one 2-conductor #14 or #12 cable may enter this box. This means that you must run to the switch box first then to this light outlet box.

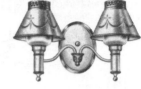

**(b)** **Box Support** - Rules 12-3012, 12-3014

**(i)** **Nail-on Type** - Most boxes, both plastic and metal, can be nailed onto a stud or joist and Rule 12-3012(5) says that supporting nails may even pass through the inside of a box provided they are hard against either the ends or back of the box so that they do not interfere with the conductors or connectors in the box. Nails must be driven in all the way - not just halfway, then bent over.

*Nails must be located in the corners and not interfere with the conductors or the connectors*

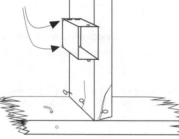

*The prongs on the right hold the box in position while the nails are driven in.*

*Drive nails in all the way. Do not bend nails.*

*Double headed concrete forming nails do this very well.*

*Boxes are usually set in the vertical not the horizontal plane. (This is another tell tale sign - amature or professional job.)*

*Lower edge of box*

*Plug outlet boxes are usually set 12 inches (300 mm) above the floor but they may be any reasonable height.*

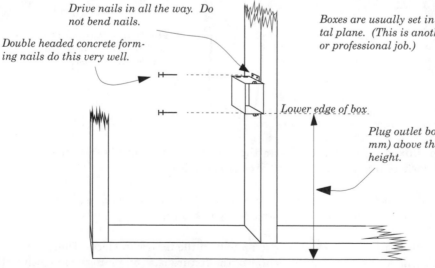

**(ii)** **Metal Gang Boxes** - Rule 12-3012(2)

Metal gang boxes may be supported with a brace, as shown below, or with wood backing.

**Note -** Metal sectional boxes must be secured with metal supports or have a header board fixed between the studs. Metal supports are the easiest to use. For metal sectional gang boxes use one of the metal side plates which were removed to form the gang box. Use the side which has the nail-on lugs and fasten one end to the back of the gang box with one of the bonding screws installed from the back of the box. The other end of the brace is nailed to the stud, as shown.

*Side of box may be used as a brace to hold the box firm*

*Metal sectional boxes*

**An alternative method** is to fasten the gang box to a wood member installed behind the box. This is usually an unhappy experience because of the many screws protruding through the back of the box.

**Caution** - For bonding of sectional metal boxes see under "Bonding of Boxes" page 96.

**(c)** **Set Flush**

**(i)** **Rule 12-3018** - Set all boxes so that they are flush with the finished surface. Pay particular attention to the feature walls of wood paneling. Don't forget to allow for the thickness of the wood strapping, in addition to the wall finish material, when fastening boxes.

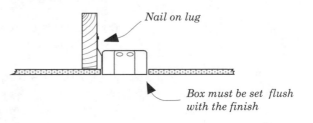

*Nail on lug*

*Box must be set flush with the finish*

*This part of the receptacle must be flush with the coverplate*
*or*
*in the case of a* **metal plate***, must project through the plate at least 0.015 in. - not likely you will find an inspector measuring how far it projects through but he is concerned that it does project through the plate. The concern is that the terminal screws in some attachment caps may contact the metal plate and cause a short circuit.*

**(ii)** **Box Extenders** - Approved box extenders must be used where the outlet box is not flush with the finish.

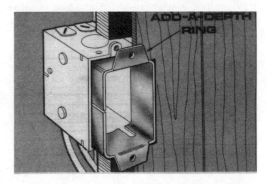

*These are extension rings for use when the original box is set a long way back from the finished surface.*

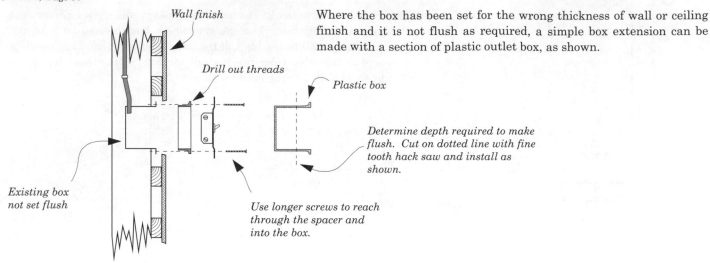

*Wall finish*

*Drill out threads*

*Plastic box*

*Existing box not set flush*

*Use longer screws to reach through the spacer and into the box.*

*Determine depth required to make flush. Cut on dotted line with fine tooth hack saw and install as shown.*

Where the box has been set for the wrong thickness of wall or ceiling finish and it is not flush as required, a simple box extension can be made with a section of plastic outlet box, as shown.

**(d)     Bonding of Boxes** - Rules 12-526, 10-400, 10-808(2), 10-906

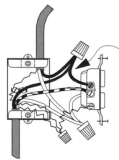

The bare bonding conductor in the outlet box must be properly connected as shown below.

**Note** - The bare wire should:

**(I)     First connect** to each box as shown.
— In metal gang boxes it connects **to EACH SECTION**. Leave one long enough to loop around a bonding screw in each section then pigtail it to the all the others.
— In plastic gang boxes it connects to each metal strap inside the box unless these straps are already joined together by the manufacturer.

**(2)     Next it connects** to each bare wire entering the outlet box. See under "Conductor Joints & Splices" on page 100 for comments on methods of joining these wires.

**(3)     Last, it connects** to the green bonding screw on the base of the plug receptacle. This connection must be made with a pigtail, as shown.

**Pigtails Required**- Rule 10-808(2) & 10-906(6) & BC Bulletin 26 - 1 - 0(1)

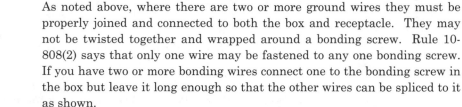

*This short length of wire from the connector to the receptacle is called a pigtail.*

As noted above, where there are two or more ground wires they must be properly joined and connected to both the box and receptacle. They may not be twisted together and wrapped around a bonding screw. Rule 10-808(2) says that only one wire may be fastened to any one bonding screw. If you have two or more bonding wires connect one to the bonding screw in the box but leave it long enough so that the other wires can be spliced to it as shown.

**(e)     Wires in Box** - Rules 12-3002(5), 12-3036(1)(c)

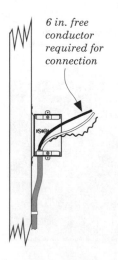

*6 in. free conductor required for connection*

**(i)  Free Conductor**

At least 150 mm (6 in.), (it is better to leave 8 inches,) of free conductor must be left in the outlet box to allow joints to be made or fixtures to be connected in a workmanlike manner.

**(ii) Cable Sheath** - Rule 2-108 - Workmanship

The outer cable sheath should not project into the outlet box more than 0.5 in. past the connector. Remove this outer sheath as required before installing the cable in the connector. This sheath is very difficult to remove properly once the cable is actually installed.

**(iii) Box Fill** - Rule 12-3036

Watch that box fill, it's tricky. This otherwise simple problem has been made difficult in the code book. We must count the number of wire connectors with insulated caps which we install in a box. We must subtract the space occupied by these connector caps from the space in the box. Of course, we are still required to note carefully the number of wires entering the box - deducting 1.5 cubic inches for each insulated #14 conductor. The bare conductor does not count. Then, the rules say the switch or receptacle in the box occupies space equal to two conductors. The tables below take all these factors into account.

The following should be carefully noted:

— Pigtails, (short lengths of wire used to connect things) do not count as box fill.

— Boxes may have internal or external cable clamps - it does not matter. The box fill is the same for both.

— Wires from light fixtures directly mounted and connected to the circuits in the box do not count as box fill.

## NOTES ON BOX FILL TABLES

### (1)  Nominal Dimensions

Don't let the nominal box dimensions fool you. These are not the actual box sizes. It should be noted that some plastic (phenolic) box manufacturers keep the dimensions of their boxes close to the nominal. It is better to work from box volume than from its dimensions. Most box manufacturers now mark the cubic volume of their boxes with a die stamp inside the box. Look for these marked boxes.

### (2)  Various Combinations Given in the Table

In some combinations the Tables allow many more connector caps than could possibly be used for the number of wires in the box. It also shows other combinations where there are not enough connector caps for the number of wires in the box. Choose a combination which will permit you to install at least the number of wires you need and at least the number of connector caps you require. For example, if we are using #14 loomex cable and intend to run a 2-wire supply cable and a 2-wire load cable into a 2 in. deep switch box and plan to make 2 joints in this box the Table says NO! It's too full. We may install only 4 - #14 wires and one connector cap in this box.

**Note** - Only the insulated wires count as box fill; the bare bonding conductors do not count. In the above example the Table requires a deeper box. The Table shows a 2.5 in. deep box may contain the 5 - #14 wires and the two splices (connector caps) we need. We do not need to provide the extra space as far as the rules are concerned but this is the combination nearest to our needs and it gives us room for a little error in our planning.

### (3)  Insulated Cap

The rule says if we use these, we must reduce the number of wires in the box. The Tables on pages 98 & 99 take all this into account.

**Note** - This applies to insulated caps of all kinds.

### (4)  Tape Insulated Joints & Splices

The rule does not mention tape insulated joints or splices - perhaps it is because they occupy less space in the box. If you are using tape to insulate splices. you may add one conductor to the box fill indicated in the table. See also under "Conductor Joints & Splices" on page 100.

If you have used insulator caps and you find you have misjudged box size; you have more "things" in a box than the rules permit you to have; simply change from insulated caps to soldered and taped splices. These do not count as box fill. See page 101 for soldering instructions.

### (5)  Bare Bond Wire Splicing

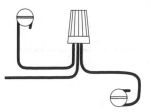

These wires are in the box but are not counted as box fill - Rule 12-3036(1).

**Note -**  The bare wires do not count for box fill but the insulated connector caps used to splice the bare bond wires do count. Rule 12-3036(2) says "every" insulator cap must be counted in box fill. Insulation is really not required on bond wire splices; a simple, bare, crimp-on connector may be used without an insulated cap and these do not count as box fill.

# ACTUAL BOX FILL PERMITTED - RULE 12-3036

| Box size and number of sections in the gang — See also Notes on page 93 | Volume cu. in. or (millilitre) | Using #14 cable this box may contain: | Using #12 cable this box may contain: |
|---|---|---|---|
| **Single gang** - metal box. Box size 3 x 2 x 1.5 in. deep. See notes page 93 | 8 (131 mL) | One switch or one plug outlets plus: — 3 3 2 Wires / 0 1 2 Caps | One switch or plug outlet plus: — 2 2 Wires / 0 1 Caps |
| **2-gang** - metal box. Each section is 3 x 2 x 1.5 in. deep | 16 (262 mL) | Two switches or two plug outlets plus: — 6 6 5 5 4 Wires / 0 1 2 3 4 Caps | 2 switches or 2 plug outlets plus: — 5 5 4 Wires / 0 1 2 Caps |
| **3-gang** - metal box. Each section is 3 x 2 x 1.5 in. deep | 24 (393 mL) | Three switches or three plug outlets plus: — 10 10 9 9 8 Wires / 0 1 2 3 4 Caps | 3 switches or 3 plug outlets plus: — 7 7 6 6 5 Wires / 0 1 2 3 4 Caps |
| **Single gang** - metal box. Box size is 3 x 2 x 2 or 3 x 2 x 2.25 in deep. See notes page 93 | 10 (163 mL) | One switch or one plug outlet plus: — 4 4 3 3 2 Wires / 0 1 2 3 4 Caps | One switch or one plug outlet plus: — 3 3 2 2 Wires / 0 1 2 3 Caps |
| **2-gang** - metal box. Each section is 3 x 2 x 2 or 3 x 2 x 2.25 in. deep | 20 (327 mL) | 2 switches or 2 plug outlets plus: — 9 9 8 8 7 7 Wires / 0 1 2 3 4 5 Caps | 2 switcvhes or 2 plug outlets plus: — 7 7 6 6 5 Wires / 0 1 2 3 4 Caps |
| **3-gang** - metal box. Each section is 3 x 2 x 2 or 3 x 2 x 2.25 in. deep | 30 (491 mL) | 3 switches or 3 plug outlets plus: — 14 14 13 13 12 12 Wires / 0 1 2 3 4 5 Caps | 3 switches or 3 plug outlets plus: — 11 11 10 10 9 9 Wires / 0 1 2 3 4 5 Caps |
| **Single gang** - metal box. Box size is 3 x 2 x 2.5 in. deep. See notes on page 93 | 12.5 (204 mL) | One switch or one plug outlet plus: — 6 6 5 5 4 4 Wires / 0 1 2 3 4 5 Caps | One switch or one plug putlet plus: — 5 5 4 4 3 Wires / 0 1 2 3 4 Caps |
| **2-gang** - metal box. Each section is 3 x 2 x 2.5 in. deep | 25 (409 mL) | 2 switches or 2 plug outlets Plus: — 12 12 11 11 10 10 Wires / 0 1 2 3 4 5 Caps | 2 switches or 2 plug outlets plus: — 10 10 9 9 8 8 Wires / 0 1 2 3 4 5 Caps |
| **3-gang** - metal box. Each section is 3 x 2 x 2.5 in. deep. | 37.5 (614 mL) | 3 switches or 3 plug outlets plus: — 19 19 18 18 17 17 Wires / 0 1 2 3 4 5 Caps | 3 switches or 3 plug outlets plus: — 15 15 14 14 13 13 Wires / 0 1 2 3 4 5 Caps |
| **Single gang** - metal box. Box size is 3 x 2 x 3 in. deep | 15 (245 mL) | One switch or plug outlet plus: — 8 8 7 7 6 6 Wires / 0 1 2 3 4 5 Caps | One switch or one plug outlet plus: — 6 6 5 5 4 4 Wires / 0 1 2 3 4 5 Caps |
| **2-gang** - metal box. Each section is 3 x 3 x 2 in deep | 30 (491 mL) | 2 switches or 2 plug outlets plus: — 16 16 15 15 14 14 Wires / 0 1 2 3 4 5 Caps | 2 switches or 2 plug outlets plus: — 13 13 12 12 11 11 Wires / 0 1 2 3 4 5 Caps |
| **3-gang** - metal box. Each section is 3 x 2 x 3 in deep | 45 (737 mL) | 3 switches or 3 plug outlets plus: — 24 24 23 23 22 22 Wires / 0 1 2 3 4 5 Caps | 3 switches or 3 plug outlets plus: — 19 19 18 18 17 17 Wires / 0 1 2 3 4 5 Caps |
| **Single gang** - plastic box. These boxes usually have their volume clearly marked. | 16 (262 mL) | One switch or one plug outlet plus: — 8 8 7 7 6 6 Wires / 0 1 2 3 4 5 Caps | One switch or plug outlet plus: — 7 7 6 6 5 5 Wires / 0 1 2 3 4 5 Caps |
| **Single gang** - plastic box. These boxes usually have their volume clearly marked. | 18 (294 mL) | One switch or one plug outlet plus: — 10 10 9 9 8 8 Wires / 0 1 2 3 4 5 Caps | One switch or plug outlet plus: — 8 8 7 7 6 6 Wires / 0 1 2 3 4 5 Caps |

# Light Outlet Boxes, Junction Boxes, Other Boxes.

| Box dimensions | Volume Cubic in Millilitres | Light outlet boxes Maximum combination wires and caps using #14 wire | | | | | | | Light outlet boxes Maximum combination wires and caps using #12 wire | | | | | | |
|---|---|---|---|---|---|---|---|---|---|---|---|---|---|---|---|
| 4 x 1½ in. deep metal octagonal Box | 15 (245 mL) | Wires 10 | 10 | 9 | 9 | 8 | 8 | | Wires 8 | 8 | 7 | 7 | 6 | 6 | |
| | | Caps 0 | 1 | 2 | 3 | 4 | 5 | | Caps 0 | 1 | 2 | 3 | 4 | 5 | |
| 4 x 2⅛ in. deep metal octagonal box | 21 (344 mL) | Wires 14 | 14 | 13 | 13 | 12 | 12 | 11 | Wires 12 | 12 | 11 | 11 | 10 | 10 | |
| | | Caps 0 | 1 | 2 | 3 | 4 | 5 | 6 | Caps 0 | 1 | 2 | 3 | 4 | 5 | |
| Shallow saucer type box. Limited use | 5 (81 mL) | Wires 3 | 3 | 2 | | | | | Wires 2 | 2 | | | | | |
| | | Caps 0 | 1 | 2 | | | | | Caps 0 | 1 | | | | | |
| Plastic light outlet box. Courtesy Nu-tek | 26 (426 mL) | Wires 17 | 17 | 16 | 16 | 15 | 15 | 14 | Wires 14 | 14 | 13 | 13 | 12 | 12 | |
| | | Caps 0 | 1 | 2 | 3 | 4 | 5 | 6 | Caps 0 | 1 | 2 | 3 | 4 | 5 | |

Note 1 - The above table is based on the fact that these boxes are used for light outlets and as junction boxes. They will not contain any devices other than wires and connector caps.

Note 2 - See also under "(b) Light Outlet Boxes" on page 60 regarding the use of plastic type boxes for light outlets.

Code Table 22

| Size of Conductor AWG | Usable Space Required for Each Insulated Conductor Cubic Inches (Cubic Centimetres) |
|---|---|
| 14 | 1.5 (24.6) |
| 12 | 1.75 (28.7) |
| 10 | 2.25 (36.9) |
| 8 | 2.75 (45.1) |
| 6 | 4.5 (73.7) |

**(f)**   **Conductor Joints & Splices** - Rules 4-034(4), 10-808(2), 12-506(1) & BC Bulletin 26 - 1 - 0(1)

**(i)**     **The illustration** below shows a number of different kinds of outlets and the different connection methods required by code in each case.

*Home run to panel*

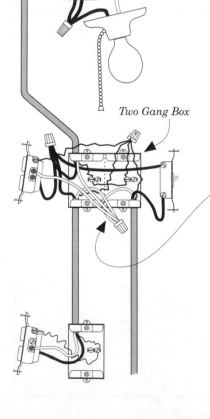

**Neutral wire in 3-wire cable** - *Rules 4-034(4) & 26-700(14) require a pigtail in every case. Without the pigtail both neutral wires would need to be connected to the receptacle. With such a connection anyone removing the receptacle would automatically interrupt the power to other loads downstream.*

**Hot wires** - *also require a pigtail, see BC Bulletin 26-1 - 0(1).*

**Bare Bond wires** - *Rules 10-808(2) & 10-906(6) requires a pigtail whenever a circuit continues on to supply other outlets downstream so that the receptacle can be removed **without disconnecting** downstream outlets from ground. Connect one bonding conductor to the box by taking the shortest route. Do not cut the wire, leave it long enough to make proper splices with other bond wires and a pigtail as shown.*

*3-wire cable*

**Neutral Wire** - *This is still 3-wire cable and therefore, Rule 4-034(4) requires a pigtail.*

**Hot Wires** - *One connects directly to the receptacle the other is spliced black to black to supply other loads down stream.*

**Bare Bond Wires** - *Rules 10-808(2) & 10-906(6) require a pigtail because the circuit continues on to supply other outlets downstream.*

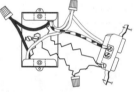

*Sometimes an electrician will leave longer lengths of free conductor . He will complete the splice with a connector cap. Later, when he installs the receptacle he will simply loop the bare wire around the bonding screw . This eliminates the need for a pigtail and it is just as acceptable.*

*2-wire cable*

**Neutral Wires** -*Pigtails are required here because this is a pull-chain type light fixture which has provision for terminating only one neutral wire. Ordinary keyless light fixtures usually have provision for terminating two neutrals and two hots. Where such fixtures are used pigtails are not required unless you are using 3-wire cables or you have more than two neutrals or two hots. Using pigtails to make any of these connections may not always be required by Code but it is still the much better way because it eliminates a lot of strain on the fixture or receptacle termination points.*

**Hot Wires** - *See under neutral wire above.*

**Bond Wires** - *This light fixture does not require a connection to the bond wire but all the bond wires must be spliced together as shown .*

*Two Gang Box*

**Neutral Wires** - *A pigtail is required to join the three neutrals and make the connection to the receptacle.*

**Hot Wires** - *A pigtail is required to connect the two devices and to splice the two hot conductors together. Make sure the hot conductors are connected to the brass coloured screws.*

**Bare Bond Wires** - *The bare bond wire in the supply cable should be left long enough to connect to the bonding screw in each box then continue on to a wire connector where all the other bare wires are spliced together. A pigtail is required here to connect the receptacle. Do not forget to connect the bond wire to each section of a multi-section metal gang box. One piece metal gang boxes require only one bond connection but multi-gang boxes consisting of a number of sections must have each section connected to the bond wire as shown.*

**(ii)**      **Joints & Splices In Boxes** - Rule 12-506(1)

Joints may be made only in outlet boxes or junction boxes.  Junction boxes should be used very sparingly because you can get into more trouble with the Inspector when he finds them.  Junction boxes may not be buried in the walls or ceilings.

**(iii)**      **Solder or Mechanical Joints & Splices** - Rules 10-808(2), 10-906(2), 12-112

**Solder** - This is probably the best possible method of splicing circuit conductors.

It takes longer to make solder joints.  Use a non-corrosive paste, usually 50/50 solder (50% tin 50% lead) for easy flowing and a minimum amount of heat.  Then apply scotch electrical tape.  Build up a layer of tape equal to the insulation thickness of the conductor.  This is needed, not for dielectric strength, but for mechanical protection.

**Be sure to melt solder on wire.**

**Caution** - Do not solder **bonding** conductors - crimp-on type may be used.  Taping is not required.

Don't try to cheat if you want to live to a ripe old age.  If you are using the soldering method, use it, don't think you can get away with just twisting the wires together, then taping them without soldering the joint -  your Inspector will find out.

**Crimp-on** -   These are good if properly installed.  Don't just gimble the connector with your pliers or side cutters and hope the Inspector will not see it.  That is poor workmanship and is rejectable according to Rule 2-108.  Use an approved crimping tool or use the twist-on type wire connectors.

**Twist-on Insulator Caps -** There are a number of different types and sizes of twist-on wire connectors available. You must use the correct size to make a good electrical connection.  Check the marking on the carton to determine the number and size of wires permitted in each connector.

**(g)**      **Junction Boxes**

**Accessibility** - Rules 12-3016(1), 12-112(3) - They must remain accessible.  This means they may not be hidden inside a wall or ceiling or similar place.

**Head Clearance** - Rule 12-3016(2) - Where junction boxes are installed in an attic or crawl space, there must be at least 900 mm (35.4 in.) vertical space above this box to provide access for maintenance.

*Junction box may be located here only if head clearance is 1 m (39 in.) or more*

**Where To Use** - Use junction boxes sparingly, only where you absolutely have to.  Usually all your joints are made up in light, switch or plug outlet boxes.

*If a junction box is placed here it must face down in order to remain accessible. It must extend through the ceiling finish and a coverplate is required.  Like a tombstone, it will always be there to remind everyone of the error in your wiring job - not a good location.*

## 21   LIGHTING FIXTURES

**(a)**    **Boxes Flush?** - Rule 12-3018

Check first if the boxes worked out flush with the wall or ceiling finish.  If not, see page 95 for box extenders.

**(b)**    **Connections**

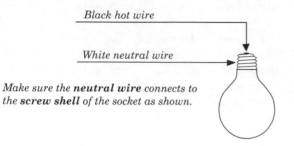

*Black hot wire*

*White neutral wire*

*Make sure the **neutral wire** connects to the **screw shell** of the socket as shown.*

Rules 30-314, 30-602 - When connecting light fixtures be sure to connect the neutral white or grey wire to the screw shell of the lamp holder and the black or hot wire to the center pin. The threaded portion of the lamp base must not be energized because of the danger of shock to a person replacing a lamp.

**(c)**    **Bathroom Light & Switch** - Rules 10-400, 30-322 and its Appendix, page 395

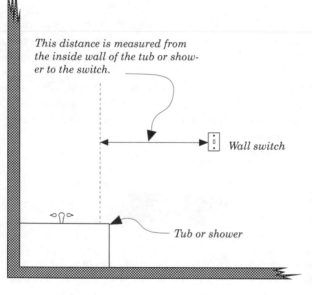

*This distance is measured from the inside wall of the tub or shower to the switch.*

*Wall switch*

*Tub or shower*

**Light Fixtures** - may be pendant type, such as swag lamps, provided that all the metal on the fixture is properly grounded.

**NOTE** - The metal chain on chain-hung fixtures may not be used to ground the fixture - Look for fixtures which have a separate grounding conductor run (threaded) through the chain to each light socket.

**All switches** must be kept out of reach of a person in a tub or shower, Rule 30-322(3).  The Appendix for this Rule, on page 395 in the Code, says this means they must be at least 39.4 in. (1 m) away from a tub or shower.  Although the rule does not say this the wording in the Appendix to this rule suggests that this is a horizontal measurement and that it is measured from the "inside edge" of the bathtub as shown.

**Heat Lamps** - Rules 30-200, 62-110(1)(2) - Like any other recessed light fixture, bathroom heat lamps can be a very real fire hazard if improperly installed.  See page 64 for details on recessed light fixture installation for a heat lamp.

**Caution -**    Care should be taken to locate the fixture so that it cannot radiate heat directly onto the upper edge of the door when it is left in the open position, see page 64.  The rules do not specify any distance, however, a safe horizontal distance may be at least 12 inches from the heat lamp to both the door and shower rod.  The reason for this is that any clothes or towels left hanging on the door or on a shower rod may be too close to the fixture and could become overheated and cause a fire.

**(d)**    **Fluorescent Fixtures** - Rule 30-310

Where this type of fixture is mounted end to end in a continuous row as in valance lighting the loomex cable (NMD-90) may enter only the first fixture.  It must enter the fixture so that it need not run past the ballast.  The connection from there to the other fixtures must be made with type A-18, GTF, R90 or similar types of wire.  Care should be taken to see that all the fixtures in the row are properly grounded both for safety and for satisfactory operation.

**(e)**    **Basement Lighting Fixtures** - Rule 30-322(2) This Rule has been revised.

**Pull chain type light fixtures are no longer permitted** in wet or damp locations such as near laundry tubs, plumbing fixtures, steam pipes, or other grounded metal work or grounded surfaces in  basement or similar areas unless the fixture is approved and marked for use in wet locations. Light fixtures in these locations must be controlled by a wall switch.

**(f)**     **Low Ceiling**- Minimum Height of Lighting Fixture - Rule 30-314

Where fixtures are installed in a crawl space or attic, where there is less than 2.1m (82.7 in.) headroom, the fixture shall be flexible type or be guarded.

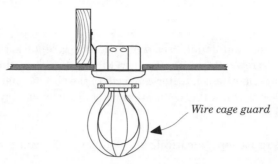

*Wire cage guard*

**(g)**     **Closet Fixtures**- Rule 30-204(2)

Fixtures may not be of the pendant, (suspended) type, nor of the exposed, bare lamp, type.. They should be located away from any possible contact with stored items in the closet. See the illustration on page 64.

## 22 PLUG RECEPTACLES

**(a)**     **Boxes Flush?** - Rule 12-3018

Check first if the boxes worked out flush with the wall or ceiling finish. Check especially the outlets in feature walls. If they are not flush, see page 95 for box extenders.

**(b)**     **Polarization of Plug Receptacles**

This is an important detail. You will notice the receptacle has a brass terminal screw and a chrome plated terminal screw. Be sure to connect the black or sometimes the red wire to the brass terminal screw and the white neutral conductor connects to the chrome plated terminal screw. The Inspector has a little tester he uses to check this connection without removing any cover, etc. If you have connected incorrectly he will find it.

**(c)**     **Type of Plug Receptacle** - Rule 26-700(2) and Diagram 1, page 326 in the code

Polarized type receptacles must be used for all plug outlets except clock outlets.

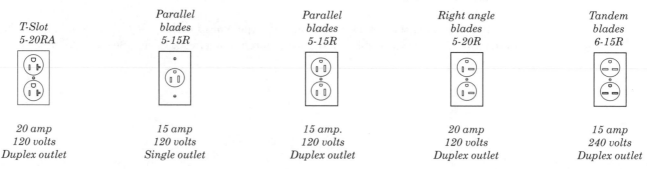

| T-Slot 5-20RA | Parallel blades 5-15R | Parallel blades 5-15R | Right angle blades 5-20R | Tandem blades 6-15R |
|---|---|---|---|---|
| 20 amp 120 volts Duplex outlet | 15 amp 120 volts Single outlet | 15 amp. 120 volts Duplex outlet | 20 amp 120 volts Duplex outlet | 15 amp 240 volts Duplex outlet |

**The T-Slot receptacle** is newest member of the family. These will take both the 15 amp parallel blade attachment cap and the 20 amp right angle blade, they are interchangeable now. The T-Slot receptacle must be wired with 20 amp wire and 20 amp breaker at 120 volts.

**15 amp. 240 volt plug receptacles** are non-interchangeable with the 120 volt receptacles. Single pole circuit breakers used to supply these outlets must be equipped with a tie-bar connecting their operating handles together or use a two-pole breaker. Fuses, if you are using a fuse panel, must have switch or common pull arrangement as used for water heater or dryer, Rule 14-010, 14-302.

> **Split Receptacle** - Note the kind of connection and the type of circuit breakers required for split receptacles. See pages 40, 78.

**(d) Grounding & Bonding** - Rules 10-808(2), 10-906

> The bare wire in each outlet box connects first to the box, then to the plug receptacle in every case as shown. In the case of sectional metal boxes the bare wire must connect to the bonding terminal in each section. Note that a pigtail is required so that the plug can be disconnected without opening the bonding connection to other outlets downstream.

*One of the bare bonding wires must be connected to the bonding screw in the outlet box then, without cutting it, splice it to the other bonding wires in the box as shown.*

**(e)**      **Bathroom Plug Receptacle** - Rule 26-700(11)

Bathroom plug outlets must be either:

**(i)**      **G.F.I. type** receptacle; or

**(ii)**      **A standard type duplex plug receptacle** provided it is supplied with a G.F.C.I. type circuit breaker at the panel. This breaker is called a Class A Ground Fault Circuit Interrupter.

**(f)**      **Outdoor Plug Receptacles** - Rules 26-724(a), 12-3022, 26-702

Receptacles exposed to the weather must be equipped with spring loaded or threaded cover plates to prevent moisture from entering.

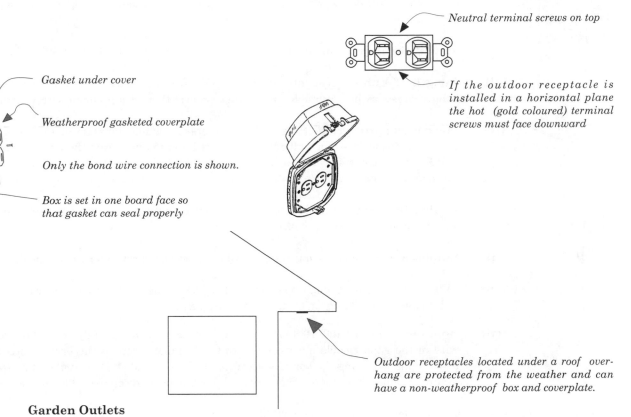

*Gasket under cover*

*Weatherproof gasketed coverplate*

*Only the bond wire connection is shown.*

*Box is set in one board face so that gasket can seal properly*

*Neutral terminal screws on top*

*If the outdoor receptacle is installed in a horizontal plane the hot (gold coloured) terminal screws must face downward*

*Outdoor receptacles located under a roof overhang are protected from the weather and can have a non-weatherproof box and coverplate.*

**(g)**      **Garden Outlets**

Where outdoor outlet boxes are free standing as in a garden area for decorative lighting the outlet must:

- Be in a weatherproof box - use an F.S. box or equal.
- Be equipped with cover plates held in place with 4 screws.

- Be very well grounded.
- Be above grade.
- These plug outlets must be G.F.I. type or use a standard receptacle supplied with a GFI type breaker. These are outdoor plug outlets, therefore they may be supplied with the outdoor plug circuit as described on page 88.

The supply cable may be direct buried NMWU #14 depending on the length of run. Depth of burial and mechanical protection must be provided as shown on page 119 for a similar installation.

Rigid steel conduit may be used to protect the cable where it is exposed above ground. Drive a wood or metal post into the ground to support the outlet box.

## 23 HEAVY APPLIANCES - RANGES, DRYERS, GARBURATORS ETC.

### (a) General Information

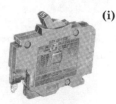

**(i)**    **System Capacity** - Rule 8-108 - Before installing additional electrical loads, such as a range, furnace, etc. to a new or an existing service, make sure there is sufficient space in the panel for the branch circuit breakers required to serve the new load. Connecting two or more branch circuits to one fuse or breaker is not approved. Often it is necessary to replace only the branch circuit panel, not the service itself. In any case, the current carrying capacity of the service conductors must, in no case, be less than 60 amperes, Rule 8-200(1)(b)(ii). See also Table of Service Sizes, page 12 of this book.

**(ii)**    **Control** - Rule 14-010(b) - requires that all 240 volt appliances, such as a range etc., must be provided with a device which will simultaneously disconnect both of the hot conductors at the point of supply.

**Circuit Breakers require** a tie-bar to fulfill this requirement. Rule 14-302(b)(i).

**(iii)**    **Length of Run** - Any length up to 30 m (98 ft.) is usually acceptable for heavy appliances. Longer runs may be acceptable too but they suggest there is a problem with the service location.

**(iv)**    **Mechanical protection** - Rule 12-518 - requires mechanical protection for loomex cable where it is run on the surface of a wall etc. and within 1.5 m (59 in.) from the floor. To comply with this rule, most Inspectors require a flexible conduit installed over the loomex cable supplying a furnace, garburator, etc.

**(v)**    **Cable Strapping** - Rule 12-510 - Cable must be properly strapped within 300 mm (12 in.) of cable termination and every 1.5 m (59 in.).

**(vi)**    **Staples and Straps** - used to support cables must be approved for the particular cable involved.

**Note**    Where cables run through holes in studs or joists they are considered properly strapped. See also page 55 for details on strapping requirements.

**(vii)**    **Bonding** - Rules 10-400, 10-404 - All equipment must be adequately bonded to ground. The bare wire in the supply cable must connect to the bonding screw in the branch circuit panel and to each appliance, using the bonding screw or the bolt provided. It is not enough to wrap the wire around a cable connector or cover screw. Too much depends on a good connection

### (b) Garburator - Rules 28-106(1), 28-200, 28-600

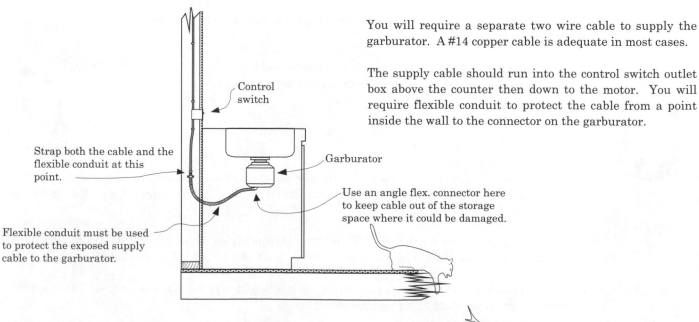

You will require a separate two wire cable to supply the garburator. A #14 copper cable is adequate in most cases.

The supply cable should run into the control switch outlet box above the counter then down to the motor. You will require flexible conduit to protect the cable from a point inside the wall to the connector on the garburator.

Control switch

Strap both the cable and the flexible conduit at this point.

Garburator

Flexible conduit must be used to protect the exposed supply cable to the garburator.

Use an angle flex. connector here to keep cable out of the storage space where it could be damaged.

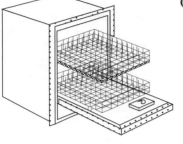

**(c)** **Dishwasher** - Rules 28-106(l), 28-200

This is a motor and heating load. These usually operate at 120 volts, therefore, a 2-wire cable is required. Unless you are absolutely sure your dishwasher can be served with a #14 cable you should install a #12 copper and 20 amp breaker. You will require a separate circuit. This cable may be run directly into the connection box on the dishwasher. Make sure that the bare wire is connected to the bonding terminal.

**(d)** **Domestic Ranges**

**(i)** **Free Standing Type** - Rules 8-300; 26-744; 26-746

Freestanding electric ranges must be cord connected. The plug receptacle required for this connection is a 3 pole, 4 wire grounding type as shown below.

**Note** This applies in every case. If for any reason a range is being replaced with a new or another used one, it must then be cord connected.

Cable size ................................................#8NMD90 copper
Outlet box size ...................................4 $^{11}/_{16}$ x 4 $^{11}/_{16}$ x 2 $^1/_8$
Plug receptacle rating ..............................................50 amp.
Rating of fuses or breakers............................40 amp. each

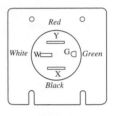

*Range receptacle*

*Free Standing Range*

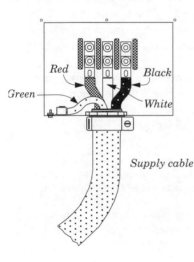

*Red* *Black*

*Green* *White*

*Supply cable*

**Note** - Rule 12-3012(3) says this outlet box must be fastened to a solid member directly behind the box or be supported on two of its sides. If possible locate the box in a stud space where it can be secured to both the plate and a stud, or if both sides of the wall will be finished the box may be supported as shown below.

*Secure a short length of 2 x 4 to the range or dryer box then secure the combination to the bottom plate as shown.. Once the gyprock is in place on both sides of the studs the box will be held firmly in place.*

**Notes** There are 3 rules to watch for:

**(1)The range outlet box** must be located very near the mid-point on the wall behind the range,

AND,

**(2)This range outlet box** must not be higher than 130 mm (5.1 in.) above the floor to the center of the outlet box,

AND,

**(3)This range outlet box** must be carefully positioned so that when the receptacle is finally installed, the ground pin will be either on the right hand or the left hand but not at the top or the bottom.

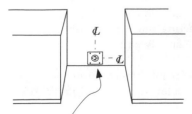

*Set box 5.1 inches (130 mm) floor to centre of the box. The ground pin must be in either the 3 o'clock or 9 o'clock position but may not be in the 12 o'clock or 6 o'clock positions. Make sure the front cover mounting screws, on the box, are in the correct position to allow the receptacle to be mounted properly.*

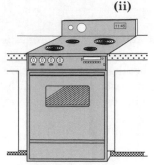

**(ii)    Drop-in Type**

This is a conventional range but it is not free standing.  It is fitted into the kitchen cabinets.

Cable size  .................................................... #8 NMD90 copper
Outlet box size ............................................. box not needed
Flexible conduit size (If required) ............... ³/₄ inch
Rating of fuses or breakers ......................... 40 amp.

This unit is not cord connected.  The #8 NMD90 cable may be run directly into the connection box.

> **Note** -  The supply cable must be protected with 3/4 inch flexible conduit for the last 3 feet or so at the range if it is subject to mechanical damage.

**(iii)    Built-in Type** - Separate units - Rule 26-744

Main cable size ............................................................... #8NMD90 copper
Flexible conduit size (If required) .................................... ³/₄ inch
Cable to oven size .......................................................... #10 NMD90
Flexible Conduit size (If required) ................................... ¹/₂ inch
Rating of fuses or breakers ............................................. 40 amp. each

**Note** - The above sizes are sufficient for the average 12  kw. range

**Separate Built-in Cooking Units** - Rule 26-746(3) says that the two units, the cooking top and the oven, "shall be considered as one appliance".  See also Rule 8-300(2).  Then notice that Rule 26-744(1) says that an electric heating appliance "shall have only one point of connection for supply".  These two rules therefore,will not permit us to run a separate supply cable from the panel to each unit.

Rule 26-742 was revised again to limit the #10 copper taps from the junction box to the oven and the cooking tops, to 25 ft each, as noted in the illustration below.  If a longer tap is needed then it must be the same size as the main range supply cable, in most cases this is #8 copper.  This change is consistent with other rules which allow a smaller tap without overcurrent protection for certain loads.

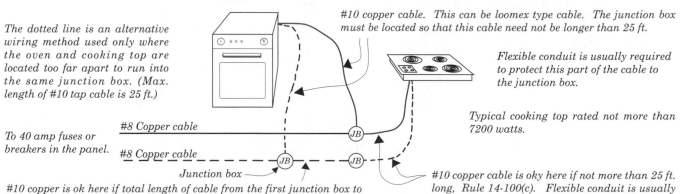

*The dotted line is an alternative wiring method used only where the oven and cooking top are located too far apart to run into the same junction box. (Max. length of #10 tap cable is 25 ft.)*

*#10 copper cable.  This can be loomex type cable.  The junction box must be located so that this cable need not be longer than 25 ft.*

*Flexible conduit is usually required to protect this part of the cable to the junction box.*

*Typical cooking top rated not more than 7200 watts.*

*#8 Copper cable*

*To 40 amp fuses or breakers in the panel.*

*#8 Copper cable*

*Junction box*

*#10 copper is ok here if total length of cable from the first junction box to the cooking top is not more than 25 ft. If it is more than 25 ft. this portion between junction boxes must be # 8 copper, Rule 14-100(c).*

*#10 copper cable is oky here if not more than 25 ft. long,  Rule 14-100(c).  Flexible conduit is usually required to protect exposed parts of this cable.*

It should also be noted that the manufacturer of electric ranges is not required to provide overcurrent protection for the individual elements on the cooking top, or the oven, nor are we, as installers, required to provide that overcurrent protection when we install these units.  Ranges which have a plug outlet for use with smaller appliances will have a 15 amp fuse or breaker protecting that circuit only.  The only protection provided for the range elements is the 40 amp breaker in the supply panel.

**Cable protection** - Flexible conduit is usually required on these cables for mechanical protection where they are subject to mechanical damage, even though they are in a cabinet below the range, Rule 12-518.

**Grounding** — If you do not connect the bare ground conductor properly at the panel and at the range, one day the chief cook may not be alive to greet you with a kiss at the end of a busy day.

**(e)**    **Gas Range** - Rule 26-712(d) says that if the piping for a free-standing gas range is installed then we must also install a 15 amp plug outlet in that space for the range. This plug outlet must be located the same as the 50 amp plug for an electric range as shown on page 107. This range plug may be supplied from the kitchen eating area plug circuit as shown on page 83.

**(f)**    **Dryers** - Rules 26-744(2)&(3)

Electrical dryers must be cord connected, they may not be hard wired. Install a 3 pole, 4 wire grounding type plug receptacle behind the dryer location.

If for any reason a hard wired dryer is being replaced with a new or another used one, the rules require a plug outlet be installed at the dryer location.

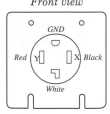

*Front view*

*30 amp Dryer*

> Cable size ..........................................#10 NMD90 copper
> Outlet box size ......................4 11/16 x 4 11/16 x 2 1/8 in.
> Plug receptacle rating ...........................................30 amp.
> Rating of fuses or breakers .........................30 amp. each

These sizes are sufficient for most dryers, i.e. dryers with ratings not greater than 7200 watts.

**Note**    Rule 12-3012(3) says this large box required for the dryer receptacle must be fastened to a solid structural member directly behind the box or on two of its sides just as described on page 107 for the range outlet box.

The bare grounding conductor must be properly connected at the panel and at the dryer to ensure safety to the operator.

**(g)    Water Heater**

**(i)    Circuit** - Rule 26-750(4) - requires a separate circuit with sufficient capacity to carry the maximum possible load that may be connected at one time by the thermostat. Most tanks are provided with 2 - 3 kw. elements, which totals 6000 watts, however, the internal thermostat control allows only one of these elements to operate at one time. See Notes 9 & 10 on page 13 for more details on this control arrangement.

> Cable size................#12 NMD90 copper
> Flexible conduit size..................$^7/_{16}$ inch
> Rating of fuses or breakers.......20 amp.
> Note - Fuse must be Type P or DRule 14-610

Note cable strapping. If this is not possible tape the flex cable to the loomex cable at this point.

**Note** - These sizes refer to water heaters with ratings from 3 kw. (3000 watts) up to 3.8 kw. (3800 watts).

**According to Rule 8-302(2)** a water heater is usually considered a **continuous load**. In that case the supply circuit must not be loaded to more than 80% of the rating of the breaker or fuse supplying it. A 3 kw. water heater draws 12.5 amps at 240 volts but the largest **continuous load** permitted on a 15 amp circuit is 80% or 12 amp. We therefore require 12.5 x 10/8 = 15.6 amp. This means we need a 20 amp breaker or fuse and #12 copper cable.

Position tank so that the nameplate remains accessible, Rule 2-118.

Use 7/16 inch flexible conduit over the supply cable.

**Rule 4-034(1)** permits a 2-conductor loomex cable to be used to supply a 240 volt load. When this is done the white wire is not used as a neutral but is hot. Wherever this white wire is visible, as in a junction box etc. it must be painted with black non-metallic paint, or better still, just wrap it with black electrical tape.

**Location of Hot Water Tank** - Rules 2-118 & 26-750(3) Locate the tank carefully; the supply connections, service covers and nameplate data must all be accessible after completion of the building.

**(ii)** **Cable Protection** - Rules 12-518, 12-1004 - Protect the hot water tank supply cable with $^7/_{16}$ inch flexible conduit where exposed to mechanical injury.

**(h)** **Furnace (gas or oil)** - Rule 26-806(1) & Bulletin 26-1-0-(4) - This rule has been officially interpreted, by Bulletin 26-1-0-(4), to mean that the supply cable to the furnace must not be with a 3-wire cable, but that **it must be a separate two wire cable all the way back to the panel.**

### Gas Furnace

Cable size ..............................................#14 copper
Flexible conduit size ............................$^7/_{16}$ inch
Fuse or breaker size..............................15 amp.

### Oil Furnace

Cable size ..............................................#12 copper
Flexible Conduit size ............................$^7/_{16}$ inch
Fuse or breaker size..............................20 amp.

**(i)** **Disconnect Switch** - Rules 26-806(5)(6)(7), 28-600

A disconnect switch is required for each furnace.

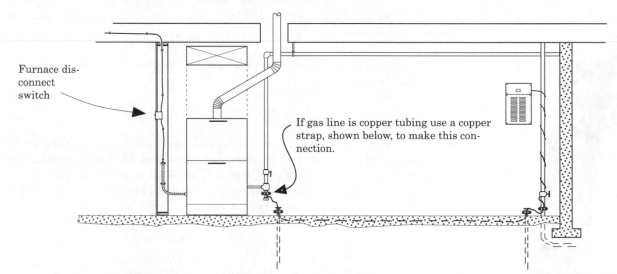

**Location** - A circuit breaker in a branch circuit panel may serve as disconnect switch provided it is located between the furnace and the escape route.

*In this case the circuit breaker in the panel is accessible without having to pass the furnace. This is an acceptable location for the disconnect switch*

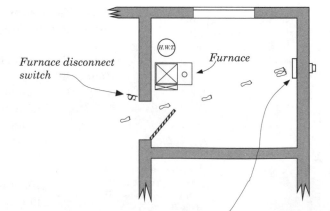

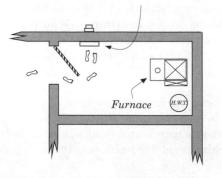

*The branch circuit breaker in this panel may not serve as the furnace disconnect switch because the escape route is past the furnace. The furnace disconnect switch must be located as shown.*

**(ii)** **Protection** - Rule 26-806 - The loomex supply cable should be run in a $^7/_{16}$ inch flexible conduit for the last few feet near the furnace where it is less than 1.5 m (59 in.) above the floor or where it is subject to mechanical damage.

**(iii)** **Bonding** - Rule 10-400 - Be sure to connect securely the bare bonding conductor in the supply cable to the bonding terminal in the furnace connection box.

**(iv)** **Gas Piping**- Rule 10-406(4) - All interior metal gas piping used to supply the furnace, fire place, or other appliance, must be bonded to the nearest grounded cold water pipe or to the service grounding electrode as shown on page 110. In that illustration the service grounding conductor continues on from the last ground rod to the gas line at the furnace. Do not cut the grounding conductor, simply run it through the ground clamps and then on to the last clamp on the gas line.

Use 2 bolts - do not try to do this with one bolt.

This strap may be used for bonding receptacles to steel pipe or copper tubing.

**Caution** - The gas lines used today are not like the rigid steel pipe we used to see in the good old days. Gas lines used today are of copper and in some cases of soft copper. Do not use an ordinary ground clamp on any copper gas lines because it may damage the pipe. Rule 10-614(2) allows us to use a copper strap to make this bonding connection. See illustration.on the left.

**(i)** **Kitchen Fan**

Cable size ....................................................#14 NMD90 copper
Flexible conduit size (If required)............$^7/_{16}$ inch
Fuse or breaker rating ..............................15 amp.

**(i)** **The kitchen fan** need not be on a separate circuit. It may be on a general lighting or plug circuit but it may **not be** on any special kitchen appliance circuits, Rule 26-722. It is counted as one outlet when determining circuit loading.

**(ii)** **Cable Protection** - Rule 12-518 - Protect loomex cable with $^7/_{16}$ inch flexible conduit where it is exposed to mechanical damage. This includes that portion of the cable which is exposed inside the cabinet where it may be subject to damage. Flexible cable must terminate in a flex connector at the fan and be strapped or taped to the loomex cable before it emerges from the wall.

**(iii)** **Grounding** - Rule 10-400 - Because it is near grounded objects it is very important to connect the bare ground wire securely to the ground terminal in the fan connection box.

**(j)** **Vacuum System** - Rule 26-710(m) requires that if piping for a central vacuum system is installed a plug outlet must be provided for the unit. Rule 26-720(e) requires that this plug outlet be supplied with a separate circuit used for no other load.

**(k)** **Hydromassage Bathtub**

**(i)** **CSA Certified Units** - Make sure the unit you install has one of the certification marks illustrated on page 2. This may seem like a picky point but in fact it is extremely important for your safety.

**(ii)** **Separate Circuit Required** - Rule 28-106(1) - This is a motor load, therefore, the rules in Section 28 must be applied. For the rough wiring stage run a separate 2-wire loomex cable to the motor location. Later when the unit is actually installed you will need to install a disconnect switch at the motor location.

**(iii)** **Disconnect Switch Required** - Rules 28-600, 28-602(3)(e).- These rules require a disconnect switch for this motor. This may be a standard wall switch, such as is used to control light outlets. Don't forget, the ampere rating of this switch must be at least 125% of the ampere rating of the pump motor.

**Note** This is not a hot tub. It is a hydromassage unit only. A hot tub usually has an electric heating element as well as a pump.

One more thing - do not forget to provide access to this motor and its disconnect switch for maintenance purposes.  See the illustration below

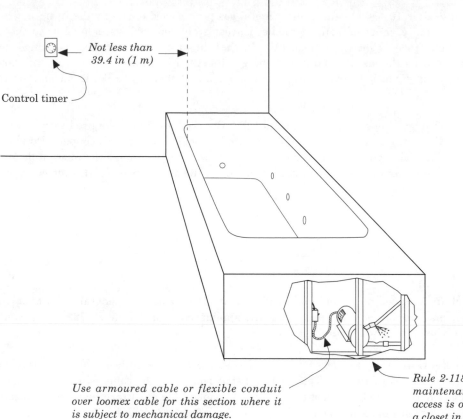

Control timer

*Not less than 39.4 in (1 m)*

*Use armoured cable or flexible conduit over loomex cable for this section where it is subject to mechanical damage.*

*Rule 2-118 requires ready access to this motor for maintenance.  Often this tub is located so that access is obtainable through a removable panel in a closet in an adjoining room.*

**(iv)**  **G.F.C.I. Required** - Rule 68-300 - This motor circuit must be protected with a G.F.C.I. type circuit breaker.  There is no exception to this rule.  Because this is a motor load this special circuit breaker **may not** also supply any other load.

**(v)**  **Lights, Switches and Plugs** - Rule 68-304 - The usual rules for lights, switches and plugs in bathrooms also apply to this special bathroom.

**(vi)**  **Control of Pump Motor** - Rule 68-302

— **Timer is not Required** - Rule 68-302(1) was revised to delete this timer.  The rule now requires only a simple wall switch properly rated, (125% of motor full load amps) to control this pump motor.

— **Location** - Rule 68-302(2) - The control switch must be at least 1 m. (39.4 in.) away from the tub.  This is a **horizontal** measurement from the outside wall of the tub, (the rule says "from the wall of the hydromassage tub") to the control switch.  There is an exception - where the control switch is an integral part of a properly certified factory built hydromassage bathtub it may be closer than 1 m from the tub.  In fact, in that case, the control switch may be on the tub itself, easily accessible to anyone in the tub.  *(Do these factory people know something the rest of us do not know or do they just use better switches?  Maybe they use better bonding methods or maybe they just use better arguments).*

## 24  ELECTRIC HEATING - baseboards only.

**(a)**  **Heat loss calculations** - Check if your Building Code or local electric power utility requires a heat loss calculation. This is a special method of calculating heat loss based on the type of construction, the quality of building insulation and the geographical location of the house. This is a fairly accurate method of determining the size of heating elements needed in each room. If a heat loss calculation is required the organization requiring it will normally advise you on the calculation methods they want you to use and will provide you with the necessary forms.

**(b)**  **Rough Floor Map Required**

The Electrical Inspector will want a rough sketch of the floor plan of your house showing:

— The location of heaters
— The rating of each heater
— What circuit it is on
— Size of supply conductors used and,
— The rating of breakers

Be sure your sketch is accurate and clear - easy to follow. Your Inspector will want it for that first rough inspection. See also page 60 for details on drawing a floor plan and how to identify each circuit.

**(c)**  **Branch Circuits** - Rule 62-108

Branch circuits which supply electric heaters may not be used to supply any other load.

**2-Wire Cables** - Electric heaters are usually connected for 240 volts - no connection to the neutral. Rule 4-034(l) permits a 2-wire loomex cable with one black and one white wire to be used for these loads.

**(d)**  **Breakers** - Tie-bars - Rule 14-302(b)(i)

Two single breakers require a tie-bar when used to supply 240 volt appliances such as heaters. The tie-bar is used to mechanically connect the operating handles of the two breakers so that they operate as one.

**(e)**  **Circuit Loading** - Rule 62-114(7) & (8)

## 20 Amp Circuit Breaker, #14 Copper Cable, Maximum Load Permitted is 3600 Watts

The actual wattage rating and the number of heaters used need not be as shown provided the sum of the rating of all the fixed heaters on the circuit does not exceed the maximum permitted for that circuit.

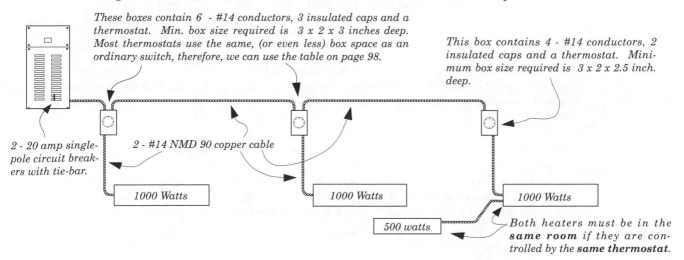

*These boxes contain 6 - #14 conductors, 3 insulated caps and a thermostat. Min. box size required is 3 x 2 x 3 inches deep. Most thermostats use the same, (or even less) box space as an ordinary switch, therefore, we can use the table on page 98.*

*This box contains 4 - #14 conductors, 2 insulated caps and a thermostat. Minimum box size required is 3 x 2 x 2.5 inch. deep.*

*2 - 20 amp single-pole circuit breakers with tie-bar.*

*2 - #14 NMD 90 copper cable*

1000 Watts

1000 Watts

1000 Watts

500 watts

*Both heaters must be in the **same room** if they are controlled by the **same thermostat**.*

The rules regarding electric heating were changed in the 1990 Code. We may now use the full ampacity of the cables supplying electric baseboard heating. A #14 copper conductor may carry 15 amps x 240 volts

= 3600 watts of heating load. To make this possible the rule was changed to permit 20 ampere breakers ahead of the #14 copper circuit conductors. This change in the rules was based on the fact that fixed heating loads are just that , they are fixed, they do not change. This is in contrast to other branch circuits which supply plug outlets or lighting outlets where the total load is constantly changing and is unpredictable. The above illustration showing a 15 amp heating circuit, and following illustration showing a 20 amp heating circuit, show the circuit loadings permissible under the changed rules.

**Maximum Length** - Maximum length of supply cable to the first heater in the circuit should not exceed 82 ft. (Approx. 25 m). After this first heater the load is smaller and length of run is not usually a problem.

The maximum load permitted with #14 copper cable must not exceed 15 amp. The 20 amp breaker shown protecting this cable is permitted because this is a fixed load. Maximum circuit load, (in watts) must not exceed conductor ampacity multiplied by the circuit voltage. For example, a 15 amp conductor operating at 240 volts could supply 3600 watts of electric baseboard heating.

**Caution** - Do not bundle these cables, maintain separation as described on page 53.

**Note**     Under the **old rules** we would not have been permitted to use a 20 amp breaker; 15 amp was the max rated breaker allowed for a #14 copper cable. With that old arrangement the maximum load permitted was only 2880 watts.

## 30 Amp Circuit Breaker, #12 Copper Cable, Maximum Load Permitted is 4800 Watts.

**Maximum Length** - Maximum length of supply cable to the first heater in this circuit should not exceed 100 ft.(Approx. 30 m)  After the first heater the load is smaller and length of run is not usually a problem.

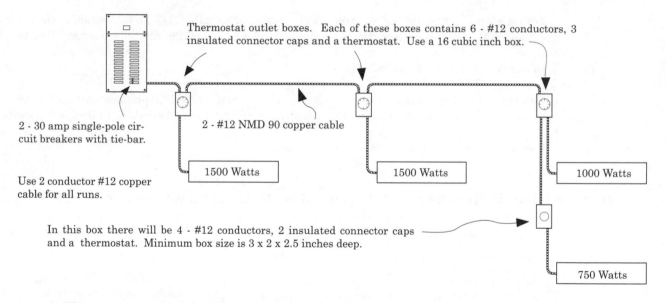

Thermostat outlet boxes. Each of these boxes contains 6 - #12 conductors, 3 insulated connector caps and a thermostat. Use a 16 cubic inch box.

2 - 30 amp single-pole circuit breakers with tie-bar.

2 - #12 NMD 90 copper cable

Use 2 conductor #12 copper cable for all runs.

1500 Watts

1500 Watts

1000 Watts

In this box there will be 4 - #12 conductors, 2 insulated connector caps and a thermostat. Minimum box size is 3 x 2 x 2.5 inches deep.

750 Watts

**The maximum load permitted** with #12 copper cable must not exceed 20 amp. The 30 amp breaker shown protecting this cable is permitted because this is a fixed load. Maximum circuit load must not exceed conductor ampacity multiplied by the circuit voltage. In this case it is  20 amps  x  240 volts  = 4800 watts.

**Note** - In the above illustration Rule 62-114(4) will permit #14 copper cable to be used between the thermostat and the heater provided that that cable length is not more than 24.6 ft (7.5 m). This distance is not measured as the crow flies, but is actual cable length. That maximum length of 24.6 feet. worked just fine about 30 years ago when we built smaller houses but in today's much larger houses the rooms are larger, and the 24.6 feet maximum length is simply not enough in many cases. Any taps longer than 7.5 m must be made with #12 copper cable.

**It is still permissible** to use a 15 amp breaker and #14 copper cable to supply 2880 watts or a 20 amp breaker on #12 copper cable supplying 3880 watts but there is no need to do so now. It should be noted that the rules always did permit the cables to carry their full rated current, the trouble was the restriction placed on the breaker supplying the cable. It could only be loaded to 80% of its rating. That has not changed either. What has changed, to make this greater loading possible, is Rule 62-114(8) which permits higher rated breakers for the #14 and #12 cables when they supply fixed heating loads.

**Caution** - Do not bundle these cables, maintain separation as described on page 53.

**(f)   Thermostats**

**(i)   Location** - Rule 62-202 requires a thermostat **in each room** where electric heating is installed. All the heaters in a room must be controlled by a thermostat located in that room.

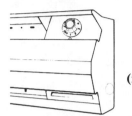

**Location In Bathrooms** - The rules do not specifically require the control for electric heaters in a bathroom to be at least 1 m (39.4 in.) **horizontal** distance from the tub or shower stall, however, that is better. It should not be possible to operate the thermostat **from any position in the tub.**. Watch this in the rough wiring stage - make provision for the thermostat.

**(ii)   Rating** - Rule 62-118(1) - Those thermostats which are connected directly into the line and control the full load current must have a current rating at least equal to the sum of the current ratings of all the electric heaters they control.

**(iii)   Type - A single pole thermostat** which does not have a marked "off" position is acceptable on a normal 240 volt heating circuit.

**Background** - Rule 62-118(2) accepts thermostats whether they are marked with an indicating "off" position or not, it does not matter. This sub-rule merely indicates that if a thermostat has a marked "off" position that it must then open, (in that case only) both hot conductors of the controlled heating circuit. If the thermostat only indicates a high and a low position with graduated markings between, it need not open all ungrounded conductors of the circuit. This means that the heating circuit is always hot (energized) but open until the thermostat calls for heat.

**(g)   Outlet Boxes** - Rules 12-506, 12-3002(6)

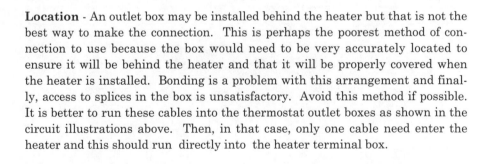

*Electric Space heater*

**Location** - An outlet box may be installed behind the heater but that is not the best way to make the connection. This is perhaps the poorest method of connection to use because the box would need to be very accurately located to ensure it will be behind the heater and that it will be properly covered when the heater is installed. Bonding is a problem with this arrangement and finally, access to splices in the box is unsatisfactory. Avoid this method if possible. It is better to run these cables into the thermostat outlet boxes as shown in the circuit illustrations above. Then, in that case, only one cable need enter the heater and this should run directly into the heater terminal box.

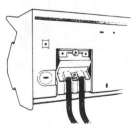

The double cable connector in some heaters is an advantage when there are two or more heaters in the same room as shown in the illustration on page 113.

**(h)   Cable Protection - Rule 12-518**

Where part of the cable is run exposed to mechanical injury, use a short length of EMT conduit or flexible conduit to protect the cable. Be sure to terminate the metal conduit in an approved manner so that it is grounded.

(i)    **Bathroom Heat Lamp** - Rule 62-108(3)

Heat lamps in bathrooms are normally supplied from general use lighting or plug outlet circuits. They may not be supplied from electric heating circuits. The reason is that the heat lamp is not the only heating provided in a bathroom, it is a supplementary heat source for a specific purpose. The control switch for a heat lamp in a bathroom must be at least 1 m (39.4 in.) from the outside face of a tub or shower. See above under "Location in Bathrooms" for details.

(j)    **Grounding & Bonding** - Rules 10-400, 10-906

The bare grounding wire (the Code now calls this a bonding wire) in the supply cable must be securely connected to the fixture with the grounding terminal screw in each fixture.

# 25 ELECTRIC HOT AIR FURNACE - Rule 62-208

Installing an electric hot air furnace is not as difficult as it may appear. By carefully following these basic instructions, you can do it and save.

**(a)      Clearances** - Rule 62-208

This rule does not specify any minimum clearance but it does draw attention to two basic clearances required.

**(1)  From Combustible Surfaces** - Observe all the clearances specified on the furnace name plate and,

**(2)  For Maintenance** - Do not install your furnace in a small confined space unless it is designed and marked for installation in an alcove or closet. There must be sufficient clearance to allow removal of panel covers and for maintenance work.

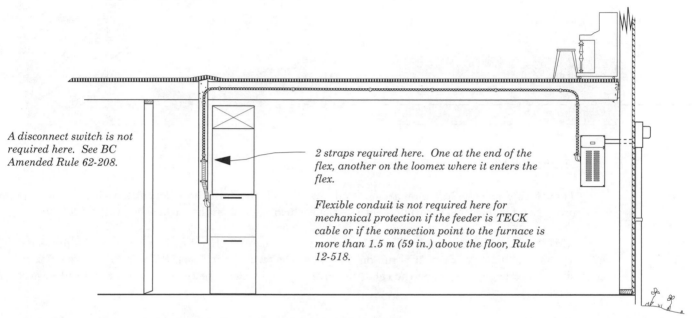

*A disconnect switch is not required here. See BC Amended Rule 62-208.*

*2 straps required here. One at the end of the flex, another on the loomex where it enters the flex.*

*Flexible conduit is not required here for mechanical protection if the feeder is TECK cable or if the connection point to the furnace is more than 1.5 m (59 in.) above the floor, Rule 12-518.*

**(b)      Supply to Furnace** - Rule 62-114(6)&(7)

Below is a greatly simplified table of sizes. Use this table to determine the rating of the furnace supply cable and circuit breakers.

**Note** - The table also takes into account the current drawn by the fan motor.

| Your Furnace Nameplate Rating | Fuse or Circuit Breaker Rating | Size of supply conductor to furnace | |
|---|---|---|---|
| | | Using Copper | Using Aluminum |
| 5 KW | 30 Amp | #10 NMD90 (Loomex Cable) | #8 NMD90 (Loomex Cable) |
| 10 KW | 60 Amp | #8 NMD90 (Loomex Cable) | #6 NMD90 (Loomex Cable) |
| 15 KW | 100 Amp | #4 NMD90 (Loomex Cable) | #3 NMD90 (Loomex Cable) |
| 20 KW | 125 Amp | #3 NMD90 (Loomex Cable) | #2 NMD90 (Loomex Cable) |
| 25 KW | 150 Amp | #2 NMD90 (Loomex Cable) | #0 NMD90 (Loomex Cable) |
| 30 KW | 175 Amp | #1 NMD90 (Loomex Cable) | #00 NMD90 (Loomex Cable |

The above Table is based on Chromalox SPEC. sheet CCSL 266.4. dated Oct. 18/82

**(c)      Furnace Disconnect switch** - Rule 62-208

Rule 62-208 does not require a disconnect switch at the electric furnace.

**(d)** **Wiring Method**

**NMD-9O cable.** This cable may be used if the size you need is available. All the usual rules for running loomex cable apply to this cable, i.e. strap it, protect it, and terminate it in approved cable connectors.

**Teck Cable** (copper) may also be used to supply the furnace. This is a tougher cable and it costs a lot more but it may not need any additional protection from mechanical injury.

Dry type cable connectors may be used indoors.

**Note**    Peel off only the PVC outer sheath, and only at the connector, so that it (the dry type connector) is clamped directly onto the metal armour.

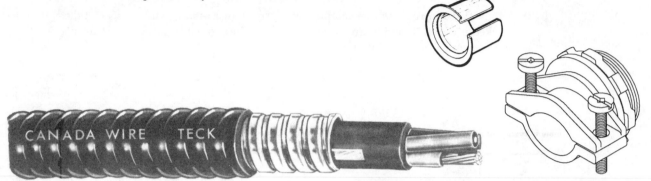

**(e)** **Mechanical Protection Required**

**Teck Cable** has an aluminum armour and can take a little abuse, however, if there is any doubt, provide protection for the cable especially those sections which are run on the surface below the 5 ft. level.

**NMD7 or NMD-90 - Loomex Cable** - has no armour and therefore must always be protected from mechanical damage where it is run on the surface below the 5 ft. level. Rule 12-518. Use a flex conduit, sized large enough to allow the cable to move freely, for those sections where mechanical protection is needed.

**Note** - This flex conduit must then terminate in a flex connector at the furnace.

Consider using an angle connector at the furnace because this cable, and the flexible conduit, may not be bent sharply without damaging it.

**(f)** **Thermostat Control Wiring**

Table 19 in the Code lists only one cable acceptable for low voltage thermostat control work. That is type LVT cable. Truth is, Table 19 does list a type ELC cable for Class 2 wiring but Rule 16-210(3) says it may not be used for heating control (thermostat) circuits. So we are stuck with having to use LVT cable only.

**Strapping** - Whatever staples or straps you use to support this small cable make sure they do not damage the sheath. Staples should be driven in only till they contact the cable. When a staple is driven in too deeply and short circuits the conductors, it turns the furnace on and there is nothing to shut it off, automatically, except the high limit safety device inside the furnace. The thermostat cable is important - install it carefully.

**(g)** **Grounding** - Rules 10-400, 10-600

Make certain the grounding conductor is properly connected with approved lugs, at each end. Look for a separate grounding lug in the furnace connection box and in the service panel.

# 26 DRIVEWAY LIGHTING

**(a)**     **Conduit System** - Conduit is very seldom used for this work. It is difficult to properly terminate the conduit at either end. Don't forget, a grounding conductor must be drawn into the conduit along with the circuit conductors to ground the light standard.

    **Polyethylene pipe** is usually permitted for this installation provided we use it only for the underground portion and the cable we use is an underground cable such as NMWU or NMW10 loomex cable. The riser at the house must be rigid metal conduit or rigid PVC pipe.

**(b)**     **Direct Burial** -Rule 12-012

    **Depth of Burial** - Type NMWU (or the old NMW10) loomex cable, size #14, may be used as shown in the illustration. It must be buried to a depth of 600 mm (23.6 in.) or if it passes under a roadway or driveway, to a depth of 900 mm (35.4 in.)..

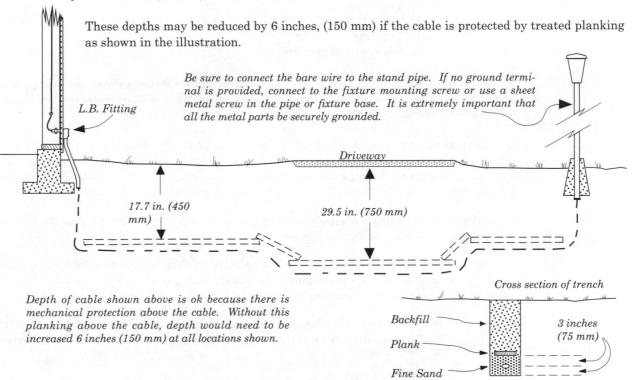

These depths may be reduced by 6 inches, (150 mm) if the cable is protected by treated planking as shown in the illustration.

*Be sure to connect the bare wire to the stand pipe. If no ground terminal is provided, connect to the fixture mounting screw or use a sheet metal screw in the pipe or fixture base. It is extremely important that all the metal parts be securely grounded.*

*L.B. Fitting*

*Driveway*

*17.7 in. (450 mm)*

*29.5 in. (750 mm)*

*Cross section of trench*

*Depth of cable shown above is ok because there is mechanical protection above the cable. Without this planking above the cable, depth would need to be increased 6 inches (150 mm) at all locations shown.*

*Backfill*

*Plank*

*Fine Sand*

*3 inches (75 mm)*

1     **Sand or earth - may be used but note the stuff is to be screened with #6 mm ($^1/_4$ in.) screen.** Cables should lie on 75 mm (3 in.) thick bed of this screened sand or earth and have a further 75 mm (3 in.) thick blanket of screened sand placed on top of the cables.

2     **Treated Planking** - 2 inch untreated cedar planking is acceptable in most cases. The Rule says a 38 mm (11/2 in.) treated plank is required. Check with your Inspector before you use untreated planks.

3     **Section of Conduit** - This is to protect the cable from damage.

    Rule 12-012(5) requires that this conduit terminate in a vertical position approximately 300 mm. (11.8 in.) above the trench floor. The cable must continue on downward, as shown, to allow movement during frost heaving.

    **Size of Conduit** - is not critical. It should be large enough so that cable can be drawn in easily and without damage to the insulation.

    **Type of Conduit** - may be rigid metal conduit or P.V.C. but may not be EMT, Rule 12-1402, 22-500.

**(c)**     **Grounding & Bonding** - Rules 10-400, 10-906

    It is very important that the ground wire be securely connected to the lamp standard.

# 27 TEMPORARY CONNECTION TO PERMANENT BUILDING - Rule 2-014

It is really a permanent type of service connection but it is on a temporary basis until the wiring is entirely completed. Many of the building contractors ask for this connection to speed up the finishing work. Check with your Inspector before attempting to prepare the installation for such a connection.

**(a)**      **Requirements for Connection**

To obtain this connection, in most districts the following is required.

**Service** - Service must be entirely complete, including;

- Meter backing
- Meter blank cover
- Dux seal in last fitting, where required. See pages 29 and 32.
- Service grounding
- Waste pipe bonding, (Note: both septic and soap systems, if they are in metal pipe, must be bonded to ground.)
- Panel covers must be installed.

**Permits** - must be complete, that is, they must cover the entire installation, including such appliances as range, water heater, dryer, furnace wiring etc. even though these appliances are not yet installed at the time the temporary connection is required.

**One branch circuit** must be completed by installing all fixtures, plates etc. but leave all other circuits disconnected from their circuit breakers in the panel unless these too are entirely completed. Do not energize any circuit which runs through an outdoor outlet box unless it is entirely complete with fixtures, fittings, plates, covers etc. It is better to choose a circuit which has all its outlets facing indoors.

**In addition**, most localities require a temporary connection permit (or TCP) before the Inspector can authorize the power utility to connect the service.

> **Building** - In some localities it is necessary to close the building for this connection. That is, it must have doors and windows installed before the service can be authorized for connection. Check this with your local Inspector.

> **Identify House** - The house number should be posted in a conspicuous place on the house. This is to help the Inspector and the power utility connection crew to identify the correct house quickly.

> **Completion** - When the installation is entirely complete, notify the Inspection department immediately. The Inspector requires written notification (this may be a permit stub properly signed and dated or a special form may need to be filled in). If the temporary permit expires before the installation is completed, you will need to renew this connection permit.

**Special Cases. Check with your Inspector first.**
**For Underground Services Only**

> It is not always necessary to frame the whole building, (i.e. put on the roof and outside sheathing to get a temporary to permanent connection) as described above. Often it is possible to have the building contractor erect only a small portion of the permanent wall where the permanent service (meter base and service panel) is to be located. The permanent meter base and service panel along with one or more plug outlets may then be installed on this partial wall. A temporary wooden enclosure similar to that described for temporary construction service on page 123, must be built to protect this electrical equipment from the weather and small prying and inquisitive fingers from getting hurt.

> **Service Grounding** - Permanent service grounding should be installed. This usually consists of 2 - 3 m(118 in.) rods 3 m (118 in.) apart. Don't forget to connect the water piping system when it is installed. See page 48 for more detailed instructions.

> **Note** - This is only a temporary connection for construction purposes and is subject to immediate disconnection if the terms of use are changed or when the permit expires.

## 28 TEMPORARY POLE SERVICES - Section 76 in the Code & BC Bulletin 6-3-0

**(a)        Minimum Service Size**

> Wire size.......................................................................#10
> Conduit size ........................................................3/4 inch
> Circuit breaker or Fuse ratings ............15, 20 or 30 amp.

**Circuit Breaker or Fuse Rating** - Rule 28-200 & Table D16, page 456 in the Code - Where the temporary power pole will supply a motor load, such as carpenters power saws, the circuit breakers or fuses may be 20 amp. or for the larger power saw loads, may be as high as 30 amp. even though the receptacle is rated for only 15 amp.

**(b)        Pole Requirements** - Guide only - check with your Inspector.

**(i)        Solid** - It must be a pole or solid timber.  Laminated timber is not acceptable.

**(ii)        Size** - Minimum size is 152 mm by 152 mm (6 in. by 6 in.) timber, or if a round pole is used, it must be at least Class 6 with a 152 mm. (6 in.) diameter top.

**(iii)        Length** - Minimum length is 5.2 m (17.0 ft.).  This provides for 1.2 m. (47.2 in.) in the ground and a minimum 4.0 m. (13. 1 ft.) above ground.  This is acceptable only where lines are short and the Hydro pole is on your side of the road.

See page 19 for minimum clearance required for a service line which must cross over buildings, roadways or walkways.

**(iv)        Gain** - Two shallow saw cuts approximately 2 inches apart, with wood chip between removed, marking the pole 3.6 m. (142 in.) from butt end.

**(v)        Bracing** - as required to offset the pull of the Hydro lines.  This should be done with 50 mm x 100 mm. (4 in. x 2 in.) lumber attached as high as possible and should make an angle approximately 30 degrees with the pole.

**(c)        Meter Base**

**(i)        Height**- maximum 1850 mm (72.8 in.), minimum 1650 mm (64.9 in.), final grade level to center of meter.

**(ii)        Blank Cover** - Hydro may require a temporary cover on the base until they can install a meter.

**(iii)        Connection** - Connections are as shown on page 122.

**(d)        Service Equipment**

**(i)        Circuit Breaker Type** - This is the preferred type of equipment for temporary construction services.

**Note**        Rule 14-302 requires a double pole breaker with single handle be used.  Two breakers with a tie-bar on the handles is not acceptable for this purpose because this is a service switch.

**Fuse Type** — Rule 14-204 - Non-interchangeable type fuses only may be used . This means that fuse adapters must be installed in the standard fuse sockets in the switch and panel.  These adapters are available in different sizes or current ratings.  Once a particular adapter has been installed, say a 20 amp. size, only a 20 amp. fuse will fit this socket.

**Please note:** In some districts only circuit breaker type equipment is permitted.  You should check with your local Inspector before proceeding.

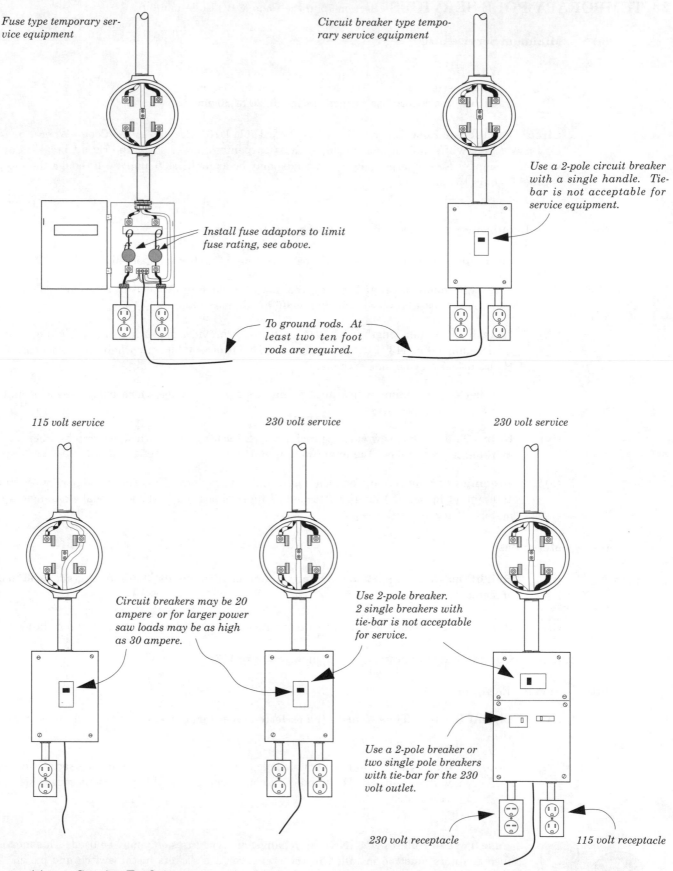

*Fuse type temporary service equipment*

*Circuit breaker type temporary service equipment*

*Use a 2-pole circuit breaker with a single handle. Tie-bar is not acceptable for service equipment.*

*Install fuse adaptors to limit fuse rating, see above.*

*To ground rods. At least two ten foot rods are required.*

*115 volt service*

*230 volt service*

*230 volt service*

*Circuit breakers may be 20 ampere or for larger power saw loads may be as high as 30 ampere.*

*Use 2-pole breaker. 2 single breakers with tie-bar is not acceptable for service.*

*Use a 2-pole breaker or two single pole breakers with tie-bar for the 230 volt outlet.*

*230 volt receptacle*

*115 volt receptacle*

**(e)**     **Service Enclosures**

**Standard Non-Weatherproof Type** - Non-weatherproof service equipment may be used if it is installed in a solidly constructed **weatherproof box.** This box may be of lumber or plywood not less than 20 mm (3/4 in.) in thickness with hinged door and lock. If practicable, the door should be hinged at the top.

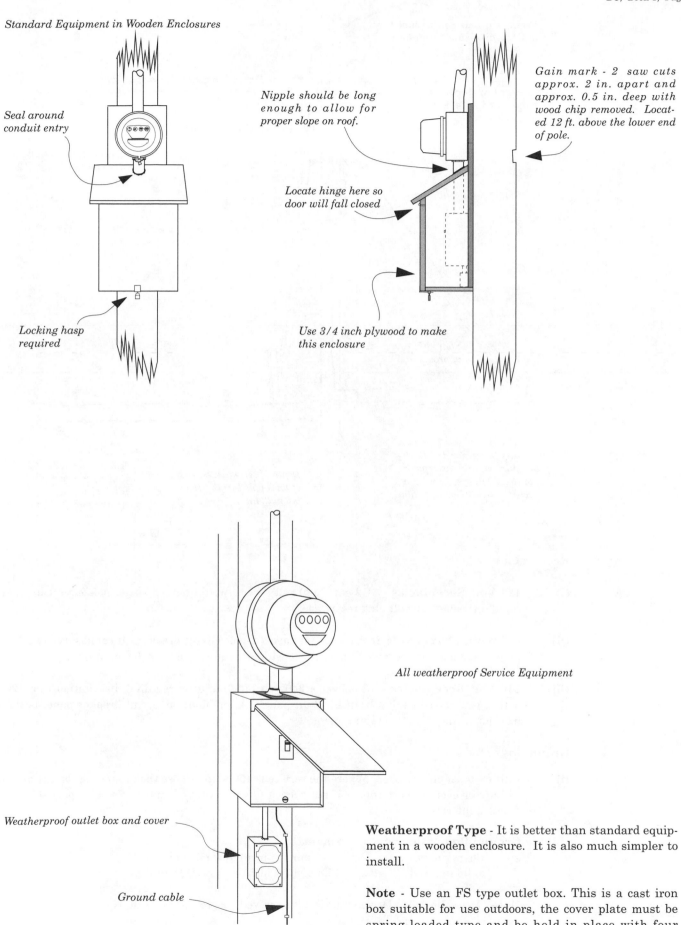

*Standard Equipment in Wooden Enclosures*

Seal around conduit entry

Locking hasp required

Nipple should be long enough to allow for proper slope on roof.

Locate hinge here so door will fall closed

Use 3/4 inch plywood to make this enclosure

*Gain mark - 2 saw cuts approx. 2 in. apart and approx. 0.5 in. deep with wood chip removed. Located 12 ft. above the lower end of pole.*

*All weatherproof Service Equipment*

Weatherproof outlet box and cover

Ground cable

**Weatherproof Type** - It is better than standard equipment in a wooden enclosure. It is also much simpler to install.

**Note** - Use an FS type outlet box. This is a cast iron box suitable for use outdoors, the cover plate must be spring-loaded type and be held in place with four screws. Use a gasketted cover plate over the receptacle as shown, Rule 26-702(2).

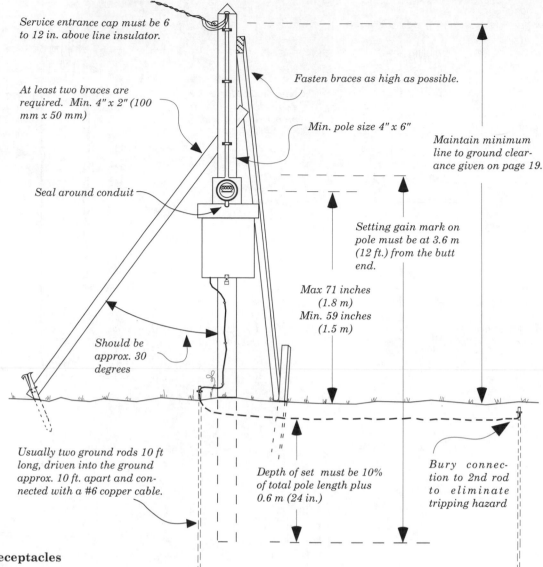

*Service entrance cap must be 6 to 12 in. above line insulator.*

*Fasten braces as high as possible.*

*At least two braces are required. Min. 4" x 2" (100 mm x 50 mm)*

*Min. pole size 4" x 6"*

*Maintain minimum line to ground clearance given on page 19.*

*Seal around conduit*

*Setting gain mark on pole must be at 3.6 m (12 ft.) from the butt end.*

*Max 71 inches (1.8 m) Min. 59 inches (1.5 m)*

*Should be approx. 30 degrees*

*Usually two ground rods 10 ft long, driven into the ground approx. 10 ft. apart and connected with a #6 copper cable.*

*Depth of set must be 10% of total pole length plus 0.6 m (24 in.)*

*Bury connection to 2nd rod to eliminate tripping hazard*

### (f)    Receptacles

**(i)**    **120 Volt Receptacles** - A 2 wire, 120 volt service would have a single pole circuit breaker. It could serve one 120 volt plug receptacle.

**(ii)**    **A 3-Wire, 120/240 Volt Service** would have a 2-pole circuit breaker. It could serve two 120 volt plug receptacles or one 240 volt receptacle without requiring a branch circuit panel.

**(iii)**    **240 Volt Receptacles** - Whenever a 240 volt plug outlet is required, in addition to a 120 volt outlet, you must install a branch circuit panel. A combination circuit breaker panel is the best way out of this awkward requirement.

### (g)    Grounding

**(i)**    **Cable** - must be of copper. Where the service is 100 amp. or less the grounding conductor may be #4 bare or even #6 bare copper if not subject to mechanical damage. See also page 48 for more detailed information.

**(ii)**    **Ground Rods** - Minimum size required.
Copper rods........................ 12.7 mm ($^1/_2$ inch) by 3 m. (118 in.)
Solid iron rod ....................15.8 mm ($^5/_8$ inch) by 3 m. (118 in.)

**Note** - Use solid rods - Driven pipe is not approved for grounding, Rule 10-702.

**(iii)**    **How Many Rods?** - In most localities 2 rods driven 3 m (approx. 10 ft.) apart, are required. In others you may need more to provide adequate grounding for the service.

# 29 PRIVATE GARAGE & FARM BUILDINGS

**(a)**    **Overhead Supply Lines**

**(i)**    **Insulation of Wire** - Rule 12-302 - Conductors must have weather proof insulation. Triplex cable is normally used today. Rule 12-318.

**(ii)**    **Elevation of Wire** - Rule 12-304 - Overhead lines must be out of reach as shown on page 19 and have the line to ground clearances given on page 19.

**(iii)**    **Roof Crossing** - Overhead lines may cross a roof provided the minimum line clearances given on page 19 are maintained.

**(iv)**    **Triplex Type Cable** - Rule 12-318 - A single 15 amp. branch circuit may be run to a building as shown below. The simplest method is to use a triplex cable. This consists of two insulated conductors wrapped around a bare messenger cable. In some cases the bare messenger, in triplex cable, may be used as the bonding conductor between the two buildings.

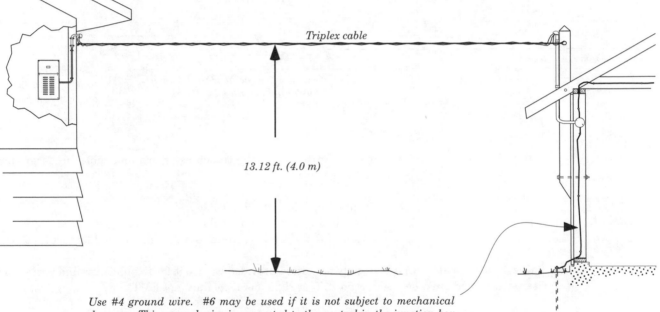

*Triplex cable*

*13.12 ft. (4.0 m)*

*Use #4 ground wire. #6 may be used if it is not subject to mechanical damage. This ground wire is connected to the neutral in the junction box above and to a ground rod below. If there is a metal water system in this building the ground conductor must be connected to it not to a ground rod.*

Two 15 amp. circuits may be run overhead as shown but if more circuits are needed a sub-panel is required in the out-building.

**(v)**    **Grounding** - Rule 10-208 - The neutral must be bonded to ground at each building. If this building **does not house livestock** the bare messenger in the triplex cable may be used to ground the circuits. If the building is used for livestock the circuits must be grounded at the building as shown in the illustration. This grounding conductor is usually #4 bare copper. A #6 conductor may be used if it is not subject to mechanical damage, Rule 10-806. The connection may be made in the first junction box. Do not use solder for this connection. Normally, only one ground rod is required for each sub-service.

**(b)**    **Underground Supply Lines** - Rule 12-012

**Cable Type** —is NMWU - Table 19 (This is the old NMW10)

**Cable Size** — is #14 but for long runs, above 15 m. (50 ft.), #12 is recommended.

**Cable Depth - without a protecting plank above the cable**

600 mm (23.6 in.) under pedestrian only area.
900 mm (35.4 in.) under vehicular trafflc areas.

**Cable Depth - With a protecting plank above the cable as shown below.**

450mm (17.7 in) under pedestrian only area.
750 mm (29.5 in.) under vehicular traffic areas.

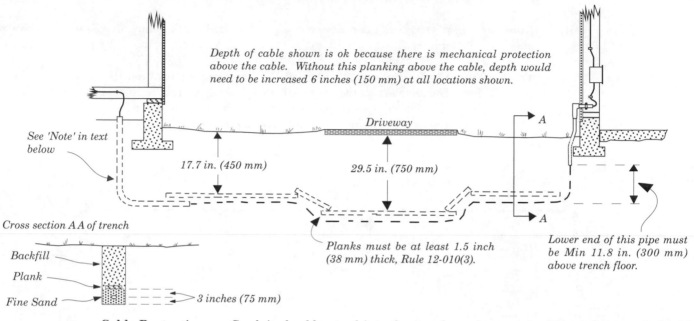

*Depth of cable shown is ok because there is mechanical protection above the cable. Without this planking above the cable, depth would need to be increased 6 inches (150 mm) at all locations shown.*

*Driveway*

*A*

*See 'Note' in text below*

*17.7 in. (450 mm)*

*29.5 in. (750 mm)*

*A*

*Cross section AA of trench*

Backfill
Plank
Fine Sand

3 inches (75 mm)

*Planks must be at least 1.5 inch (38 mm) thick, Rule 12-010(3).*

*Lower end of this pipe must be Min 11.8 in. (300 mm) above trench floor.*

**Cable Protection -** Conduit should extend into the trench as shown and cables underground should be protected as follows:

75 mm(3 in.) of sand below cable
75 mm(3 in.) of sand above cable.
38 mm( I 5 in.) plank above the sand. (Not nominal but actual thickness).

**Polyethylene water pipe** is usually permitted provided we use it for the underground portion only. The riser at each end must be either rigid PVC or rigid metal conduit, not EMT.

**(c)**     **SUB-PANELS** - in a garage or similar building.

Wood and Metal Lathe

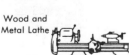

Where the load in the garage or other separate building requires more than two 15 amp. circuits, or where you wish to provide for future load additions, a sub-panel may be installed.

**Sizes**   Where plug outlets are used to supply power tools in a private garage or workshop it is recognized that there will normally be only one man working these tools at any one time. Therefore, even if you have a number of large power tools it is unlikely that more than one tool would be used at any one time. For this reason, when we are calculating the feeder size for this panel, we need to concern ourselves with only one machine, the one with the largest electrical load.

Power Saw

Drill Press

**#10 Sub-Feeder** - If there is no fixed electrical heating load and no electric welder load a #10 NMD-90 (copper) cable may be sufficient. This cable could supply a 30 ampere load at 240 volts. It could supply a $1^1/_2$ HP power tool at 240 volts, one circuit for lighting and one for plug outlets. The panel should be large enough for present loads plus some reserve capacity for future load additions.

**LARGER LOADS** - such as welders or fixed electric heaters would require more power and therefore a larger cable. A #8 NMWU (copper) cable will supply 40 amperes at 240 volts. This is large enough to supply a small private garage type welder, one circuit for lighting and one or more circuits for plug outlets. If the full load current of the welder was say 20 amps, then the circuit breaker supplying the 40 ampere NMWU sub-feeder cable could be as high as 60 amperes. Obviously, the load may not be greater than 40 amperes on this 40 ampere cable but because the biggest load is either a welder load or a motor load the code permits the ampere rating of the main supply breaker to be greater than the cable rating.

**WOODWORKING SHOP** - A 40 ampere NMWU copper feeder cable supplied with a 60 ampere circuit breaker in the main panel could serve a 3 HP 240 volt motor in the shop. There would be sufficient capacity left to supply garage lighting and a number of branch circuits for plug outlets.

**THE BIG ONE** - A #6 NMWU (copper) feeder to a garage or workshop is better but it may be more than is necessary in most cases. If you have an unusually large load, or the length of this feeder to the 2nd building is say 80 ft or more, you should consult your local Electrical Inspector for advice.

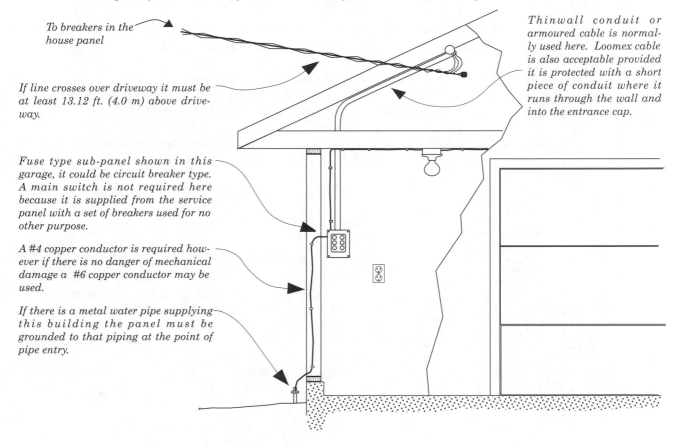

To breakers in the house panel

*Thinwall conduit or armoured cable is normally used here. Loomex cable is also acceptable provided it is protected with a short piece of conduit where it runs through the wall and into the entrance cap.*

If line crosses over driveway it must be at least 13.12 ft. (4.0 m) above driveway.

*Fuse type sub-panel shown in this garage, it could be circuit breaker type. A main switch is not required here because it is supplied from the service panel with a set of breakers used for no other purpose.*

*A #4 copper conductor is required however if there is no danger of mechanical damage a #6 copper conductor may be used.*

*If there is a metal water pipe supplying this building the panel must be grounded to that piping at the point of pipe entry.*

**Grounding** - Rule 10-208 - says the neutral must be grounded at each building which houses livestock but for all other buildings Subrule (b) suggests that grounding can be brought in with the sub-feeder conductors. If this sub-feeder is run underground direct from the service panel it is easy to bring a grounding conductor with the feeder but when the supply feeder is run overhead it may be much more difficult. While all that is possible there is yet another possible problem with that arrangement. If there is a metal piping system entering this building it must be bonded to this incoming grounding conductor. This is too complicated. The normal arrangement is as shown.

This grounding conductor is usually a #4 bare. A #6 grounding conductor may be used if it is not subject to mechanical damage, Rule 10-806. This grounding conductor must be connected to the neutral bus in the first switch or branch circuit panel in the second building. If the neutral in that switch or branch circuit panel is not already bonded to the enclosure you will need to bond it as shown for services on page 48.

**Ground Rods** - Normally, only one 3 m (10 ft.) ground rod is required for each sub-service panel in a separate building.

# 30 DUPLEX DWELLINGS

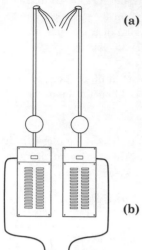

**(a)**  **Separate Service Conductors** - Rules 6-104 & 6-200 - In duplex dwellings each suite may be served with separate service equipment as shown.  The meter base, conduit sealing & draining, the service panel and all the instructions for grounding would be exactly the same as that given in the appropriate sections in this book for a single family residence.

**Note**  The two entrance caps must be located close together so that only one Hydro service drop is required.

**(b)**  **Common Service Conductors** - Rule 6-200(2) - This rule permits a two-gang meter base to be used in a duplex dwelling without a main switch ahead of it

¡*Both services must ¡be grounded to the ¡same grounding ¡electrode.*

**Note -**  The main service conductors must be large enough to carry 100% of the calculated load in the heaviest loaded suite plus 65% of the calculated load in the other suite plus the heating and air conditioning loads.  See sample calculation below.

**(i)**  **Calculation** - If both units of the duplex are to be served from a common service the size of the conductors to each suite should be as follows:

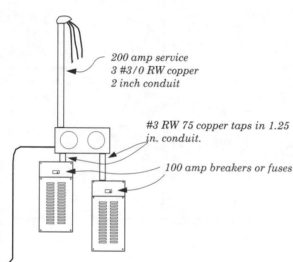

*200 amp service
3 #3/0 RW copper
2 inch conduit*

*#3 RW 75 copper taps in 1.25 in. conduit.*

*100 amp breakers or fuses*

**Sample Calculation** - Identical load in each suite.

**Basic Load** 102.2 m² (1100 sq.ft.) floor area

First 90 m² (968.4 sq.ft.) ......................5000 watts
Next 12.2 m² (131.6 sq.ft.) ...................1000 watts
10 kw.range ...........................................6000 watts
4 kw. dryer.............................................1000 watts
3 kw. water heater ...............................750 watts

Total  13750 watts

Electric heating                                    7000 watts

20750 watts

$$\frac{20750}{240} = 86.4 \text{ amps}$$

Each suite requires  100 amp. service panel with 100 amp. breaker.

#3 RW75 copper wire in 1¼ in. suite service conduit.

## Main service size calculation

13750 watts at 100% ......................................................................... 13,750 watts
13750 watts at  65% ......................................................................... 8,937 watts
Heating total is 14000 watts
10,000 at 100% ................................................................................. 10,000 watts
7000 at  75% ...................................................................................5,250 watts

37,937 watts

$$\frac{37937}{240} = 158. \text{ amps total calculated load}$$

Main service size is 158 amps

**(ii)**     **Metering and Service Conductors** - Normally the suite service panels can be installed within a few feet of the meter base, as shown above. Rules 6-206(1)(e) & 6-208 limit service conductor length inside the building to "as close as practicable". This means just through the wall, about 10 inches long. See also page 24 for some exceptions to this minimum length inside a building. On the outside of the building these runs may be a bit longer but the total length of each individual suite feeder must not exceed 24.6 ft (7.5 m). This is measured from the meter base terminal to the suite service breaker, it is the actual length of that feeder. The reason for this limit of 24.6 feet is that these suite feeders are smaller than the main service conductors, see Rule 14-100(c).

**(iii)**     **Service Equipment** - The service equipment in each suite normally consists of a combination service panel as shown.

**(iv)**     **Service Grounding** - In this case the service grounding conductor must run into the duplex meter base. These meter bases usually have provision for the grounding conductor connection and for bonding the neural to the meter enclosure. See also under "Grounding" on Page 48.

    **Size of Grounding Conductor** - may be determined from the List of Materials, page 8 in this book.

    **Note**     The size of this grounding conductor is related to the current carrying capacity of the main service conductor.

# 31 REWIRING AN EXISTING HOUSE

### (a)    Electrical Service Panel

**Old Panel** - If you are adding load to an existing panel in an old house but have no more breaker or fuse spaces you will need to install an additional sub panel and feed it from breakers in the existing panel. Before you do this, make sure the service equipment is adequate to supply the new load. Use the table on page 12 to determine size of service needed for all the load. If there is sufficient spare capacity, reroute two of the existing circuits to a new panel located nearby. This will free up space for two breakers for a sub-feeder to supply the new panel.

**Change Service panel** - This will cost a bit more but it may be the only solution if the old stuff is too small. Don't forget that if you change the panel you must upgrade the whole service, not the branch circuit wiring but the service. The reason for this is the new service may require larger conductors, conduit, meter base and grounding. It may also be necessary to find a more acceptable location for the new panel, meter base or service entrance cap. It may also be that all of these items are satisfactory and all that is needed is to replace the old panel with a larger one.

All this may sound expensive and indeed may be but don't forget this is the most important part of your installation. This is what protects all the circuits in the house and this is where that enormous hydro electric capacity is limited to a safe value. To compromise here is to compromise with minimum safety.

**Caution** - Even if it looks harmless, Don't take chances. **Before any work is begun you should make sure that that part of the system you will be working on is, in fact, not energized.** If you are changing your service equipment have Hydro crew disconnect your service before you begin work.

Where a service has been changed the Inspector will usually check for:

- **Entrance cap** - Re: height and location, page 21.

- **Size of Service Conduit & Conductors** - This may have been large enough at one time but may be too small now. See under "Service Size", page 7.

- **Meter Location etc**. - Accessibility and distance from the front of the house. page 38.

- **New Panel** - Must comply with new Code re: ampacity, number of circuit positions and number of 2-pole positions available for 240 volt and 3 wire circuits, page 44.

- **Service Grounding** - Size of conductor, condition of run, connected to old abandoned water service? Must comply with current regulations, see page 48.

- **Service Bonding** - Rule 10-406(3) - Older houses may have metal waste pipe system which may not have been bonded. In that case the Code requires a bonding connection between the metal waste piping and the service grounding electrode, or to the nearest bonded cold water pipe.

### (b)    Branch Circuit Wiring

**Additions or Changes To The House.** - All new wiring must comply with current regulations. The information on branch circuit wiring, given in this book, does apply to any new additional wiring.

**Existing wiring** - The Inspector will not normally require the existing finished areas to be rewired except as may be necessary for minimum safety. He will, however, require upgrading of branch circuit wiring where the walls have been opened to make other structural revisions or additions to the house. He has the knowledge and the experience to guide him in his assessment of your installation. He will ask for minimum changes to the existing wiring to make your home reasonably safe. The fact is - it's your safety he is concerned about and you want him to be concerned about that.

**Replacing Old Plug Receptacles** - Subrules 26-700(7)(8) & (9) - If you are fixing up an old house you may find the branch circuit wiring is with single insulated conductors supported on insulator knobs, (this is called knob and tube wiring) or, it may be the wiring consists of old type loomex cable which did not have a bonding conductor in the cable. In either case all the plug outlets will be ungrounded type. The Code permits us to use **grounded** type receptacle in these **ungrounded** outlet boxes provided we do one of the following things:

*Use 2 bolts - do not try to do this with one bolt.*

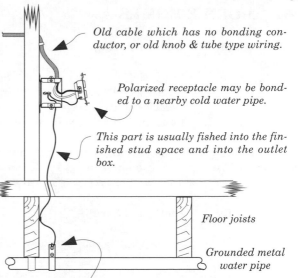

*This strap may be used for bonding to steel pipe or copper tubing.*

1 Install the new grounded type plug receptacle, (it could be a GFCI type but does not need to be) and bond it as shown in the illustration on the right. The illustration shows an outlet in a finished wall where you may need to fish a new bonding conductor down through the floor into the basement area where connection can be made to a grounded cold water metal pipe. A #14 solid copper conductor with green insulation may be used. It must be installed where it will not be subject to mechanical damage. The clamp may be an ordinary ground clamp or you may use a copper ground strap arrangement shown on the left; or

2 Install a GFCI type **circuit breaker** in the panel then use grounded type receptacles in all the outlets on this circuit as shown in the top circuit in the illustration below; or

3 Install a GFCI type **receptacle** as shown in the lower circuit below. Make sure the connections are correct so that all the other downstream receptacles will also have GFCI protection. The illustration shows new additional outlets added to this existing circuit. In some difficult cases this may be a good solution but the rule does not clearly say it may be so done, therefore, you should check first with your Inspector.

*Old cable which has no bonding conductor, or old knob & tube type wiring.*

*Polarized receptacle may be bonded to a nearby cold water pipe.*

*This part is usually fished into the finished stud space and into the outlet box.*

*Floor joists*

*Grounded metal water pipe*

*This bonding conductor is usually fished into the basement where it is connected to a nearest, grounded cold water pipe.*

*Use a GFCI type circuit breaker in the panel and standard grounded type receptacles in the outlet boxes.*

*There is no connection to the bonding terminal on these receptacles.*

*To other existing outlets on this, unbonded, 2-wire circuit.*

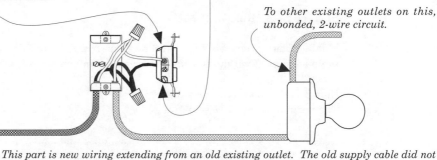

*Old existing wiring. There is no bonding conductor in these cables.*

*This part is new wiring extending from an old existing outlet. The old supply cable did not have a bonding conductor but the new cable does. In this case the bond wires in the new cable must not be connected to anything in any of these outlets on this circuit. It s best to cut these bonding conductors very short or tape them up so that they cannot contact anything in the outlet box; Rule 26-700(10).*

*Power supply leads must connect to the line terminals.*

*GFCI type Receptacle*

*Downstream outlets must be connected to the load terminals.*

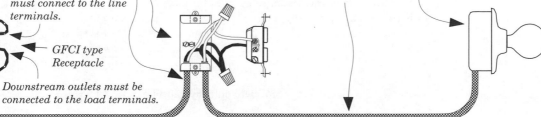

*Pigtails are required as shown, BC Rule 26-700(14).*

**Note**  Part of the lower circuit in the illustration above is new work, ie. these are new outlets extended from an old existing circuit. Subrules 26-700(7)(8) & (9) do not refer to new extensions to old existing installations, they refer only to existing outlets. However, Subrule (9) says there must not be any bonding connection between plug receptacles unless the bonding connection is complete all the way back to the panel. In this case it is not complete, the supply cable to the first outlet box has no bonding conductor, therefore, the bond wires in all of the outlet boxes must be left completely disconnected from the boxes, the receptacles and from other bond wires. Crazy? no not really. When the bonding conductor connects these receptacles together a fault on one outlet will also appear on all the other outlets connected together and that could be very dangerous.

**Electrical Permit** - make sure your electrical permit is adequate to cover the work done.

## 32 MOBILE HOMES

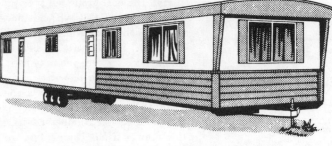

(a) **C.S.A. Marking**

The mobile unit must have a C.S.A. label or a label applied by one of the other certification agencies noted on page 2. If your unit does not have such a label you are in deep trouble. Sometimes it is lost in a move or for one reason or another it is gone. This approval label is one of the first things the Inspector will look for. If it is not there he cannot authorize a service connection. Your local inspection office can advise you on the procedure for replacing a lost certification label.

(b) **Electrical Permit**

An electrical permit must be obtained before any electrical work is done.

Note    If this mobile unit is on private property and you are personally going to occupy it, you are usually permitted to obtain a permit and do the work; or

If this mobile unit is to be occupied by someone in your immediate family, you are usually permitted to obtain an electrical permit and do the work; but

If this unit is for rental purposes to someone other than the immediate family then the wiring must be installed by an electrical contractor; and

If this unit is to be connected in a mobile home park the work must be done by a certified electrical contractor. The owner would not normally be permitted to do this work nor to take out a permit.

(c) **Service Size** - Rule 72-102(1)

Mobile homes are treated the same as a single family dwelling as far as service ampacity is concerned. See the table on page 12 for quick sizing of service equipment.

Rule 8-200, Floor area - **less** than 80 m$^2$ (861 sq.ft.)
The normal load will be something like this.

| | |
|---|---|
| Basic | 5000 watts |
| Range - (12 kw. range) | 6000 watts |
| Water heater - (3 kw tank) | 750 watts |
| Dryer — (4 kw. unit) | 1000 watts |
| Quick Steam Tap — (500watts) | 0 watts |
| Furnace — (gas or oil) | 0 watts |
| Freezer | 0 watts |
| Dishwasher | 0 watts |
| Fridge | 0 watts |
| Total | 12750 watts |

12750 divided by 240volts = 53.1 amps.

The code requires a 60 amp. service for this load.

Note    It really does not matter if the range, dryer, water heater and furnace are all gas - the fact is, the minimum service size is still 60 amp. for any size floor area up to 80 m$^2$.

**Larger Floor Area** - Where the floor area **is** 80m$^2$ (861 sq. ft.) or larger the minimum size service acceptable by Code is **100 amps**.

Unfortunately, the rules make no distinction between a single family house and a mobile home. The same rules used to determine the size of a service in a house are also applied in determining the size of service in a mobile home.

We all know that the calculated load in this unit is much less than 100 amp. The extra service ampacity is usually intended for future load changes. In single family houses there is always the possibility of finishing a basement, adding a sauna or large power vacuum etc. In a mobile home such changes are difficult, very costly and rare. But the minimum service size is the minimum service size - it's the law.

# (A)  SINGLE UNIT IN MOBILE PARK

### (a)        Connection Box in Mobile Home Park

A typical connection box in each lot in a mobile home park.

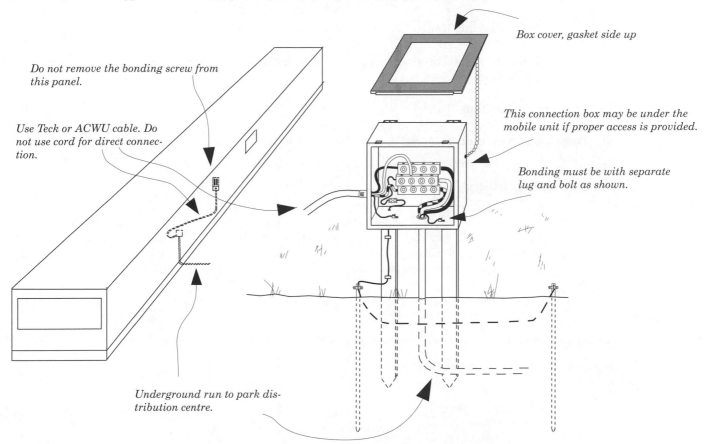

*Do not remove the bonding screw from this panel.*

*Use Teck or ACWU cable. Do not use cord for direct connection.*

*Underground run to park distribution centre.*

*Box cover, gasket side up*

*This connection box may be under the mobile unit if proper access is provided.*

*Bonding must be with separate lug and bolt as shown.*

Connection to this box can only be made by a certified electrical contractor. Neither the owner of the mobile unit nor the mobile park operator (or owner) may make this connection unless they have a valid Certificate of Qualification to do this work.

**An electrical permit** must be obtained before connection is made.

**Cable Connector** - The cable from the mobile unit must connect to the box with a connector approved for the particular cable you are using.

**Conductor Terminations in Box** - Watch this carefully - most of the problems are right here.

-        **Don't skin back too much insulation** - only enough to make good connections.

-        **If the box does not have** a terminal strip as shown - use only approved connectors to make the splices. This is an extremely important detail when aluminum conductors are used. In that case use only connector lugs **marked approved** for aluminum and make sure the conductor surface has been cleaned and an inhibitor has been applied.

-        **Bonding** - Terminate the grounding conductor in an approved lug which is separately bolted to the box. Don't try to use a bolt or screw already used for some other purpose.

-        Clean the Surface under the bonding lug to ensure a good electrical contact.

# (B) SINGLE UNIT ON PRIVATE PROPERTY

### (a)    Basic Requirements

#### (i)    Permission to Place Mobile Home

More and more of our freedoms are being taken away from us.  Before you move a mobile unit onto your own property, it is best to find out first if that would be permitted by local by-law.  In some cases you will be required to produce some kind of proof of approval from the local authorities before the Electrical Inspection department will issue an electrical permit for connection.

#### (ii)    Consult Hydro - Rules 6-206(1) & 6-114

Before any work is done the power utility should be consulted to determine which pole service will be from.

### (b)    Connection Methods

There are several connection methods you may choose from - each has its problems, pitfalls and advantages.

#### #1    DIP SERVICE

As shown below, only the meter is on the pole.  The service conductors dip underground to a point under the panel where they rise and enter the service box in the mobile unit.  This means the service conductors do not have fuse protection until they enter the panel.  It means there is no quick easy shut-off, except by removal of the meter when the moving truck arrives.

**Note** - Meter only on service pole.

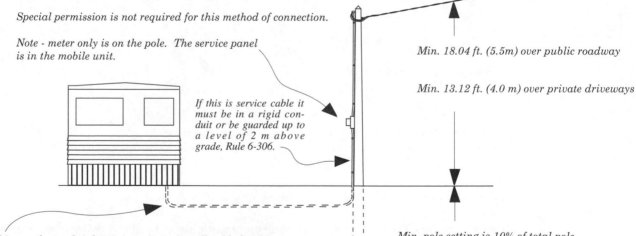

*Special permission is not required for this method of connection.*

*Note - meter only is on the pole.  The service panel is in the mobile unit.*

*If this is service cable it must be in a rigid conduit or be guarded up to a level of 2 m above grade, Rule 6-306.*

*Min. 18.04 ft. (5.5m) over public roadway*

*Min. 13.12 ft. (4.0 m) over private driveways*

*Min. pole setting is 10% of total pole length plus 0.6 m. (23.6 in.)*

*This may be conduit but it is easier to install cable for this run.*

*Remember, in this case you are installing a SERVICE cable and therefore much more care must be taken.  Rules 6-206(e) & 6-208(1) require the service conduit or cable to be as short as possible, usually just through the exterior wall.   However mobile units are CSA certified electrical loads and these usually arrive on site as fully finished, they are not built on site.  Therefore if they are equipped with service supply conduit running down into the crawl space the service connection will likely continue to be acceptable as shown above.  Note that if your existing supply cable is too long for the new connection you may be required to cut it to length, coiling the access cable in the crawl space below the unit may not be acceptable, but actually burying it in the ground below the crawl space may be.  Check this point with your local Inspector.*

**#2   MAST ON MOBILE UNIT**

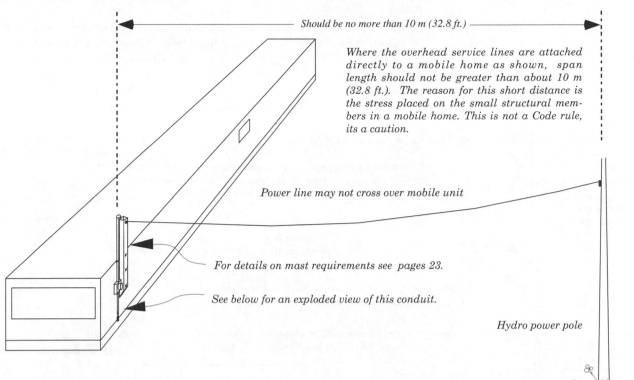

*Should be no more than 10 m (32.8 ft.)*

*Where the overhead service lines are attached directly to a mobile home as shown, span length should not be greater than about 10 m (32.8 ft.). The reason for this short distance is the stress placed on the small structural members in a mobile home. This is not a Code rule, its a caution.*

*Power line may not cross over mobile unit*

*For details on mast requirements see pages 23.*

*See below for an exploded view of this conduit.*

*Hydro power pole*

**Note** - It is often difficult to provide adequate mast support on a mobile unit. For this reason length of this overhead service drop should be as short as possible.

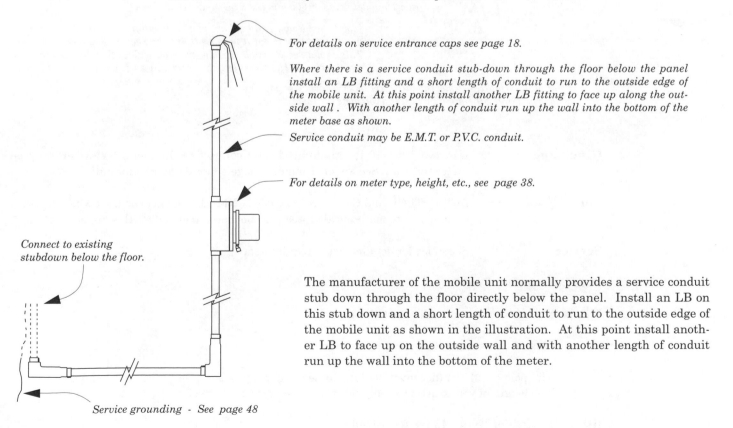

*For details on service entrance caps see page 18.*

*Where there is a service conduit stub-down through the floor below the panel install an LB fitting and a short length of conduit to run to the outside edge of the mobile unit. At this point install another LB fitting to face up along the outside wall . With another length of conduit run up the wall into the bottom of the meter base as shown.*

*Service conduit may be E.M.T. or P.V.C. conduit.*

*For details on meter type, height, etc., see  page 38.*

*Connect to existing stubdown below the floor.*

The manufacturer of the mobile unit normally provides a service conduit stub down through the floor directly below the panel. Install an LB on this stub down and a short length of conduit to run to the outside edge of the mobile unit as shown in the illustration. At this point install another LB to face up on the outside wall and with another length of conduit run up the wall into the bottom of the meter.

*Service grounding  -  See  page 48*

**#3    POLE SERVICE - By SPECIAL PERMISSION ONLY**

This is an outdoor service and Rules 6-206(d) 70-102(2) say special permission is required for such an installation. Special permission for these installations must be obtained before any work is done. Service ampacity is based on Rule 72-102(1) which is the same as for a house of similar size. See the table on page 12.

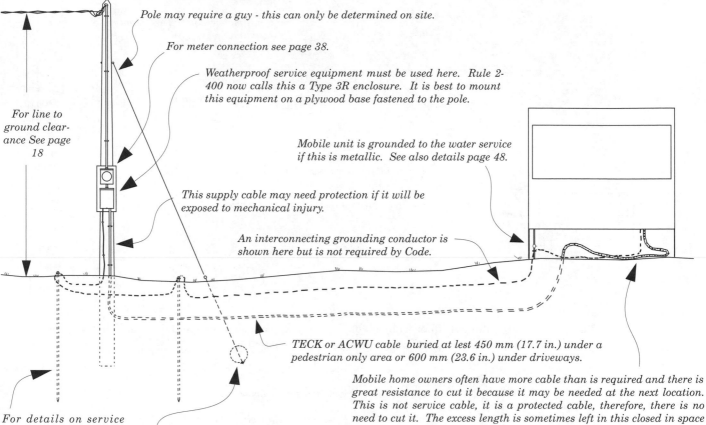

*Pole may require a guy - this can only be determined on site.*

*For meter connection see page 38.*

*Weatherproof service equipment must be used here. Rule 2-400 now calls this a Type 3R enclosure. It is best to mount this equipment on a plywood base fastened to the pole.*

*For line to ground clearance See page 18*

*Mobile unit is grounded to the water service if this is metallic. See also details page 48.*

*This supply cable may need protection if it will be exposed to mechanical injury.*

*An interconnecting grounding conductor is shown here but is not required by Code.*

*For details on service grounding see page 48.*

*TECK or ACWU cable buried at lest 450 mm (17.7 in.) under a pedestrian only area or 600 mm (23.6 in.) under driveways.*

*Mobile home owners often have more cable than is required and there is great resistance to cut it because it may be needed at the next location. This is not service cable, it is a protected cable, therefore, there is no need to cut it. The excess length is sometimes left in this closed in space*

*Dead man - usually a 1.2 m (48 inch) section of a pole. Use galvanised anchor bolt and galvanised guy wire to complete the installation.*

**Grounding -**    Use two 3 m. (10 ft.) ground rods and connect to the metal water service pipe under the unit. See under Grounding page 48 for detailed information.

**Cable Types -**    ACWU, TECK and Corflex may be used. NMWU may also be used when provided with adequate mechanical protection - not recommended for this application.

**Service -**    See index for detailed list of requirements.

**(c)    Pole Location on Property**

This is very important — consider the following:

**(i)    Near Connection Point**

The pole should be (not must be) located near the point of service connection on the mobile unit. The length of your existing supply cable will often determine this.

**(ii)    Length of Hydro Lines Required**

Note the Hydro power pole location. Hydro will usually run 30 m (98 ft.) onto your property without additional fee. Beyond this length they may be into your wallet for more money. Long runs, more than 30 m. (98 ft.) may also require additional poles and this is at your expense, usually.

**(iii)** **Crossings**

- **Crossing a Public Roadway?- Rule 6-112(2)(b)**

You may not have a choice. If the Hydro line is on the other side of the road you must cross the road with the line. Clearance required is 5.5 m. (18.04 ft.) minimum above roadway. It may require a long pole to do this.

- **Crossing a Driveway?**

Avoid crossing driveways if possible. If you must cross, the minimum line to ground clearance is 4.0 m. (13.12 ft.) above a driveway. This is generally considered the minimum height even if there is no garage or carport, only a driveway.

- **Crossing a roof?**

Do not cross the roof of any building including the roof of the mobile unit unless you can provide the clearances required by Rule 12-310. See page 19 for a simplified list of required clearances.

**(d)** **Pole Requirements - Check with your Inspector**

**Types** - Cedar, fir, lodgepole pine are usually acceptable. If you go into the woods to cut down a tree to make a pole, observe the following picky points:

I - Make sure it is straight and has the correct dimensions - see below under 'length'.

2 - Remove all branches, leaving a smooth surface.

3 - Remove all bark.

4 - Cut a gain mark 3.6 m. (142 in.) from butt, as shown below.

5 - Apply an effective treatment to both ends to retard rotting.

**Note -** It may be possible to use a sawn timber instead of a round pole. It is not recommended and before you try it, check with your Inspector.

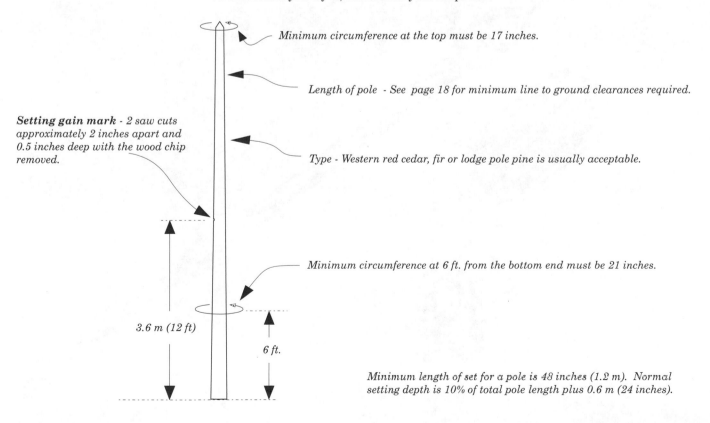

*Minimum circumference at the top must be 17 inches.*

*Length of pole - See page 18 for minimum line to ground clearances required.*

***Setting gain mark** - 2 saw cuts approximately 2 inches apart and 0.5 inches deep with the wood chip removed.*

*Type - Western red cedar, fir or lodge pole pine is usually acceptable.*

*Minimum circumference at 6 ft. from the bottom end must be 21 inches.*

*3.6 m (12 ft)*

*6 ft.*

*Minimum length of set for a pole is 48 inches (1.2 m). Normal setting depth is 10% of total pole length plus 0.6 m (24 inches).*

**Size** - Must be minimum Class 6 pole. This means it must be:

1 - Minimum 17 inches (430 mm) circumference at the top of the pole. This is minimum, it may be larger.

2 - Minimum 27.6 inches (700 mm) circumference 6 ft. (1.8 m) from the butt end for a 7.7 m (25 ft.) pole. Longer poles must be even larger in circumference.

**Length** - Two factors must be considered.

1 - **Length of pole above ground.** This is simply line to ground clearances given on page 19. Add to this the expected sag in your line, AND the:

2 —**Length of pole set into the ground.** In most cases this is 1.2 m (47.2 in.). Where the pole length above ground must be greater than 6 m (19.7ft.) the length of pole set into the ground must be increased. The normal setting in depth is 10% of total pole length plus 0.6 m.

**Guy Lines** - When Required? This must be determined on site. A very rough thumb rule is as follows:

If the length (of pole above ground) is 4 5m (14.75 ft.) or less and the length of span for the Hydro lines is say 10 m. (59 ft.) a guy is likely not required. If the dimensions are greater than these, it is very likely you will need to guy the pole.

- **Type of Guy Wire** - must be galvanized cable. Do not try to use ordinary wire rope or clothes line cable.

- **Size** - 5/16 in. guy wire would be sufficient in most cases.

- **Dead Man** - This is usually a 4 ft. length of log buried to the same depth as the pole setting. Use a long galvanized anchor bolt as shown below

# 33   PRACTICE EXAMINATION for CERTIFICATION

In the official examination you are not permitted to use your own code book or bulletin book. The examiner will provide unmarked copies of these books to you. He will also supply writing paper for your calculations.

Use all the time allowed for the exam. This is not a test to determine who finishes first but who finishes best.

Don't guess where True or False answers are required. A penalty may be assessed for each incorrect answer. Therefore, you could lose not only the marks for the question but also an equal mark as a penalty.

The theory behind this is that if you knew the correct answer, you would have given it but since you gave an incorrect answer you must have have been guessing. Therefore, if you don't know the correct answer, leave it blank unless you are very good at Russian Roulette.

**TYPICAL EXAMINATION QUESTIONS**

| | SECTION 1    TRUE or FALSE | True | False |
|---|---|---|---|

*Allow 2 points for each correct answer and subtract 2 points for each incorrect answer.*

I.   A CSA enclosure 3R may be used indoors where subject to drops of falling liquid due to heavy condensation.............. ____ ____

2.   A standard duplex receptacle may be installed in a bathroom provided the circuit is GFCI protected.............. ____ ____

3.   The neutral must be bonded to the meter base in every case without exception .............. ____ ____

4.   The plug outlet on the bathroom light fixture is acceptable to the code for the bathroom plug.............. ____ ____

5.   A diesel fuel pump at a service station is considered less hazardous than a gasoline fuel pump .............. ____ ____

6.   The grounding conductor running around a pool must connect to the reinforcing steel of the pool in at least 3 equally spaced points around the pool.............. ____ ____

7.   The metal supply conduit from the deck box to an in-ground pool light fixture may be used to ground the fixture .......... ____ ____

8.   The rules permit the G.F.C.l. type receptacle in the bathroom to also serve the outdoor plug outlet.............. ____ ____

9.   2 or more loomex cables may be run in contact with each other without affecting their ampacities .............. ____ ____

10.   The Electrical Code specifically states that where two or more smoke alarms are installed they shall be interconnected to sound together .............. ____ ____

11.   There is no limit to the length of service conduit if it is run on the outside surface of the building.............. ____ ____

12.   A grounding conductor is not required in seal-tight flex provided it is smaller than 1 inch.............. ____ ____

I3.   The secondary of a 24 volt Class II transformer need not be grounded when the primary is 120 volts and all the secondary wiring is run overhead outside of buildings according to Rule 6-112.............. ____ ____

14.   Plug outlets may be located between 60 in.( 1.5 m) and 118 in.(3 m) of the inside wall of a swimming pool provided they are protected with a G.F.C.l. of the class A type.............. ____ ____

I5.   TWH conductor is rated for 75 C and therefore may be used in conduit for fire alarm system wiring.............. ____ ____

16.   Conductors of any size or colour may be painted white and used for neutral conductors except in the case of service conductors.............. ____ ____

17.   The disconnect for an electric hoist must be accessible from the ground or from the floor below the hoist.............. ____ ____

18.   The plug outlet for the door opener in a garage may be supplied with a garage lighting circuit.............. ____ ____

19.   A telephone jack, if located in a bathroom, must be at least 1.2m from a tub or shower.............. ____ ____

20.   Electrical metallic tubing must be securely fastened in place within 39.4 inches of each outlet box, junction box. cabinet or fitting.............. ____ ____

21.   A 60⁰ C conductor could not carry any current at all in an ambient temperature of 60 C.............. ____ ____

22.   Underground wiring to the dispensing pumps at a gas station must conform to code requirements for Class I. Zone 2 hazardous location wiring methods.............. ____ ____

23.   If the pump and hot tub are at least 3 m apart G.F.l. protection is not required for the pump.............. ____ ____

24.   A circuit supplying a combination heat lamp (maximum rating 300 watts) and exhaust fan may also supply other outlets.............. ____ ____

25.   Sectional boxes are now approved for use embedded in concrete.............. ____ ____

26. Set screw type EMT couplings and connectors may be used underground provided the conduit is not buried below permanent moisture level ......................................................................................................................................... _____  _____

27. An electrical permit is required for all small jobs such as a furnace, range or dryer connection ...................................... _____  _____

28. The wiring for fire alarm systems may not be drawn into conduits used for other circuits. They must be kept entirely separated except at point of supply............................................................................................................... _____  _____

29. It is the responsibility of the Electrical Contractor to ensure that all the electrical equipment he connects has been properly certified by CSA or by one of the other equipment certification agencies ......................................... _____  _____

30. The service conductors for a 60 amp. service in Prince George may be #6TW provided the demand load is not more than 55 amp............................................................................................................................................................ _____  _____

31. All the outdoor plug receptacles on a single family dwelling, which are accessible from grade level, must be supplied with a circuit used for no other purpose ...................................................................................... _____  _____

## SECTION TWO- FILL IN THE BLANK SPACES.
*Each question is worth 2 points.*

1. Minimum permissible radius of TECK cable bends is ____ the internal diameter of the cable.

2. Junction boxes may be installed in attics, ceiling spaces or crawl spaces provided the head room, vertical clearance, is _____

3. Is a disconnect switch required for a fixed sign ____

4. Where low voltage conduit is buried underground it shall be at least _____ below the surface where it is subject to vehicular traffic and _____ where not subject to vehicular traffic.

5. The rated secondary open circuit voltage of a sign transformer shall not exceed ____ volts.

6. Where NMS cable is run through studs, joists or similar wooden members, the outer surface of the cable shall be kept at least _____ from the nailing edges of wooden members or be protected.

7. Where light fixtures are mounted less than _____ above the floor they must be guarded or be flexible.

8. The maximum number of light or plug outlets permitted on a circuit is _____

9. The minimum wiring method for Class I, Zone I location is ____

10. The maximum baseboard heating load that may be connected to a #14 copper conductor is _____ watts

11. Outlet boxes must be set flush with the surface finish except that in the case where the finish is non-combustible type the box may be set back ____

12. The minimum size bonding conductor for a spa is ____

13. The maximum fixed heating load that may be connected to a 30 amp. 240 volt branch circuit breaker, using #12 copper conductors, (in a residence) is ____ watts.

14. The service entrance cap shall be so located that open conductors are above windows etc. or not less than ____ from windows or similar openings.

15. The minimum distance between an electrical meter and a gas meter is _____

16. Meter bases shall be installed so that they are not more than _____ not less than _____ from grade level to center of base.

17. The service equipment shall be installed so that the top of the top breaker is not more than ____ above floor level.

18. The conductors used to supply ceiling light outlets shall have an insulation rating of ____ C.

19- The minimum size of copper grounding conductor permitted for a UFER (concrete encased electrode) grounding electrode is _____

20. The maximum current that a #14 NMD7 copper cable, which is rated for 90 degrees C. may carry is ____ amp.

## SECTION THREE ADDITIONAL QUESTIONS

Write your answers on a separate sheet of paper

Marks

2   I.   May the service neutral for a single family dwelling be bare (uninsulated)?

2   2.   May flexible cord be used as a substitute for fixed wiring?

2    3.    What does the term "readily accessible" mean?

5    4.    Calculate the maximum expected expansion in a 12.2 m straight run of 3/4 in. PVC conduit located where the temperature will vary between +115F to -30F.

5    5.    What size conduit is required for the following combination of copper conductors; 12 #12TW, 3 #6TW and 3#10TW.

     6.    An apartment has 8 suites. The floor area in 4 suites is 45 m² (484 sq.ft.). Each has a 9 kw. range. a 3 kw. water heater, a 4 amp. gas furnace. The remaining 4 suites are 79 m² (850 sq.ft.) each and each has a 12 kw. range, 3 kw. water heater, 4 amp gas furnace and a 5 amp 120 volt garburator. The house load consists of one 4 kw. dryer and 1 kw. of light. Electric service is 120/240 volt, single phase.

         Calculate the following:

5      a    Main service load in amperes.

5      b    Small suite feeder load in amperes.

5      c.    Large suite feeder load in amperes.

5      d.    Minimum number of branch circuit spaces required by code for      (i) Small suite.
                                                                                                       (ii) Large suite.

4      e.    Main service conductor size required.

2      f.    Sub-feeder size to small suite.

2      g.    Sub-feeder size to large suite.

2      h.    Main service ground.

10    7.    A single family residence has a floor area of 2000 sq. ft. including breakfast room and laundry room. There are two 1/3 hp. 110 volt motors in the basement hobby workshop. There will be a 12 KW range, 3 KW water heater, 4 KW dryer, an 11 amp. 120 volt dish washer and a 3 amp. garburator. Air conditioning is with a 1200VA unit. There are 70 plug outlets and 20 light outlets. There is also a 4 KW sauna, 8 KW electric heating and a 4 KW hot tub heater. Calculate the minimum service size required by code. Service is 120/240 single phase.

     8.    Calculate the wiring requirements for a 5 hp. single phase, 230 volt totally enclosed, non-ventilated motor with Class B insulation for a power saw on a construction project.

2      a.    What size wire and conduit is required for this load?

2      b.    What size code fuse is required?

2      c.    What size overload protection is required?

2      d.    What other motor protection does the code require?

2      e.    What is the purpose of the protection required by (d)?

2      f.    Would #8 TW copper be acceptable if run into the motor terminal box.

5    9.    a.    What is emergency lighting?

5        b.    Describe fully one method of providing emergency lighting.

5    10.    Describe fully how you would install a recessed light fixture.

2    11.    Does the code require the nameplate on electrical equipment to remain accessible after installation?

2    12    a.    What is the minimum service cap height permitted by code.

2        b.    What is the minimum height of service drop wires over a public roadway?

2    13.    a.    When using 3-wire loomex cable, would it be permitted to connect both the black and the red wires in this cable to different breakers in the panel but to the same bus?

2        b.    Give a reason for your answer to question (a).

2    14.    a.    What is the maximum rating of the overcurrent device for a lighting branch circuit in a residence?

2        b.    What is the maximum rating of the overcurrent device for a branch circuit supplying polarized outlets in the kitchen if the wiring is #12 loomex (copper)?

     15.    You are asked to connect a 46 amp. (primary current) manually operated transformer type welder which has a duty cycle of 80% in a non-hazardous area in an existing building of combustible construction in Quesnel. The service is 120/240 volt, single phase.

2      a.    What is the minimum size copper feeder required by code if TW insulation is used?

2      b.    What is the minimum size aluminum feeder required by code if TW insulation is used?

2      c.    If this feeder can be concealed within the building structure, will the code permit it to be NMD7 or NMW-90?

2    16.    a.    What is an EYS fitting?

2        b.    Where is it used?

2    17.    When wiring barns or stables may NMD7 cable be used?

     18.    You are to install the wiring for the lighting and small motors in a machine shop. The service is 120/240 volt, single phase. The building is of frame construction.

2      a.    Would the Code permit NMS cable to be used for lighting and plug outlet wiring in this building?

2      b.    Could NMS cable be used to supply the 2 hp. lathe and the 2 hp. compressor motors?

4    19.    Two circuits are run side by side but in separate conduits. One is #6 R90 copper, the other is #6 TW copper. They are both of equal length and both carry full rated current. Which circuit will have the greatest I R loss?

2    20    When connecting end to end mounted fluorescent light fixtures may R90 wire be used?

3    21.    What is the maximum I R loss permitted on an emergency circuit when unit equipment is used?

2    22.    Where must the bathroom light switch be placed.

23. You are asked to replace a 500 watt electric heater with a 1000 watt heating unit on an existing circuit. The circuit, you discover, already supplies 3 other 500 watt heaters, which are on the same thermostat, and another 500 watt heater in the bathroom on its own thermostat. The load is supplied with 90 degree NMD7, #14 copper cable which is connected to a pair of 15 amp. breakers.

2     a. Would the regulations permit the larger heater to be connected to this circuit?

2     b. Because the rules permit overcurrent protection for electric heating circuits to be 125% of the fixed load and because 90 degree cable has been used, would it be permitted to replace the 15 amp. breakers with 20 amp. breakers?

2  24. Is a nurses call system a Class II circuit?

2  25. Must the air conditioning load always be included in the calculations for service size?

2  26. May PVC be run in a wall where it is enclosed in insulation?

2  27. How many outlets may be on a 15 amp circuit (not including any appliance outlets)?

2  28. Must the fridge receptacle and it's circuit be split type in every case?

2  29. Is it permitted to cut new holes in the meter base (not round type) for conduit entry?

4  30. What is the maximum length of service conductors permitted inside a building?

10  31. An existing 30 amp, 240 volt machine is supplied with 2 #10 copper conductors in 3/4 inch conduit. It is intended to install another 20 amp machine and supply it with 2 #12 TW conductors pulled into the same 3/4 inch conduit. Would it be permitted to do this? Give reasons.

     32. A building has 2200 sq. ft. of office space and 20,000 sq. ft. of warehouse space. There is also a 3 kw. water heater in the office area. There will be a gas boiler supplied from the warehouse panel for heating. There are three 4 amp motors on circulating pumps and seven 4 amp motors on unit heaters. All motors are 120 volt, single phase. Service is 120/240 single phase. Calculate conductor sizes for:

2  a. The main service.

2  b. The sub to office.

2  c. The sub to warehouse.

2  d. What is the calculated service demand load in amperes?

That, was a tough exam!

**Note** - The official exam usually includes a few questions on permit rates in your region. It will also ask questions on who may apply for an Electrical Permit, and in general, the limitations of an Electrical Permit.

EXAMINATION ANSWERS

## SECTION ONE ANSWERS

1. T Rule 2-400(2)
2. T Rule 26-700(11)
3. F Rule 10-516 re. to services only. Meters in subfeeders in an apart. build. are not service equipt..Rule 10-204(1)(d) prohibits neutral bonding in these bases. See also Rule 10-516(3) re: grounding devices.
4. F Rule 26-710(k).
5. F Rule 20-002(l) refers. to "other similar volatile flammable liquids".
6. F Rule 68-058(2)
7. T If in the same structural section, Rule 68-058(5).
8. F Rule 26-724(a)
9. F Rule 4-004(10)
10. F The Building Code requires this.
11. T Note Rule 2-108 re: Workmanship and cost of material usually controls this.
12. F Rule 12-1306
13. F Rule 10-114(a)
14. T Rule 68-064(2)
15. T Section 32 does not specify min. insulation temp.
16. F Rule 4-028(4), 4-030 & 4-034
17. T Rule 40-008
18. T Rule 26-724(b)
19. F Rule 60-400(2) Tele jacks not permitted in bathrooms.
20. T Rule 12-1404
21. T Tables based on 30 C ambient plus 30 degree rise.
22. F Rule 20-004(8) - Class I. Zone I.
23. T Rule 68-068(7)(c).(Outside of pool enclosure)
24. T Rule 62-108(3)
25. F Rule 12-3010(2)

26. F Rule l2-1402(l)(c).
27. T Regulation Governing Permits and Fees.
28. T Rule 32-102(3)
29. T Rule 2-024.
30. F Rule 12-102(2)
31. T Rule 26-724(a)

## SECTION TWO ANSWERS

1. 6 times external diameter, Rule 12-614(l)
2. 900mm. Rule 12-3016.
3. Yes, Rule 34-100.
4. 600mm, 450mm,Rule 12-012(1)&(2), Table 53
5. 15000 volts, Rule 34-300(2)
6. 32 mm, Rule 12-516, page 56.
7. 82.6 in. (2.1 m), Rule 30-314
8. 12, Rule 12-3000
9. Rigid metal conduit or cables approved for hazardous locations, Rule 18-106(1)
10. 3600 watts, Rule 62-114(6)(7)(8), Page 113
11. 6 mm, Rule 12-3018
12. #6 copper, Rule 68-402(1)
13. 4800, page 114
14. 1 m, Rule 6-112(3) page 22.
15. 900 mm, Rule 2-322
16. 1500mm 1800 mm page 35
17. 1.7 m, 67 inches, page 47.
18. 90°, Rule 30-408(1).
19. #4, Rule 10-702(2)(a), Table 43
20. 15, Table 2

# SECTION THREE ANSWERS

I. Yes, Rule 6-308
2. No, Rule 4-010(3)
3. Page 9 in the Code book.
4. First change F to C. then, 12.2 m x 62.8°C x 0.052 mm = 39.8 mm.
5. 1 1/4 inch, Tables 8, 9, 10.
6. a. 196.9 amps.
   b. 42.7 amps
   c. 48.9 amps
   d. (i) 8 circuits, Rule 8-108(3)(a)
      (ii) 8 circuits
   e. 3/0 RW75, 250 MCM RW75
   f. #6 RW75,#6 R90
   g. #6 RW75,#6 R90
   h. #3 copper, aluminum not permitted - Rule 10-802
7. 126 amps. Note 1 sq.ft. = 0.0929 m² & for Hot Tubs see Rule 8-200(1)(a)(v)
8. a. #8 R90 copper in 3/4in. conduit direct to motor. Length between motor starter and motor termination must be minimum 1.2 m (47.2 in.), see Rule 28-104.
   b. 90 amp.
   c. 35 amp.
   d. Magnetic starter, Rule 28-400
   e. Rule 28-400, page 469 of Code.
   f. No, Rule 28-104
9. a. These are lights which automatically give minimum illumination in specific areas when the normal power supply to the building fails.
   b. An emergency lighting system may consist of two or more lamps directed to light specific areas of a room. The power supply for these lights consists of a metal enclosure which contains batteries, charging equipment, control equipment and a relay which is kept connected to the building power supply. In the event of normal power failure this relay becomes de-energized, falling into the open position, thereby closing a set of contacts which complete the circuit through the lamps and batteries. In this way the emergency lighting system is operating the moment after normal power failure. Rule 46-300.
10. Page 62.
11. Yes, Rule 2-118
12. a. 3.5 m plus 150 mm = 3650 mm, Rules 6-112(2) & 6-116(b)
    b. 5.5 m page 19
13. a. no
    b. The red and black wire must be connected to give 240 volts in order to balance the load on the neutral. If this is not done the neutral conductor would have to carry the combined load of the two 120 volt circuits.
14. a. 15 amp, page 53
    b. 20 amp, page 83
15. a. #8, Rule 42-006(1)(a)
    b. #6, Rule 42-006(1)(a)
    c. Yes, Rule 12-504
16. a. A conduit seal used in hazardous locations.
    b. Rule 18-108(1)&(3)
17. No, Type NMW or NMWU is required, Rule 22-204
18. a. Yes, Rule 12-504
    b. Yes, Rule 28-100
19. The R90 conductors because they carry more current, Table 2
20. Yes, Rule 30-310(2)(a) & (b), Note, must have 600 volt rating. See also Subrule (3) if loomex is used.
21. 5% , Rule 46-306
22. 1 m (39.4 in.) from the tub or shower, page 67.
23. a. No, Rule 62-114(6)
    b. Yes, page 108
24. No, Rule 16-010
25. No. Rule 8-106(4)
26. No, Rule 12-1102(2), page 30
27. 12, Rule 12-3000(1)
28. No, Rules 26-712(d)(i) & 26-720(a), page 80
29. Not if base is located outdoors. Yes if the base is indoors. All holes to be below any live parts inside base. This is the same as any switch or gutter in which we may cut holes.
30. As short as possible. See page 24 for exceptions.
31. No, conduit fill is okay, Tables 8,9 and 10 but conductor ampacity is only 80%. Rule 4-004(1)(c)
32. a. #3 R90 copper
       #1 R90 aluminum
    b. #6 R75, #4 R75
    c. #6 R75, #4 R75
    d. 103.4 amperes

Okay we did it!

To find out the percentage points do this:

(a) Add all the marks for all the correct answers; then
(b) Add all the marks for the incorrect "True or False" answers only; then

Your formula should look like this;

$$\frac{a \text{ less } b}{\text{Total points possible}} \times 100 = \underline{\quad}\% \text{ or } \frac{a - b}{264} \times 100 = \underline{\quad}\%$$

# INDEX